The Battle for British Islam

The Battle for British Islam

Reclaiming Muslim Identity from Extremism

SARA KHAN

with Tony McMahon

SAQI

Published 2016 by Saqi Books

Copyright © Sara Khan and Tony McMahon 2016

Sara Khan and Tony McMahon have asserted their right under the
Copyright, Designs and Patents Act, 1988, to be identified as the authors of this work.

ISBN 978-0-86356-159-7
eISBN 978-0-86356-164-1

A full CIP record for this book is available from the British Library.

Printed and bound by CPI Group (UK) Ltd, Croydon, CR0 4YY

Saqi Books
26 Westbourne Grove

To my daughters, Maryam and Hannah

Stand up for something, even if it means standing alone. Because often the one who flies solo has the strongest wings.

She who is brave is free.

CONTENTS

ACKNOWLEDGEMENTS

I would like to thank all the people I interviewed for this book. I am indebted to each person who was willing to share insights and experiences with me. Many of these people are doing incredible work.

A special thanks to Rashad Ali and Usama Hasan, who were always at the end of a phone or email.

I would also like to thank my mother-in-law, Hamida, and my sister-in-law Afshan who both helped take care of my children as I devoted my time and energy to this book. I thank my husband, Mohsin, for his long-standing patience, encouragement and support in all that I do; and my brother Anis and sister-in-law Mehwish for their continual support and help. You have always been there for me no matter what time or day.

A special thank you to my younger brother, Adeeb, for supporting me in the early days, and Kalsoom Bashir for her friendship, laughter and love of cake, which kept us both sane in times of darkness.

Finally, I am forever indebted to my parents. You gave me the best gifts one can give a daughter: an education and independence. And to my sister, Sabin, who encouraged me to believe in myself. She is one of the most remarkable, resilient and awe-inspiring women I know.

A NOTE ON TERMS

Many of these terms hold different meanings for different people. Here are the definitions that will guide usage in The Battle for British Islam.

Extremism

The primary focus will be on Islamist extremism and other forms of Muslim extremism, though the far Right of British politics will also be covered. My definition of extremism includes any who incite violence, hatred or discrimination for political, religious or ideological causes. This can often include undermining the rule of law and democracy.

Extremism is not just about violence. In the twenty-first century, universal human rights norms should be the means by which we judge extremism. My definition is also based on contemporary Muslim scholarship on notions of citizenship and equality.

Moderate

The label 'moderate Muslim' is ambiguous and subjective and will be avoided in this book. Individuals of all faiths should be judged on whether they subscribe to accepted human rights and values.

Conservative

Conservative interpretations of Islam should not be conflated with extremist belief, as it often is. Muslims may hold certain conservative opinions on homosexuality, for example, and be protected under Article 9 of the European Convention on Human Rights guaranteeing religious belief. However, although the legislation recognises the right to make one's religious belief manifest, there are limitations to what is allowed. This especially applies when hate, discrimination or violence are advocated in the name of religion.

Conservative Islamic interpretations should not be considered to be especially authentic. Liberal interpretations are just as valid. Historically, Islamic jurisprudence has always produced diverse opinions; conservative interpretations have to take their place among many equally other legitimate views that exist in Islam.

Islamism

Islamism is a political ideology; it is not synonymous with the faith of Islam. Islamism defines Islam as a socio-political system and advocates an expansionist Islamic state governed by sharia law. There are different types of Islamism. Some are violent, others not.

Non-Muslims

'Non-Muslims' refers to people outside the Muslim faith. It is a crude term, used reluctantly for the purposes of this book as alternatives were considered too clumsy or long-winded.

ISIS

Daesh, Islamic State, ISIS and ISIL have all been used in the media to describe the so-called Islamic State. ISIS is still a commonly used term, and we have used it in this book. This does not suggest any recognition of the ISIS claim to be an Islamic state.

Islamophobia

Islamophobia is a problematic and loaded term. Used as originally intended, it is there to protect or defend Muslims from abuse, attacks and discrimination. However, in recent years it has been extended by some to include a prohibition on criticising Islamist ideology and shutting down discussion on theological matters within Islam. Alternative terms have been used in this book to characterise attacks, hatred or discrimination against Muslims.

INTRODUCTION

A tumultuous crisis has engulfed contemporary Islam as the faith struggles to escape the clutches of extremists. News of Muslim terrorists murdering and engaging in suicide bombing, claiming that their actions are 'Islamic', has become a daily occurrence. Many Muslims painstakingly and repeatedly stress that these acts of terror have no justification in the Islamic faith. Other Muslims disagree; across the world thousands have joined Islamist terror groups. ISIS's leader Abu Bakr al-Baghdadi rebuffs the notion that Islam is a peaceful religion. Instead he asserts *'Islam was never a religion of peace. Islam is the religion of fighting.'*[1]

In this highly divisive environment, what can be agreed on is that the word 'Islamic' clearly means very different things to Muslims across the world. The result is a furious battle to claim or reclaim what Islam stands for in the twenty-first century. The controversial idea of a clash of civilisations, between Islam and the West, is continuously debated. But the real clash taking place now is within Islam. It is pitting Muslims against each other with competing claims of what values and principles the faith stands for. The consequence of this bitter conflict will impact on not just the lives of over a billion Muslims but all of us, and future generations.

Often the focus of this battle is analysed with primary reference to terrorism. In an era of global Islamist extremism, this is inevitable. From Boko Haram in Nigeria, to Tehreek-e-Taliban in Pakistan, al-Qaʿida, al-Shabaab in Somalia, and of course ISIS, Muslims and non-Muslims alike are being murdered. The sheer brutality and scale of Islamist terrorism engulf us all. That is the case whether the atrocities occur in a concert hall in Paris, at Friday prayers at a mosque in Nigeria or at a funeral in Baghdad. We are not seeing any diminution to this violent threat. The unfortunate truth is that Islamist-inspired terrorism, for the time being at least, is here to stay.

The battle within Islam, however, encompasses much more than just the challenge of terrorism. At its heart is a conflict of ideas and a question as to whether Muslims believe Islam is reconcilable with pluralism and human rights. Or do Muslims, instead, hold religious supremacist ideas over and above notions of equality and citizenship? These debates are taking place every day in communities, mosques, homes and on social media across the UK as well as around the world. These disputes among British Muslims define the battle for British Islam.

There are just under 3 million Muslims in the UK. While only a fifth of the UK's population as a whole is under fifteen, this age group makes up a third of Muslims in Britain.[2] The term 'British Muslim' does not adequately reflect the ethnic, sectarian, linguistic, class and ideological diversity of this faith group. South-Asian Muslims still dominate the ethnic profile of British Muslims (68 per cent), but this heterogeneous section of society also encompasses Arabs, Somalis, Kurdish, Kosovans, Turkish, Afghan, English, Welsh and many more.[3]

The same heterogeneity exists in the workforce. Unemployment is higher among Muslims than any other religious group and particularly among women. At the other end of the scale, it is estimated that there are more than 10,000 Muslim millionaires in Britain, with liquid assets of more than £3.6 billion. There are 13,400 Muslim-owned businesses in London, creating more than 70,000 jobs and representing just over 33 per cent of Small to Medium Enterprises in the capital alone.[4] Research has also indicated that, of all faith groups, British Muslims donate the most to charity.[5]

Most opinion polls among Muslims evidence a strong endorsement of being British. A study by the think tank Demos showed that British Muslims tend to be more patriotic than the average citizen.[6] This may be the case, but a parallel trend over the past twenty-five years has seen some British Muslims become ever more conservative on social and equality issues.[7]

More worryingly, hundreds of British Muslims have pledged allegiance to terrorist groups. Despite being born and raised here, some have been convicted of planning to carry out atrocities in the UK, in the hope of killing ordinary Britons, whom they perceive to be the enemy. This has brought an uncomfortable reality to the fore: rather than an identity crisis, there appears to be an identity catastrophe among a small but significant section of Britain's Muslims.

Ever since I was a teenager, I have witnessed how Islamist extremism has wreaked havoc on the lives of British Muslims. In my work over the past eight years as co-founder and director of Inspire, a counter-extremism organisation, I have seen at first hand how this ideology has ripped families apart, turning daughters against mothers and sons against fathers. It has robbed kids of their childhood and their promising futures, and has even groomed teenagers to be killers.

It has encouraged intolerance and the dehumanisation of both non-Muslims and other Muslims, furthering sectarianism, acts of excommunication and even violence. Islamist extremism provokes anti-Muslim hatred and creates polarised communities; yet despite the damage it causes it continues to thrive among some Muslims in the UK.

The seemingly unstoppable growth of puritanical and Islamist ideology in Muslim communities troubles me deeply. I still meet many young Muslims who believe that Islamism is authentic Islam. What it actually represents is a politicised ideology that has emerged mainly in the twentieth century. Islamism advocates the belief of an expansionist Islamic state governed by sharia law. Rejecting 'man-made' concepts such as gender equality and democracy, Islamists also often endorse *hudood* punishments, with the death penalty for adultery and apostasy.

Since the nineteenth century, an austere and puritanical form of Islam known as Salafism has also grown in popularity across the world. The Salafists desire a return to what they regard as the ways of the earliest followers of Islam through a literal reading of Islam's religious texts. Both Salafism and Islamism have won over an increasing number of the younger generation as they seek to define their identity in a post-9/11 world. As will be seen in this book, the reason for the growth of these ideologies is the relentless activism of Salafi and Islamist groups on campuses, in communities and on social media. While promoting a compelling victimhood grievance narrative to this 9/11 generation, both Salafism and Islamism present themselves to these young people – who increasingly view themselves through the prism of their faith identity – as 'normative' or orthodox Islam.

The spectrum of Islamist extremism is wide. Not all Islamists advocate violence, but what many Islamists share is an ideological worldview. Core assumptions about the ultimate goal of creating a caliphate, the codification of sharia law, gender inequality and an opposition to internationally recognised human rights are shared across this Islamist spectrum. As a result of its growing influence, interpretations of Islam that were once regarded as fringe and extreme have now become mainstream.

This book seeks to examine how Salafi-Islamism has become such a major influence within British Islam, crowding out voices that advocate a more reconciled British Muslim identity. In contrast with the situation in the 1990s, a process has been under way since the dawn of the new millennium in which previously competing strands of opinion – Salafism and Islamism – have become intertwined.

Salafi-Islamists seek to influence not only British Muslims but also wider society, engaging with unions, academics, the media and even politicians. The situation would not be so dire if there was an equally strong counter-movement that could provide an alternative to puritanical and Islamist ideologies, but this is currently not the case. The phenomenon and activism of Salafi-Islamism are not well understood amongst Britain's Muslims and non-Muslims; too many believe they represent Islam outright. But understanding the dynamics of this movement is fundamental to grasping the direction of travel of British Islam.

Inevitably there is much trepidation among non-Muslims about Islam and Muslims. They wonder if this religion can ever be compatible with the British way of life. This was borne out by a March 2015 survey conducted by the YouGov-Cambridge Programme revealing that over half of British voters (55 per cent) believed 'there is a fundamental clash between Islam and the values of British society', compared with just 22 per cent who said Islam and British values were 'generally compatible'.[8] Such emotional responses are further exploited by the far Right to nurture anti-Muslim hatred.

However, the unifying sentiment across both sides of the argument is fear. Non-Muslims fear the threat of terrorism, particularly from home-grown Muslim extremists. These extremists appear to despise Britain and its values, despite having been born and raised in this country. Muslims worry about being viewed as a suspect community and about what the future holds for them and their children in Britain, fearing rejection by their home country due to the actions of a minority. They worry that they too could be killed by Islamist terrorists. They see on the one hand increasing sectarianism and hard-line interpretations of Islam within Muslim communities, and on the other hand growing anti-Muslim prejudice.

This does not point to a bright future. There is a real problem with young people drifting to ideological extremes: some white kids gravitate to the far Right and some Muslim kids to Islamist views. The former speak the language of white supremacism while the latter speak disdainfully about the 'filthy *kuffar*' (non-believer). This shows the emergence of a worrying symbiotic relationship between Islamist extremism and far-Right extremism. As the former gains a footing, so does the latter – both feeding off fear and hate. The result is an increasingly divided and potentially violent society. It is incumbent on people on both sides to halt this drift to extremism.

It is therefore of critical importance how we respond to these puritanical and Islamist extreme ideologies. My organisation Inspire has for a number of years engaged with the Government's Counter-Terrorism 'Prevent' strategy as a civil society group. Our anti-ISIS campaign #MakingAStand, launched after the declaration of ISIS's so-called Islamic State, was an example of a Prevent project that was aimed at empowering Muslim women. My direct involvement with Prevent enables me to share my observations of this arm of the Government's counter-terrorism strategy, both negative and positive, and I do so in an independent capacity outside of my role as director of Inspire.

The 'Prevent' strategy aims to stop people becoming terrorists or supporting terrorism, but it has attracted much public criticism. Prevent has often been described as 'toxic'. A perception exists that it seeks to criminalise British Muslims, spy on Muslim children and close down debate within school classes. So much can be written about the achievements and shortcomings of Prevent. My focus in this book, however, is an area that has not been discussed enough, which is how British Salafi-Islamists have led and delivered a highly effective strategy to derail Prevent on account of their own ideological beliefs and for reasons of self-preservation.

Despite the urgent need to prevent people from being drawn into either far Right or Islamist extremism, what has become obvious is that engaging in the counter-terrorism and counter-extremism arena is akin to walking into a minefield. It is a deeply divided and polarised space where everybody has a strong opinion on the best way forward. Entering the fray results in being attacked by all sides.

While I have been working with countless schools, Muslim communities and statutory agencies championing human rights and challenging extremism, my work as director of Inspire has resulted in me experiencing abuse, harassment, threats, online stalking and character assassination on a scale even I could never have imagined. I have seen British Islamists and extremist Muslims regularly denigrating counter-extremist Muslim voices on their social media platforms with the hope of pushing these voices to the fringe of

British Islam. At the same time these extremists claim that they 'represent the vast majority of British Muslims'. If this is the case, then British Islam faces a calamity.

As a Muslim countering Islamist extremists who justify hatred and violence in the name of my faith, I am accused of being an 'Islamophobe'. I am a 'sell out' or a 'native informant' because I have delivered projects supported by the UK authorities to dissuade young Muslims from joining ISIS. Speaking out against institutions in this country that have bowed to pressure from the Islamists has led to my being declared an apostate, alongside my two young children.

When I turned to liberals and some on the Left for solidarity, instead I found painful rejection; some had clearly allied themselves with Islamists. Those on the Right wondered why I even bothered to be a Muslim in the first place when my faith was so 'backward'. The leading light of New Atheism, Richard Dawkins, tweeted in October 2014 that there was nothing to 'reclaim' in Islam after I wrote a national newspaper op-ed about the ISIS murder of British aid worker Alan Henning by the notorious British terrorist 'Jihadi John'.

> *You pick your peaceful verses, but ISIS can find verses to justify their vile acts. Why not just give up your faith and join the 21ˢᵗ century.* [9]

Finding myself in such a predicament often left me wondering: why struggle when the odds are stacked up against you? The situation seemed hopeless. Yet while navigating my way through this hostile terrain, I have realised that clarity at a time of confusion has never been more important. Sections of the Left and Right are both wrong. Muslim voices championing human rights are needed, otherwise the extremists are the ones who will be left to define British Islam. The Left, Right and liberals need to realise that, if they want to prevent our society becoming more polarised, they must stand with Muslims who are fighting Islamism. This also means understanding how the flourishing of identity politics in Britain today fosters a sullen insularity and hampers the development of a British Islam, as it instead bolsters Islamists and far-Right ideologies.

Those Muslims who believe in engaging fully with British society, supporting gender equality and human rights, condemning violence in the name of religion, promoting inter-faith dialogue and standing against all forms of sectarianism within Islam, find themselves a beleaguered group these days. No insult is out of bounds in the bully pulpit of social media. Even violence and threats towards their person seem to be regarded as an acceptable form of discourse. But they soldier on, providing valuable community services in our country, such as youth leadership courses and hate-crime monitoring, as well as rebutting the arguments of Islamist ideology. They often pursue this work with the minimum of financial and moral support.

My motivation, first and foremost, in writing this book is a sense of obligation and principle as a Muslim. Throughout my life, Islam has been and continues to be a core part of my identity and has framed my humanistic outlook. I care deeply about the direction of travel that contemporary Islam finds itself in and the violence and ugliness that are often justified by Muslims. Truth be told there were times when the actions of ISIS and the inhumanity of Muslim extremists rocked my own faith. In their pursuit of hate and violence, not only are these extremists helping to create a divided British society, they are also toxifying Islam, turning the faith whose cornerstone advocated compassion, mercy and justice into a religion of death, despair, inhumanity and brutality.

I firmly agree with the sentiment by theologian and academic Khaled Abou El Fadl:[10]

> *It is a profound injustice for a Muslim to remain oblivious, when his or her religion and tradition are being hijacked and corrupted. In part, this is a question of love and loyalty: if Islam is supposed to be a universal moral message to humanity but this very same message has become associated in the minds of many human beings with violence and ugliness, what are the obligations and*

duties of a Muslim toward his religion? I believe that if a Muslim loves his religion and is loyal to it, his first and foremost obligation becomes to save and reclaim his faith.

My second reason for writing this book is this: because I have spent my life working with Muslim communities and in particular young Muslims, I care passionately about their future. So many of Britain's Muslim youth are incredibly aspirational, positive and thoughtful. Whether their involvement is in the arts, youth politics, music or drama, I am always left feeling optimistic for the future, despite the numerous challenges and pressures that face them from all sides. These young hopefuls belong to Britain, and Britain belongs to them.

I have worked with young Muslims whose lives have been ruined by predatory radicalisers who have sought to destroy their future by enticing them towards extremism, through binary and falsely constructed paradigms of identity and belonging. I feel it is imperative that we do what we can to help them. These promising young people, who have so much to contribute to our country, are being let down. They suffer from a lack of strong and visionary Muslim leadership, a disconnect from mosques, a rising Islamist movement in the UK, alongside growing anti-Muslim hatred. As a mother it pains me greatly to see this happen; we cannot allow it to continue.

My co-author is Tony McMahon, an independent consultant who has worked with civil society groups and Government on projects concerning youth safeguarding and community cohesion. We met in late 2013 and this book evolved from conversations about why so many young people were going to Syria. We share a deep concern on this issue and wanted to examine the roots of the problem. Over a two-year period we have pooled our expertise and knowledge into this book.

While recognising the huge challenges that lie ahead I hope to share my understanding of a British Islam that opposes extremism and rejects the dehumanisation of others. Muslims must define what Islam stands for in the contemporary era. Equally, non-Muslims have an essential role to play in supporting Muslims who are on the frontline speaking out against Islamist extremism. To do so will place us all on the side of human rights and pluralism in recognition of our shared humanity.

I write this book with a call for reason and hope, because I believe we can forge a better path to a future based on human rights, shared values, compassion and co-existence, prizing such aspirations over discrimination, hatred and supremacy. The question is whether we are brave enough.

This is the battle for British Islam.

ONE

RACE TO YOUR CALIPHATE: THE RISE OF ISLAMIST EXTREMISM

'Islamic Disneyland'

Muneera told Leila that living in the ISIS caliphate would be like something she referred to as an 'Islamic Disneyland'.[1] Leila, a Muslim woman in her thirties, had been assigned to be Muneera's intervention provider under the UK Government's counter-terrorism programme. Her role was to provide support to individuals at risk of joining ISIS and travelling to Syria. Her charge, Muneera (whose name we have changed), was just thirteen years old.

The teenager was a third-generation British Muslim, born and raised in the UK. Her family was originally from Pakistan but had now settled in Birmingham, Britain's second city. Her father was a mechanic in his forties, while her thirty-something mother stayed at home with the younger siblings. There was no adolescent rebelliousness with Muneera. She was very close and loving to her parents. Leila describes Muneera's home set-up as that of a regular British Asian family.

Muneera was home-schooled but had friends in the neighbourhood and was not shy or introverted. In early 2015 her mother had become acutely ill during a sixth pregnancy and the teenager, left to her own devices, retreated to her bedroom to spend a growing amount of time online. One evening she had watched a TV news report on ISIS and logged on to her new mobile phone to find out more about this so-called caliphate in Syria and Iraq.

She began asking questions on Twitter and was excited when responses began to appear along the lines of 'saw your tweet, tell you more about it'. A support network of seemingly like-minded people from all over the world swarmed round her on social media, telling Muneera not to trust the official media and the lies they spread about ISIS. Other girls chatted about how they were thinking of going to Syria and the great life that awaited them.

Bit by bit, Muneera formed a very strong friendship triangle with a fifteen-year-old girl in Wembley and a fourteen-year-old boy in Blackburn. Leila notes that they became 'really weirdly close':

> This was a fast-track radicalisation happening in just a
> matter of weeks.

The fourteen-year-old in Blackburn turned out to be a remarkably hardened terrorist operator. From his suburban bedroom in north-west England he was already plotting a massacre of army veterans at the 2015 Anzac Day parade in Australia.[2] When his case eventually went to court, the boy would be the youngest Briton to be found guilty of a terrorist offence.

It was later revealed that he had displayed an early taste for ultra-violence. His own classmates dubbed him 'the terrorist' because of his stated wish to behead his own teachers.[3] Incredibly, across thousands of miles, this boy was already radicalising an eighteen-year-old in Melbourne through an encrypted Voice-Over Internet Protocol (VOIP). VOIP allows the user to send voice information over the internet instead of the telephone.

His radicalisation target, Sevdet Besim, aged eighteen, was an ethnic Albanian teenager from Macedonia who had emigrated to Australia with his family. A seasoned Australian ISIS fighter called Abu Khalid al-Cambodi, given this name on account of his family's Cambodian roots, had drawn Besim and his friends towards ISIS.[4] Al-Cambodi's former name was Neil Prakash;[5] he was one of the top international ISIS recruiters up until his death in a US military airstrike in early 2016.[6] His online tactic was to work through various Twitter accounts, find people like Muneera or the Blackburn boy then direct them to his private messaging account for one-on-one discussions.[7] In the Blackburn boy, he had found a very willing disciple.

In court, the transcript of the youngster from Blackburn's conversations was made public. They made for grim reading. It became clear that he had transitioned with remarkable ease from experiencing raw grievance to embracing an ultra-violent Islamist ideology:

> **Blackburn Boy:** *Ok now listen. Im going to tell you what you are.*
> **Mr Besim:** *Whats that*
> **Boy:** *You are a lone wolf, a wolf that begs Allah for forgiveness a wolf that doesn't fear blame of the blamers. I'm I right?*
> **Mr Besim:** *Pretty much.*
> **Boy:** *Mashalla [what God wills].*
> **Mr Besim:** *I'm ready to fight these dogs on there doorstep. The more equipment im provided with the better but ill still go with just a knife in my hand. I want to be among those that allah laughs at...*
> **Boy:** *So listen akhi [my brother]. I want you to do this on your own. Just you no one else.*
> **Mr Besim:** *ok.*
> **Boy:** *Im here for any advice anything you may need to know that im here, I'll plan something in sha allah [God willing]. Also you will have to make a video and snd it to abu kambozz to snd to al hayat [a media arm of Islamic State].*[8]

The Blackburn youth had immersed himself in online extremist material, citing Osama bin Laden as a hero. The young terrorist became an ISIS celebrity 'fanboy', gaining 24,000 followers within two weeks of setting up a Twitter account.[9] Not only was he sending thousands of online messages to Besim down in Melbourne but he was also tweeting and messaging Muneera in Birmingham and her new friend in Wembley. In no time both girls were desperate to leave for ISIS. When this precocious young jihadist was eventually put on trial, Mr Justice Saunders who sentenced him described how chilling it was that someone who was only fourteen years old at the time could have become 'so radicalised that he was prepared to carry out this role intending and wishing that people should die'.[10]

Muneera and the girl in Wembley were increasingly enthusiastic to pack their bags and go to Syria. Leila says that Muneera told her the Blackburn boy was much more hesitant about leaving the UK, saying they should wait or take their time. In contrast, the Wembley girl was '100 per cent committed to ISIS' and determined to get to Syria as quickly as possible.

She urged Muneera to join her. The only problem for the thirteen-year-old was that her father had now become rather suspicious of her behaviour. When she begged to be given her passport, he locked it away. Muneera then went on a hunger strike in an attempt to emotionally blackmail her parents into giving her the passport, but without success.

By contrast, the Wembley girl grabbed her passport and without her parents' knowledge tried to leave the UK – on two separate occasions. However, on the second attempt she was stopped at the airport by the police. They examined her phone and discovered the many messages to Muneera. Very soon there was a firm knock on the door of Muneera's family home.

Intervention

Muneera and the Wembley girl were given an intervention provider through the Prevent counter-terrorism programme; this is pre-criminal, so they were not put on trial. Leila, as an intervention provider, works for a programme called Channel. Sitting under Prevent, Channel is about deradicalising those who have expressed sympathy for terrorist causes without crossing the line into criminality. With Muneera, this has involved getting her to express creatively what was going on in her mind when she considered joining the Wembley girl and fleeing to Syria.

A unique insight into what a thirteen-year-old is thinking when she considers fleeing to Syria is provided by a poem that Muneera wrote about the experience. She and Leila agreed to share it:

They took me towards a path I'm glad I never went
down,
At first it was a paradise,
A place where all my dreams were to come true,
I was told I'd live like a princess,
But it was all a trap I was falling into,
Thinking it's an adventure,
Painting over the real picture, Avoiding the truth,

With their lies I was drowning deep,
Convinced I was picking a rose without any thorns,
Coating every fault,
Assuming I was gathering fresh honey from a hive,
Thinking the bees will not bite,

With their bribes I was led astray,
I was believing everything said,
Not knowing I had lost my Mind,
Till I finally realise to what I was thinking at the time,
Knowing I was not all there,
The escape route was fading, yet still visible,
Now was my chance to stay away from this nightmare,
How could I have ever let this disaster overthrow?

I'm relieved to know I'm now safe,
It could have been worse,
If the star wasn't there to guide my way,
Now every day I pray,
So something like this doesn't come your way,
Hoping you will see the truth behind their lies,
And help save others from this distress.[11]

The Wembley girl took longer to deradicalise, but she and Muneera are now back at school and piecing their lives together again. Both feel angry about their experience. Their fate was a lot better than that of the Blackburn boy, whose advanced terrorist planning landed him in court and resulted in a life sentence. For the first five years he will be given a chance to demonstrate his contrition and deradicalisation; but, if the evidence is not forthcoming, he will be deemed too dangerous ever to be released.[12]

In spite of what emerged during his trial, the girls think the Blackburn boy was a pawn being controlled by jihadists in Australia. He was like a young gang member trying to impress the older males. In his trial, it was asserted that he adopted the style of an older teenager in his messages. However, here was a boy whose advice to Besim included developing a taste for beheading by testing it out on any loner he chanced upon.

Muneera was Leila's youngest-ever case. But she embodied a growing trend for ISIS to target teenage girls, grooming them online to persuade them to leave their homes.[13] Facilitators guide the girls through the process of getting to Syria and avoiding being caught. Research has shown they mix extremist messaging with cooking recipes or even images of kittens and coffee, to make life in ISIS territory seem relatively normal.[14]

Seclusion and sacrifice

In January 2015, a document appeared online titled 'Women of the Islamic State: Manifesto and Case Study'.[15] This was a conscious attempt to paint a positive picture of ISIS to potential female recruits. The all-female al-Khansaa Brigade's media wing uploaded the text in Arabic, so it is unlikely Muneera ever read this document. However, many of the Brigade's arguments would have been used to sway Muneera and other girls. This ISIS unit has become notorious for its harsh measures against other women in Syria, even for minor infractions.

In short, this document presented ISIS as an empowering force for Muslim women while condemning feminism as a 'Western programme'. The role of women is entirely distinct from men, it argued. Women are not equal, but different. Their roles are divinely ordained. They must be sedentary, secluded and preferably hidden from view, while men are the opposite, exhibiting 'movement and flux'. If roles are exchanged, 'the base of society is shaken, its foundations crumble and its walls collapse'.[16]

Even though she is secluded and hidden, a woman has a central role to play in the caliphate as a mother and wife. She can study, but only theology. The manifesto did welcome female doctors and teachers, though their education in these fields would have undoubtedly taken place outside of ISIS territory. It stressed that women are not expected to be illiterate, in spite of their constrained role. In extreme circumstances, women can fight when the situation is desperate. The ISIS document made a curious analogy with the world of film production to explain the role of a female in their self-proclaimed caliphate:

> It is always preferable for a woman to remain hidden and veiled, to maintain society from behind this veil. This, which is always the most difficult role, is akin to that of a director, the most important person in a media production, who is behind the scenes organising.[17]

To recruit young women in the West, ISIS uses its female operatives to radicalise their peer group. Leila has spoken to girls who received messages saying 'you'll be given a house' and 'you'll be treated like a queen'. The notion of a sisterhood fulfilling its religious duty, and its members supporting each other, is held out as better than life in the West. Even the prospect of finding romance with a fighter husband is on offer. The same ISIS propaganda points out he may die – but this will be a singular honour for his teenage widow.[18]

One of the most notorious female radicalisers based in Syria has been the Scottish radiography student Aqsa Mahmood, who took the name Umm Layth after fleeing her Glasgow home in November 2013. Via Tumblr and Twitter she has posted rather girly messages about life under ISIS, including food recipes and pictures of clothes shops. She advised British teenagers not to worry about shampoo and other necessities as these are available in ISIS territory; but makeup and jewellery, especially for those who intend to be married, should be brought from the West.

Mahmood, writing as Umm Layth, used the kind of language to be found in the ISIS manifesto for women. This is an example of a rallying call she sent out to girls like Muneera:

> Our role is even more important as women in Islam, since if we don't have sisters with the correct Aqeedah [creed] and understanding who are willing to sacrifice all their desires and give up their families and lives in the west in order to make Hijrah [migration to live in the house of Islam] and please Allah, then who will raise the next generation of Lions?[19]

The Scottish jihadist became a member of the al-Khansaa Brigade. Various horror stories have emerged about this brigade, including one report that a woman in the Syrian city of Raqqa was summarily executed for breastfeeding her baby in public, even though she had been doing this under her burqa.[20] It is believed that up to seventy

British women may be members of al-Khanssaa, meting out a variety of punishments for infractions of ISIS's take on sharia law.

This kind of brutality clearly takes a toll on those involved. Aqsa Mahmood's tweets eventually lost any semblance of teenage fun and descended into distinctly unpleasant ramblings.[21] After terrorist attacks on three continents on a single day saw thirty-eight people killed at a beach resort in Tunisia, a Shi'i mosque bombed in Kuwait and a man beheaded in France, Aqsa Mahmood posted a poem on her Tumblr account glorifying the acts in the cause of 'change, freedom and revenge'.[22]

Knowing that the reality of a harsher life under ISIS might get through to Muneera, her female ISIS facilitators warned her off western media, which they said were working to an agenda to denigrate Islam. They would counter stories of the beheading of female captives by alleging they were spies or asserting that the mass rape and sale in slave markets of Yazidi girls was a practice justified in Islam. (The Yazidis are an ethnically Kurdish religious group persecuted by ISIS.) Radicalisers often prey on natural teenage rebelliousness and an unwillingness to accept answers from voices of authority, be those the media or their own parents. They give this rebelliousness an Islamist dimension.

It is hard to put an exact figure on how many western-born Muslim girls have joined ISIS. One estimate is that 10 per cent of foreign recruits from Europe, the US and Australia are women. Many may have been attracted by the pseudo-empowerment that ISIS appears to offer women. Examples are the opportunity to join the all-female al-Khansaa Brigade or train at the ISIS Al-Zawra school, which mixes lessons in sewing (to mend your husband's uniform) with speeches on suicide bombing.

While this empowerment and sense of sisterhood may seem attractive, they tend to gloss over ISIS practices such as male fighters being polygamous and acquiring sex slaves, sometimes in public auctions. One Yazidi girl recounted how she had been bought by the self-proclaimed ISIS caliph himself, Abu Bakr al-Baghdadi, at a slave auction in 'a white palace... between the mountain and the sea'.[23]

The sixteen-year-old managed to escape, having witnessed Baghdadi personally torturing the US hostage Kayla Mueller, a young aid worker captured in 2013.

ISIS has even produced a manual, in a Q&A format, on how its male fighters can 'enjoy' their slaves:

> *Question 13: Is it permissible to have intercourse with a female slave who has not reached puberty?*
>
> *It is permissible to have intercourse with the female slave who hasn't reached puberty if she is fit for intercourse; however if she is not fit for intercourse, then it is enough to enjoy her without intercourse.*[24]

If Muneera had made it to Syria, she would have been forced to burn her passport. Then she would have been married off to a male fighter and introduced to her life of sedentary seclusion with possible service in al-Khanssaa. Should she have decided that this life was not what she had expected and attempted to escape, then the fate of Austrian teenager Samra Kesinovic is instructive.

In 2014, the Bosnian-heritage youth fled Vienna with her friend Sabina, ending up in Raqqa, Syria. Sabina died shortly afterwards during fighting in the city and Samra contacted her family saying she wanted to leave because of ISIS brutality. Eventually, she attempted to make her escape. According to media reports, she was caught and beaten to death by ISIS thugs in November 2015.[25]

Muneera has come to realise that she was brainwashed, comparing it to being in a hypnotic state. She is now in her mid-teens and back at school, ostensibly an ordinary pupil putting a very unfortunate episode behind her. Leila believes that what happened to Muneera was grounded in a quest for identity that made her vulnerable to Islamist propaganda. Her powers of critical thinking were not strong enough to withstand the online ideologues with their violent interpretation of Islam. They successfully played on her sense of grievance and led Muneera towards the terrorist outlook.

Bitten by the Islamist bug

Leila emphasises that anti-British and anti-Western sentiments have been professed by every one of the girls she has worked with who have been 'hit by the ISIS bug'.

> *They repeatedly hear that the kuffar [disbelievers] hate you, that Britain is a kuffar country, you cannot live there as a Muslim as God has warned that if you die in such a land you will die as a disbeliever. The kuffar hate your religion and they want to eradicate Islam.*

How have young British Muslims come to think like this?

One leading analyst posed the question in 2015: 'The roots of radicalisation?' And then answered: 'It's identity stupid.' How else, he explained, can you find a common factor among UK Islamist extremists and link 'a white Englishman from Buckinghamshire with a second generation British-Asian man born in Dewsbury and a missing family of twelve from Bradford'?[26] Strip away all the individual triggers and grievances and what you discover is a crisis of identity.

The desperate search for identity undertaken by many Muslims can lead to a cognitive opening through which the outlook of their parents' generation is rejected while extreme ideas enter. Since the 1990s, the cultural and ethnically based Islam of Muslims who arrived and lived in Britain in the post-war decades has lost ground to a globalised Islamist identity that is transnational and hostile to integration and assimilation. It dismisses British values, the nation state, democracy and gender equality as man-made concepts, because Allah – they contend – commands the faithful to fight for a caliphate, the perfect expression of Muslim rule.

Islamism forces a choice between British values and Islamic values. Muneera felt she had to reject Britain to be a good Muslim. Leila, her intervention provider, understands what her young charge was going through, having been involved in an Islamist movement when she was a student at university. Leila was a member of Hizb ut-Tahrir (the Islamic Liberation Party) (HT), a group that agitates for the return of an Islamic caliphate but rejects the ISIS claim to have established one.

In spite of its official rejection of terrorism, HT's ideology has a number of touch points with ISIS. The same can be said of other Islamist-based groups. Leila can appreciate how Muneera was radicalised because she was seduced by the idealist rhetoric of HT, which she compares to the attraction of communism in the past for many young people. Part of the appeal, Leila says, was the idea of a global struggle between Islam and the West, through which everything was viewed:

> *It was drilled in to the extent that you were made to believe it was like a matter of life or death if we didn't establish this Islamic state.*

Rashad Ali was also once a member of Hizb ut-Tahrir. Like Leila, he has used this experience of being in an Islamist movement in his work as an intervention provider. In an interview for this book, he drew on his deep understanding of how young people can become intoxicated by ideology. Over the past six years Rashad has been involved in trying to deradicalise more than 100 men and women aged between fourteen and sixty.

In common with most people involved in this line of work, he has noticed how the rise of ISIS has brought an increasing number of teenagers into his caseload. Al-Qa'ida operated as a traditional terrorist organisation with a secretive cell structure, while ISIS has been more like a movement, recruiting adherents to its ideological brand. With claims to have set up a 'caliphate', and calling on Muslims everywhere to rally to its flag, it has found hundreds of willing recruits among Britain's Muslims.

One of Rashad's cases has been a fourteen-year-old boy who openly celebrated the slaughter of journalists from the French satirical magazine *Charlie Hebdo* in January 2015. The boy was referred to Rashad through Prevent. There was also a seventeen-year-old who had been in regular contact with an uncle fighting for ISIS in Syria. The uncle was instructing his nephew online about the need to establish sharia globally and the virtues of enslaving women.

Faced with more and more radicalised teenagers, Rashad has set out to rationalise what he is facing every day. He has identified four types of radicalisation with some individuals displaying more than one type. The first are puritanical religious zealots motivated by a religiously extreme understanding of Islamic scripture. Rashad has worked with men, now back in the UK, who have fought for the extremist group al-Shabaab in Somalia as well as jihadist groups in Syria. Their ideological position is grounded in a superficial and violent reading of scripture.

The second type is driven by a political, ideological outlook that is fundamentally anti-western. The political worldview of these individuals is the primary driver ahead of their religious views. Geopolitics is presented through religious framing to further the notion of a western conspiracy against Islam. These politically inclined Islamist extremists see Islam as more of a political identity than a spiritual belief. To them, the West is systematically persecuting the *ummah* (the global Muslim community). Michael Adebolajo, who killed the British soldier Lee Rigby on the streets of London, is arguably an example of this type.

The third type is more grievance-driven, appearing not to need a political or religious narrative. Rashad has worked with young Iraqis and Afghanis who have witnessed the horror of war and in some cases have seen their parents blown up by a drone. Such exposure to violence is often enough in itself to radicalise individuals. The final type is made up of people who belong to the 'other' camp – this can include those with mental health issues or young angry males who, in a different set of circumstances, could have ended up in criminal gangs.

Mental health and radicalisation are a growing area of interest. Some psychologists argue that radicalisation should be treated as a public health issue with clear risk factors identified that might lead a troubled individual towards violent action.[27] The criminal justice system deals with those already well advanced on the journey towards becoming a terrorist, but a public health approach would block the pathways to radicalisation earlier on. The best place to intervene successfully could be in the schools and college system.

> *Focusing counter-radicalisation interventions on secondary schools and centres of higher learning could reach a wide social group at a formative stage when many young people explore modes of engaging with 'radical' and alternative perspectives and many grapple with identity issues.*[28]

Asperger's Syndrome has been cited as a contributory factor in radicalisation. That is not to say, of course, that people suffering from this condition are more dangerous than the general population. But the subject has arisen in terror-related convictions and been used as a defence for the accused. Muslim convert Nicky Reilly, a twenty-two-year old from Plymouth, tried to detonate a bomb in the Giraffe restaurant in Exeter in 2008. Like many with Asperger's he had experienced a degree of social isolation but, after converting to Islam several years before his crime, he had felt accepted by the local Muslim community.

According to his mother at the trial, he was subsequently radicalised over the internet by two men in Pakistan. 'They were telling him how to make the bomb step by step,' she said.[29] Mercifully, the bombing attempt failed. But it posed the question, discussed in similar courtroom cases, as to what extent a radicalised individual living out a fantasy or truly engaging with reality has been brought to this mental state within the wider context of suffering from Asperger's. The initial grievance, like being bullied at school, can lead to attachment to an ideology like Islamism with tragic consequences.[30]

The realisation that mental health issues can influence this process has led to the NHS employing full-time staff to identify at-risk individuals as part of the Government's Prevent programme.[31]

There are, of course, sensitivities in this area, but many psychiatric professionals believe the refusal to recognise cross-vulnerabilities such as cultural isolation, depression and a confused sense of identity can lead somebody directly into the hands of a radicalising group.[32]

Prisons of the mind

Prisons are of growing concern as centres of radicalisation in the UK. In December 2015, the Prison Officers Association made the astonishing claim that Islamist extremists were deliberately seeking custodial punishments or jobs in prisons in order to radicalise prisoners.[33] Government advice to the prison service has been to distinguish between prisoners converting to Islam, which 'can reduce the likelihood of future offending,'[34] and those showing adherence to an extremist ideology that can have the opposite effect. In order to monitor this situation, prison chaplains have a very important role to play.

Ahmed (whose name we have changed) is a Muslim chaplain in his thirties who has ministered for a number of prisons over the past ten years. He memorised the entire Qur'an at the age of thirteen and holds both an MA and PhD in Islamic studies. The prisoners Ahmed works with have been convicted of Islamist-inspired terrorism offences. In 2015, there were 143 terrorist convicts in UK jails, of which 139 considered themselves to be Muslim.[35] Like Leila and Rashad, Ahmed is at the frontline of efforts to deradicalise those brainwashed by ISIS and other Islamist-related propaganda.

Over the past two years Ahmed has spent more time working in high-security jails. This has led to encounters with ten high-profile cases, including Michael Adebolajo and Michael Adebowale, the two men found guilty and convicted of the murder of Fusilier Lee Rigby in Woolwich in May 2013.[36] He has also come in contact with members of a jihadist gang in the Midlands convicted in 2013 of attempting to attack an English Defence League rally with swords, knives, guns and a homemade bomb. The bomb was made from fireworks, 359 nails and ninety-three ball bearings.[37]

His youngest case was nineteen-year-old Brusthom Ziamani. At the age of fifteen, this individual had become interested in Islam through the medium of rap music. By March 2014 he was ready to reject the Jehovah's Witness faith of his Congolese parents, which led to his being thrown out of the family home in Camberwell, south London. Homeless, he was taken in by the now-banned Islamist group al-Muhajiroun (ALM) and given clothes and a place to stay.[38]

An ITV News report claimed that Ziamani had been converted to Islam after a chance meeting with Michael Adebowale on Lewisham High Street in south London.[39] Adebowale handed him a leaflet and the impressionable youth began his ideological journey. He ended up idolising Adebowale's co-killer Adebolajo, describing him as a 'legend' and hoping one day to pose for the camera, holding up the head of a victim he had killed.[40]

The troubled young Ziamani had boasted to his girlfriend of what he intended to do and posted Facebook messages about hating non-believers and dreaming of martyrdom.[41] In a five-page letter to his parents, Ziamani gave a very clear insight into the mind of a young British jihadist from inner-city London. He began by quoting the Qur'an on 'Jihad holy fighting in Allah's cause' before asking his parents' forgiveness for the stress he had caused them. Ziamani then referred to his 'brothers and sisters' in Iraq and Syria being raped, killed and tortured – one grievance element in his radicalisation.

His sense of identity had clearly shifted from being a Congolese Jehovah's Witness. He now identified with people in the Middle East as part of his newly found global Muslim identity while failing to notice that ISIS was perpetrating the very crimes he had mentioned. As a warrior for Islam he would 'wage war against the British Government on this soil' because 'this is Islamic States of Ireland and Britain'. His letter then echoed a familiar threat, very similar to the words of Lee Rigby-killer Michael Adebolajo, that killing Britons would be revenge for the daily deaths of Muslims.

Kill every gay, every Shia, every Les [lesbian].

We should do a 9/11 and 7/7 and Woolwich all in one day everyday for 8 yrs to dz people n be a mujahid.[42]

Remarkably, Ziamani had been questioned on camera in May 2014 about his views by the far Right group Britain First, who posted the exchange on their website, showing his refusal to answer questions about his attitude to the Lee Rigby murder.[43] Just months later, Ziamani was arrested on an east London street with a 12-inch knife and a hammer in his rucksack. He was on his way to behead a British soldier.[44]

Ziamani was Ahmed's youngest case and the most resistant to change. Like the other young people discussed above, here was another teenager committed to extremism and violence, radicalised to a deeply disturbing degree. Yet he also displayed another trait found in these youngsters – a very basic grasp of theology.

> *He is adamant that his literal and extreme interpretation of Islam is right, yet he has so little knowledge of Islam, he doesn't know any Arabic and he's been actively trying to convert people to Islam, or his version of it, in prison.*[45]

Ahmed finds that all of these convicts have a fundamental misunderstanding of Islam's religious texts. Their ideology is based on scripture but it is a selective or literal rendition to justify murder and ultra-violence. They skim the surface of Islam, fishing out what they need but never going deeper to really understand their faith. This distortion of Islam is more potent as an influence to action than western foreign policy. Ahmed says:

> *Adebolajo told me in prison straight up that killing Lee Rigby wasn't about killing him per se, but what Rigby represents, but he justified his actions on a twisted ideological worldview. He justified his actions using the*

> *Qur'an. The reality is that a toxic misunderstanding*
> *of theology has more to do with it than foreign policy.*
> *Ziamani, for example, wanted to kill because he thought*
> *he'd get a reward in the hereafter.*

Converts to Islam appear more likely to be vulnerable to extremist Islamist ideologies. One view is that some converts are vulnerable because their families often abandon them when they become Muslims, as happened to Ziamani, and they may not be accepted into mainstream mosques that can have strong ethnic affiliations. The resulting isolation makes them vulnerable to extremist influencers,[46] with radicalisation occurring as they search for identity and meaning.

Many conversions happen behind bars; the European Union's counter-terrorism coordinator Gilles de Kerchove has described prisons as 'a massive incubator for radicalisation'.[47] This could in part explain why converts have accounted for 31 per cent of jihadist terrorist convictions in the UK from 2001 to 2010, despite representing only 2–3 per cent of all Britain's 2.8 million Muslims.[48] However, many converts drawn into terrorism have no criminal background at all.

Converts and moral realignment

A similar phenomenon has been noted in the United States, where a quarter of those convicted between 1997 and 2011 of al-Qa'ida-related offences were converts. Women played a more prominent role among the converts than the non-converts, who were 97 per cent male. And converts tended to be older than non-converts.[49]

There have been many high-profile converts in the UK who have either been accused or convicted of terrorist offences. These include Samantha Lewthwaite,[50] known as the 'White Widow', who was married to Germaine Lindsay, one of the London 7/7 suicide bombers – himself another convert. February 2016 saw a group of Walsall-based converts in the headlines, as four were convicted of terrorist offences while two others had been killed in Syria and another two were still there fighting for ISIS.[51] The group included Lorna Moore, aged thirty-three, who was a trainee maths teacher brought up as a Protestant in Northern Ireland. She was married to a former supply teacher turned jihadist called Sajid Aslam, who was already in Syria. It emerged during the trial that she had complained about being treated like a slave by her husband, but was told by local Muslim leaders she would 'go to hell' if she left him. The couple had met as students at Manchester Metropolitan University in 2000, but by 2007 their stormy relationship had even led her to call in the police.[52]

Other converts have included Andrew Ibrahim, convicted in 2009 of plotting to blow up Bristol town centre. In court, he was painted as an isolated and rather odd figure 'who could only communicate with his mother through a teddy bear' and lived in a fantasy world.[53] Thomas Evans, aged twenty-five, died fighting with al-Shabaab in Somalia, with his mother reduced to identifying his body on Twitter. In his last conversation with her, Evans said if he did not come back 'I'll be in paradise.'[54]

One of the most curious converts has been Kent woman Sally Jones, who was previously the lead singer in an all-girl rock band and reputedly interested in black magic and witchcraft. In 2013 she converted to Islam and travelled to Syria with her ten-year-old son to join jihadist Junaid Hussain, whom she had met online and later married.[55] He was a leading ISIS computer hacker until his death in an airstrike in August 2015.

Jones tweeted in August 2014:

Alhamdulillah me and my husband made it to the Islamic State after being stuck in Idlib [in north-western Syria] for 7mths & are now living in the khilafah #isis...[56]

She informed her Twitter followers how much she enjoyed living under ISIS's interpretation of sharia law while also promoting hatred of Jews, Christians and the West. One tweet referenced the ghoulish execution site in Raqqa, Syria, where heads are put on public display.

You Christians all need beheading with a nice blunt knife and stuck on the railings at raqqa.... Come here and I will do it for you.[57]

A substantial number of people Rashad Ali has worked with are converts. He says they go through a moral realignment encompassing everything in life. It is not a case of merely changing their religion; converts are fundamentally altering their whole way of life, which can make them vulnerable to extremist propaganda. As they restructure and reassess their identity, some become more open to this kind of messaging.

Reasons for radicalism?

As a migrant to Britain the Muslim prison chaplain Ahmed has been shocked at the extent and spread of Islamist ideologies in the UK, and is concerned about the general ease of access to extreme and ultra-conservative interpretations of Islam. He witnesses a version of Islam in the UK which is often characterised by literal, decontextualised and puritanical teachings regularly being promoted in faith institutions and by numerous Muslim organisations.

Ahmed recalls arriving in the UK from the African continent and his initial shock at the number of preachers promoting hate-filled and extreme views. His first experience of a mosque was in London at a place of worship heavily orientated towards the ultra-conservative Sunni ideology Salafism. He had gone there for Friday prayers in the early 1990s and afterwards joined other worshippers for lunch.

They served massive portions of chicken and rice, the food was great but then I found myself being invited to take part in some classes that were taking place in the basement. They were literally training people how to fight, how to prepare for jihad. I found it shocking. One minute you're eating chicken, next minute you're being taught how to use a knife as a weapon.

Ahmed acknowledges improvements in Muslims' places of worship. He spoke at a mosque in Luton recently and was pleased to see that they have now enforced a mandatory requirement to employ an English-speaking imam, and that the Friday sermon, or *khutbah*, often takes on the challenge of ISIS. It would help if more *khutbahs* deconstructed the ways in which extremists use religious texts to legitimise violent ends. It is not enough to say that Islam is a religion of peace when clearly some are using the theological building blocks to justify war.

Some mosques have been filmed promoting extreme views, which has led to them being accused of playing a key role in the radicalisation of some Muslims. However, many mosques are largely not to blame for radicalisation but neither do they necessarily provide the solutions. The reality is that they simply do not wield enough influence over young Muslims, who often go online to find the answers they seek. As a result, the mosque of YouTube becomes more important than the bricks-and-mortar mosque in their neighbourhood.

This is a dangerous situation. If young people felt they could turn to the local mosque for answers, they might not be sucked into a radicalising vortex on social media. Ahmed believes that mosques could play a much bigger role in building resilience among young people and deepening their knowledge of Islam. Otherwise these people are exposed to preachers of varying merit on YouTube and the risk that, through social media, a radicaliser will groom them.

Leila, Rashad and Ahmed are working with those who have gone down the track of being radicalised. But the exact process involved is open to plenty of academic and expert interpretation and dispute. Some believe the overriding factors are poverty and social deprivation feeding a grievance against western society. The French economist, author and commentator Thomas Piketty pointed to the lack of life opportunities for first- and second-generation immigrants living in the unequal societies of the Middle East and the housing estates of the *banlieues* circling French cities. In this commentator's view, reducing inequality in the West and the Arab world would stem recruitment to ISIS.[58]

However, this brushes over the fact that many convicted terrorists and those who have fled to Syria come from well-educated and middle-class backgrounds, maybe more so in the UK than France. Far from being socially deprived, they have had comfortable lifestyles and have often progressed their studies to university. As several academics have noted, the correlation between poverty and terrorism is actually quite weak. So simply improving living standards or educational attainment may not result in the hoped-for reduction in terrorism.

Foreign policy is another reason given for young Muslims being radicalised. After the Lee Rigby attack, *Guardian* journalist Seumas Milne – now the Labour Party's executive director of strategy – wrote that the Woolwich murder was 'blowback' for US and UK interventions in the Arab and Muslim world. His view was that the 'terror war' abroad being waged by the West had brought bloodshed to the streets of London.[59]

Milne went on to state that the attack was not terrorism in the normal sense of an indiscriminate attack on civilians, because Rigby had taken part in multiple combat operations in Afghanistan. Milne described the UK Government's response to the Rigby murder as 'deceitful inanities' in the context of a decade of 'mass slaughter, torture, kidnapping and destruction across the Muslim world'.[60]

He has set out in other articles a prevalent view among many in the mainstream Left that ISIS is not just an accidental bi-product of military action by the West in the Middle East. Milne previously cited a 2012 secret US intelligence report that countenanced a 'Salafist principality' in eastern Syria. Milne does not assert that the UK and US directly created ISIS but that it exploited the existence of the group against other forces in the region. Essentially, he sees ISIS as fitting into an imperialist project of classic divide and rule.[61]

However, when it comes to the radicalisation of individual Muslims in the UK, grievance over foreign policy is not enough to explain the appeal of ISIS or al-Qa'ida. Positive buy-in to an ideology is also required, according to practitioners who work with those who have drifted into or are close to terrorism. There has to be a belief system present that legitimises and necessitates violence to make somebody murder in cold blood or blow themselves up.

Ideology and identity

That belief system may not be very sophisticated. Teenagers lured by ISIS might not be fluent in the history and evolution of jihadist doctrine, an example being Brusthom Ziamani mentioned above. They may know nothing about the Islamist foundations of extremist groups. As Peter Neumann, director of the International Centre for the Study of Radicalisation and Political Violence, states, what they will have been exposed to are the key ideas that the West is at war with Islam and they have a religious obligation to defend their Muslim 'brothers and sisters'.[62]

Intertwined with ideology is the whole question of identity. Those British Muslims undergoing radicalisation not only adopt a belief system, they essentially redefine who and what they are. They become something they had not been before. This new identity allows them to transform, as they see it, into a true Muslim. This can result in rejection of family, something that most Muslims would find un-Islamic. It can mean refusing to mix with non-Muslims and adopting a supremacist attitude towards them. Crucially, they come to feel that it is impossible to belong in Britain because their religious and national identities cannot be reconciled.[63]

The next step is to join or support an Islamist organisation, which may or may not advocate violence. There will be a period where the individual is exposed to the movement's ideas and may look at other groups. 'Only when an individual is convinced that the group represents the "true" version of Islam is he or she likely to join,' according to one scholar.[64] Many individuals go through this process without actually deepening their understanding of Islam. Those involved in deradicalisation are often struck by the shallowness of religious thought that they find in their subjects. It is almost as if they have picked up the basics of Islam as they have gone along.

Two British men from Birmingham – Mohammed Ahmed and Yusuf Sarwar – were arrested, tried and convicted for terrorism offences after flying out to Syria to join an al-Qa'ida affiliate, then deciding to return to the UK in January 2014. Before going to Syria they had bought *Islam for Dummies* and *The Koran for Dummies*.[65] This theological ignorance has been noted for a while. An MI5 report leaked to *The Guardian* in 2008 found that many involved in Islamist-inspired terrorism were 'religious novices' – as well as some being converts still wrestling with an understanding of their new faith.[66]

This does not mean, as one commentator suggested, that faith-based ideology has nothing to do with terrorism.[67] It means that the ideology takes root when an individual's grasp of Islam is deficient. One study of UK and US female jihadists in 2015 found that the women were driven in part by religious ideals but with a very narrow understanding of Islam. Being against the West was seen as a litmus test of the strength of their faith – a measure of authenticity.[68]

They wanted to erase their western identities. Democracy was rejected in favour of a utopian caliphate. Being friends with non-Muslims was seen as a violation of Qur'anic teachings. And a special hatred was reserved for those Muslims who were not prepared to support warlike jihad. These women were not interested in engaging thoughtfully with Islamic religious texts and the complexity of interpretations. What they yearned for was clear-cut explanations.

In its recruitment activities, ISIS has also recognised that its Muslim recruitment targets often have conflicted identities. They have been exposed to an enormous range of western, consumerist material. While rejecting the West, ISIS produces propaganda material in video and disseminated online that frequently resembles Hollywood action movies or video games. As one article put it, ISIS says to young western Muslims:

Come to Iraq and Syria and play out the same violent acts you fantasise over while playing Call of Duty, or Grand Theft Auto, and terrorise those who have bullied and discriminated against you in high school.[69]

Research by the Brooking Institution found that ISIS had released 845 audiovisual campaigns between January 2014 and September 2015, promoted through more than 46,000 Twitter accounts. At least 15 per cent of the film material took direct inspiration from real movies and games. Through its different media production arms – Al Furqan, Al I'tissam and Al Hayat – ISIS is producing specific cultural products aimed directly at different global audiences, essentially making terrorism look cool.[70] It has tapped into the hybrid identity of many young Muslims with one foot in their Islamic heritage and another in the world of modern pop culture.

Central to the ISIS and Islamist approach is a drive to divorce Muslims from loyalty to the nation state they live in and supplant that with loyalty to the 'caliphate'. This remoulding of identity through ideology is key to recruitment success.

The ISIS brand projects territorial integrity and genuine statehood. The reality is a territory in a state of constant war with ill-defined boundaries and a failure to provide basic services to the populations under its control. Millions of Syrians have fled the war zones while, at the same time, hundreds of British Muslims have gone in the opposite direction. For those potential British recruits who might have been given pause for thought by the sight of three-year-old Aylan Kurdi, a Syrian refugee found drowned on a beach, ISIS offered up an explanation. Its online magazine *Dabiq* warned that this was the well-deserved fate for Syrian Muslims who flee with their children to infidel lands.[71]

Grievance does not inevitably lead to radicalisation. Plenty of Muslims feel deeply about the suffering of people in the Middle East without needing recourse to terrorism. They may get involved in humanitarian or charitable programmes instead. But young people like Muneera, engaged in a quest for answers bound up with a questioning of their own identity, move towards a belief in the need to strike out against an enemy they come to believe is bent on destroying Islam.

That enemy is invariably 'the West', but can also include governments in Muslim countries they believe have betrayed their religion. In order to view the world in these dogmatic terms, young people like Muneera must have been exposed to one crucial ingredient: ideology. Not everybody accepts the idea that ideology underpins terrorism. Some argue that the actions of ISIS or al-Qa'ida have nothing to do with faith-based belief and that their motivation is socio-economic or purely political. To those people, terrorism is just a methodology with no underlying belief system – simply a grievance-based attack on the West. But intervention providers working directly with individuals who have drifted towards terrorism find that grievance alone is not enough to create a terrorist. Ideology is required too.

Faith-based ideology gives a minority of Muslims the direction and motivation to make a decisive leap into violent activity. The evidence for this is the propaganda output from ISIS, which is laced with Qur'anic references and appeals to scripture. The appeal to join them is framed with references to *hijra* and jihad. It is a twisting of Islam to suit a purpose. Critically, it relies on its subjects having a fairly superficial understanding of Islam but enough to land their key messages. This use of faith, even at a simplistic and crude level, is what has lured several hundred British Muslims to Iraq and Syria.

The reason some young people in Britain find the ISIS ideology attractive is in part based on the discourse that has developed within British Islam in recent years. To understand why hundreds have left these shores for Syria, one has to examine the kind of arguments and assertions that have become common currency in Muslim communities.

TWO

BRITISH SALAFISTS AND ISLAMISTS: THE GROWING CONVERGENCE

Throughout the 1990s, two ideological strands competed for the loyalty of young British Muslims looking for a globalised Islamic identity: Islamism and Salafism. The former operated more like a political party advocating a caliphate governed by sharia law; the latter called for a return to the traditions and teachings of the first three generations of Muslims during and after the time of the Prophet. They both spurned the notion of integration into British society, offering instead an identity based entirely on faith. But they were to a large extent in opposition to each other.

The student scene was a notable battleground. Salafists and Islamists competed to recruit the best young talent among Muslim students, and there were constant tussles to seize control of college Islamic student societies. Denunciatory pamphlets and leaflets were widely circulated. It was a regular occurrence for one side to tear down posters for the other's events. Frequently, Salafist meetings would be disrupted by Islamists, or vice versa. Speakers were aggressively barracked. Confrontations were expected and violence was by no means unknown.

Throughout the 1990s, the main Islamist groups in the UK were Hizb ut-Tahrir (HT), the Muslim Brotherhood (MB) and Jamaat-e-Islami influenced groups, while JIMAS (Jamiat Ihyaa Minhaaj al-Sunnah – a UK-based Muslim charity) once dominated the Salafist scene. In the years after the 1989 Salman Rushdie affair, both Islamism and Salafism grew in strength and influence, particularly among Muslim youth and students. There was not much love lost between the groups as they disrupted each other's meetings and crowded out other Muslim organisations.

British Islamists

Islamism is essentially politicised Islam – but it is not synonymous with Islam. It is a relatively modern movement that seeks to revive an Islamic global political order, a caliphate in other words. Islamists see no distinction between religion and politics. Islam for them is as much a political guide to action as an article of faith. Sharia law will govern the society they struggle for, and non-Muslims will be reduced to the status of *dhimmi* ('protected people'), paying the *jizya* (a special tax).

Islamists can employ the language of civil rights, multiculturalism and even equality to win over audiences or neutralise opposition. This is part of a multi-stage, long-term strategy to reach the goal of achieving Dar al-Islam (state under Islamic rule). In the 1950s the founder of Hizb ut-Tahrir, Taqiuddin al-Nabhani, made clear in a series of works what an Islamist-controlled society would look like. A caliph would control the state. All male Muslims over fifteen would undergo military training for jihad. The role of a woman would be as mother and wife, and the sexes would be segregated. Education would be about the forming of the Islamic personality and nothing else.[1]

Islamism was born out of the trauma of modern history.[2] The past 200 years are perceived as having been a record of failure since the British and French carved up Muslim-majority territories and shared these acquisitions between them. The task is to build on new foundations a polity based on Islamic principles. Getting there might involve gradual Islamisation or violent upheaval – or a mixture of both.[3] This is reminiscent of the twentieth-century debates among socialists about the relative merits of reform or revolution.

Prominent groups in the UK that can be placed under the Islamist umbrella are: Hizb ut-Tahrir (the Islamic Liberation Party); al-Muhajiroun (ALM) (The Emigrants); Muslim Brotherhood-affiliated groups; and Jamaat-e-Islami-inspired groups. HT has been banned from university campuses and over the years has operated under different names, such as the One Nation Society, Islamic Society, Muslim Women's Cultural Forum, Debating Society, Millennium Society, 1924 Committee, International Affairs Society and Dialogue with Islam.[4]

As regards ISIS's declaration of a caliphate in Syria and Iraq, HT believes that declaring a caliphate is an obligation on all Muslims, but thinks that the ISIS version lacks the 'required components of the state'.[5] A similar position is held by many other Islamists and politically inclined Salafists.

Al-Muhajiroun (ALM) is now an organisation proscribed by the Government. It has thrown up several front organisations to try to keep operating, including Islam4UK, banned in 2010 after it planned a demonstration at Wootton Bassett, a town in Wiltshire where crowds often gathered to welcome home the war dead flown in from the battle zones of Iraq and Afghanistan.[6] Anjem Choudary has been the standard bearer for the successor organisations to ALM since Omar Bakri left the UK in 2005.

Raffaello Pantucci, a prominent researcher into and commentator on radicalisation and security issues, estimates that individuals who have passed through ALM have been linked to twenty-three out of fifty-one terror plots carried out or intercepted by the UK police in a twenty-year period up to 2015. This includes the murder of Lee Rigby, a plot to blow up planes with liquid bombs, and a planned attack on the Ministry of Sound nightclub.[7]

Islamist groups had been present in the UK since the 1960s, but from the late 1980s faced 'a significant challenge for community support from militant Salafists who had returned to the UK after fighting in Afghanistan and regarded the Brotherhood as ineffective'.[8] In spite of this unwelcome onslaught from co-religionists, the MB continued to influence Islam in the UK by helping to set up or shape representative bodies such as the Muslim Association of Britain and the Muslim Council of Britain. The latter body was often consulted by the Government during the Tony Blair years until 2009, when dialogue was suspended over an MCB office-holder signing a declaration that appeared to condone violence against UK armed forces if deemed necessary in support of Gaza.[9]

Salafism in the UK

Salafism originated as an ideology within Islam in the late nineteenth century. Like Islamism, it was another revivalist movement believing that Muslims had to be 'purified' from historical, cultural and legalistic influences that had accrued over the centuries. Its members were prepared to throw out a whole mass of medieval and modern jurisprudence to get back to what they believed was the original message of the Prophet.

The name of this theological movement comes from *as-salaf as-saliheen*, meaning the pious predecessors or the first generation of Muslims including the direct followers of the Prophet. Salafists believe the faith is not being practised as it should be, and has been subjected to sinful *bida* (innovation).[10] Unlike Islamists, Salafists define themselves wholly through theology as opposed to calling themselves a 'political party', as HT styles itself. They seek to emulate the first three generations of Muslims so they wear Saudi-style *thobe* robes, emphasise their knowledge of scripture and Arabic, and implement strict social and moral codes.

The nineteenth-century founders of Salafism were not necessarily opposed to western ideas. Rejecting medieval jurisprudence opened up the possibility of introducing modern concepts into Islamic thought. But, instead, a puritanical rendition of Salafism has gradually taken hold, reducing it to a series of dogmas for which the founders were not responsible.

Salafism is broadly split in three ways today. First there are 'quietists' who withdraw entirely from politics and believe Muslims should focus on prayer and piety while being obedient to whoever rules their land. Then, political Salafists, who in effect drift closer to Islamism by getting involved in elections – an example is the al-Nour movement in Egypt.[11] Third, there are the jihadist-Salafists who encompass ISIS and al-Qaʻida. Advocating violent jihad against non-believers, they also regularly engage in *takfir*, that is, excommunicating other Muslims from the faith and classifying them as apostates.[12] While they are not the only Muslim group to engage in *takfir*, their willingness to execute and persecute those they excommunicate is a distinctively appalling trait.

A group called JIMAS, founded in 1984 by Abu Muntasir, spearheaded the spread of Salafism in the UK. JIMAS stood for the Jamiat Ihyaa Minhaaj al-Sunnah (Movement of the Revival of the Prophet's Way) and Abu Muntasir was dubbed the 'godfather of Salafism'.

The same year saw the launch of The Young Muslims UK by Jamaat-e-Islami influenced groups. But many British Muslims found it to be too 'liberal' in comparison with the energetic Salafism of JIMAS. The latter leading Salafist organisation was able to attract 5,000 people to its yearly annual conferences during the 1990s. These were normally held in Leicester where entire families attended gender-segregated events.[13] JIMAS nurtured a generation of preachers, some of whom are now the leading lights in British Salafism.

Abu Muntasir lived, breathed and fought for this puritanical ideological movement; he was even prepared to die for it, having waged jihad in the 1980s and 1990s fighting in Afghanistan, Kashmir, Burma, Bosnia and Chechnya.[14] In conversation during the writing of this book, he held up a picture of a younger Abu Muntasir, in boots and full combat gear sternly staring into the camera: 'I had just returned from Kashmir.'

The jihadist speakers given a platform by JIMAS inspired some young British Muslims to leave these shores for violent jihad overseas, something Abu Muntasir now bitterly regrets. It reduces the imam to tears when he considers the consequences for those who were swept up in the excitement of a jihadi variant of Salafism to the extent that they left to take up arms with al-Qaʻida or the Taliban.

Abu Muntasir eventually came to reject violent jihad after personally witnessing bloody in-fighting between rival Muslim groups and realising that local people in places like Afghanistan and Kashmir did not want foreign jihadists interfering in their affairs, a point many Syrians themselves have also stated in recent years. Today, JIMAS is a much reduced, non-jihadist organisation doing valuable work with converts and fostering inter-faith dialogue.

The coming together

In the 1990s, Islamists and Salafists went toe-to-toe fighting for recruits among those British Muslims searching for a Muslim identity that differed from that of their parents. They offered globalised ideologies that seemed purer and more authentic. As early as the mid-1990s, studies analysed the situation of younger Muslims struggling to define their mixed British and Muslim identity, with mosques seemingly unable to provide much-needed answers.

> *What you find is that a lot of mosques are culturally led. They are more interested in keeping ties of kinship and traditional values. This excludes the youth who follow in their footsteps. Many young Muslims have a dual identity. They are Muslims, but they are also British, with the British identity being more predominant. Their issues are not being addressed by most of the mosques.*[15]

Traditional ties of family and community were loosening, and individuals were becoming open to new ideas about their faith.[16] Of course, many Muslims were happy to reconcile their religion with their nationality. But others joined organisations and moved in circles where they were exposed to ultra-conservative and literalist interpretations of Islam that rejected British identity, democracy, the concept of human rights, gender equality and tolerance. These groups did not necessarily endorse terrorism, but they drove a wedge between Islam and Britishness.

HT, JIMAS and others jostled for the best talent to win over.

But, after 9/11, the dynamic between Islamists and Salafists changed dramatically. Competition between the two ideological strands began to give way to cooperation in the first years of the new millennium. At the London Central Mosque, Regent's Park, Salafists and Islamists started to meet every month under the auspices of something called the 'London Forum'. Members of Hizb ut-Tahrir sat alongside Salafists and Muslim Brotherhood types and discussed how to formulate a strategy to communicate their common objectives.[17]

In the 1990s Usama Hasan was a leading Salafist activist in JIMAS, freshly returned from military training and fighting in Afghanistan against the Soviets. His journey from jihadist to counter-extremist was recognised ten years ago when he was interviewed by BBC TV's *Hardtalk* programme on how Muslims could reject the politics of hate.[18] He attended London Forum meetings around 2002 to 2004 and believes that the post-9/11 'War on Terror' forced Salafists and Islamists into each other's arms. 'Hizb ut-Tahrir, Muslim Brotherhood, Salafists and even Islamist-inclined Sufis were coming together for the first time,' he says.[19]

These ideologues viewed the War on Terror as a war on Islam that necessitated a robust response. Surveys of Muslims at this time gave mixed signals for this emerging convergence of groups. On the one hand, most Muslims in the UK still felt patriotic about Britain – not welcome news for Islamists – but over half did not believe al-Qa'ida should be blamed for 9/11, while over a third had suffered hostility and abuse since the World Trade Center had been attacked.[20] So a ratcheting-up of tension in Muslim communities and a feeling of being under pressure among Salafists and Islamists gave impetus to this new willingness to cooperate.

Then came the 7/7 bombings in London – which Usama Hasan describes as 'our 9/11'. The revelation that those involved included Yorkshire-born British Muslims brought the media magnifying glass down on every Muslim. In response, reconciled voices set up groups to campaign against terrorist radicalisation and extremist ideology and to promote an identity that melded Britishness and Islam. Usama Hasan sums up the mood among many who were fed up with groups like al-Muhajiroun hogging the media limelight with their provocative demonstrations against the West and democracy:

It was time to speak up and speak out.

Groups promoting a reconciled Muslim civil society, like British Muslims for Secular Democracy, Radical Middle Way and Faith Matters, came into being between 2005 and 2008. Hasan believes the emergence of these groups riled the Islamists and Salafists who, taking more of their coordination online, began a fresh initiative called the Comms Group. Through it they set up new bodies and projects to push back and further their ideological positions. Hasan thinks they were motivated by a combination of strength and weakness. Within British Muslim communities, they realised that, operating in union, they could be very strong and influential. There was a job of work to be done in shoring up their ideological position and reaching out to impressionable young Muslims.

This led to a combination of previously existing organisations and the creation of new ones. Among the Islamists were Hizb ut-Tahrir and various Muslim Brotherhood-inspired organisations, while on the Salafist side emerged proselytising organisations like the Muslim Research and Development Foundation (MRDF) and the Islamic Education and Research Academy (iERA). The MRDF operated an online news service called Islam21c and the newly cooperative Salafists and Islamists received further editorial backing from a news site called 5Pillars. The most potent addition to the mix came from the formation in 2003 of CAGE Prisoners (later just called CAGE), an 'advocacy' organisation led by former Guantanamo detainee Moazzam Begg after his release in 2005. This network of groups has become a powerful influence on the discourse among British Muslims over the past five years. Together they have a formidable and powerful voice that was never theirs to command when they were divided.

Banned from speaking? Share a platform

On the Islamist side, Hizb ut-Tahrir has been around since 1986 in the UK, agitating for a global caliphate. The radical preacher Omar Bakri Muhammed – who often hit the headlines for making inflammatory remarks – set it up but departed ten years later to establish the now-banned al-Muhajiroun.

In the 1990s HT was a major fixture on university campuses and by 2003 could still attract 8,000 people to its annual conference in Birmingham. But by then its actual membership was estimated to be only about 500 across the UK.[21] In spite of its stagnation in recent years, HT is seen as having played a central role in defining Islamist ideology.

The organisation has not openly advocated terrorism in the UK as a means to creating a caliphate, so the Government has not banned it. However, since the mid-1990s HT has been regularly 'no platformed' (i.e., put on a list of people or organisations banned from addressing meetings) by the National Union of Students (NUS), on the grounds that HT has been sexist, racist and homophobic. (In 1998, when the Committee of Vice Chancellors and Principals of the Universities had consulted thirty-two colleges over complaints from Muslim, Sikh and Jewish students, the overwhelming majority reported intimidation by HT members.)[22]

The organisation is hostile to any talk of British Islam. Dr Abdul Wahid is the current chairman of the HT executive committee in Britain. He has poured scorn on the notion of a reconciled Muslim and British identity as a 'desire to twist Islam to make it conform to secular liberal values'.[23] He had an interesting take on the *Charlie Hebdo* killings in January 2015, when Islamist terrorists gunned down journalists over a cartoon depiction of the Prophet. Wahid argued that, if Muslim governments had taken diplomatic action or cut trade relations over earlier insults to the Prophet, the gunmen would not have felt 'the frustration to retaliate'.[24] In July 2015, as the Prime Minister David Cameron unveiled a counter-extremism strategy in Birmingham, Wahid told the *Guardian* newspaper that the word 'extremist' was just a secular term for 'heretic'.[25]

In that interview, Wahid asserted there was no provable link between extremist opinions and terrorism. When asked if he believed in democracy, Wahid replied that the 'caliphate we want to see is one where a ruler would be elected, accountable, not above the law'. He was then asked to comment on women being screened off from men at HT meetings and replied that it was no worse than the BBC broadcasting a programme (*Woman's Hour* on Radio 4) that was just for women.

In a 2014 article HT's media representative Taji Mustafa alleged that the schools inspectorate Ofsted was a Government tool for forcing Muslim children to adopt secular liberal values in relation to sexuality, gender relationships and supporting British troops abroad.[26] Mustafa and Wahid headlined an HT event in June 2013 after the killing of the British soldier Lee Rigby by Michael Adebolajo and Michael Adebowale. At that meeting, Wahid attacked those Muslims who had condemned the killers – especially for denying them their Islamic identity.

> First it was apologies, then condemnations and then some went further to make takfir on the perpetrators... The least we as Muslims should have done was ask Allah to forgive them for their mistakes, not call them kafir... So the secularists and moderates amongst the Muslim community went further and made takfir on the Woolwich perpetrators and began showing their support for British troops.[27]

The venue for HT's June 2013 meeting was the Waterlily, a two-hall space-for-hire in east London. Five months later, in November, it hosted one of the first major appearances of Salafists and Islamists on the same platform. The occasion was titled 'Freedom of Speech – are Muslims Excluded?' Wahid shared the stage with the then-president of the Federation of Student Islamic Societies (FOSIS), Omar Ali (in office 2012–2014). FOSIS presumably saw no issue with appearing alongside Hizb ut-Tahrir, in spite of the National Union of Students having no-platformed the organisation for nearly twenty years. The no-platform is still in place, meaning every student union affiliated to the NUS is obliged to deny HT a platform because of its extremist views.[28]

Within the National Union of Students, FOSIS is now a commanding presence at the annual conference, the biggest voting bloc by far. It accounts for about a quarter of the conference floor. A Government report on the Prevent strategy in 2011 noted that FOSIS had not 'always fully challenged terrorist and extremist ideology within the higher and further education sectors'.[29] The report urged FOSIS to make a 'clear and unequivocal position against extremism and terrorism'. It also recommended that FOSIS work closer with the National Union of Students.

That is already happening, but not with the results the Government might have intended. One NUS source claims privately that FOSIS is arguably the best-organised faction in the student movement and is flexing its voting muscle already.[30] Omar Ali anticipated this when he once said 'We have a large student bloc – we need to start using that power.' In 2016, that power contributed to the election of the first Muslim president of the NUS, Malia Bouattia, who has openly called for the dismantling of the Government's counter-terrorism strategy, Prevent.[31]

New best friends

1. Haitham al-Haddad

Proof of the new-found amity between Salafists and Islamists was the presence of the UK's leading Salafist preacher, Haitham al-Haddad, at the November 2013 Waterlily event. He was, until recently, the chairman and trustee of the Muslim Research and Development Foundation (MRDF), which has effectively displaced JIMAS as the main Salafist organisation in the UK. Haddad bases his religious authority on having studied theology for over twenty years under a former Grand Mufti of Saudi Arabia, among others, and his doctoral thesis was on Islamic jurisprudence.

The Islam21c online news website (200,000-plus followers on Facebook in April 2016) was operated by MRDF directly until September 2009, when it was spun off.[32] Haddad writes regularly for the site, which toes a Salafi-Islamist editorial line. Haddad has also been a judge on the UK's Islamic Sharia Council based in east London, dispensing rulings on areas like family law and divorce.[33]

Several universities have been urged to ban him from speaking on campus on account of his controversial views. Thousands of people signed a petition in early 2015 to stop him addressing the Islamic student society at the University of Westminster because of his strident opposition to homosexuality.[34] The University of Kent also blocked him on similar grounds after a last-minute intervention by the Vice-Chancellor.[35]

The reasons cited for these slammed doors are normally Haddad's views on gay people, whom he regards as a 'scourge'.[36] There is also his endorsement of female genital mutilation (FGM) as a religious requirement, even though this is illegal in the UK.[37] Media reporting of these remarks (after he was allowed to speak at London's School of Oriental and African Studies in 2014)[38] led the Islam21c site to claim that an attack on his FGM views was an attempt to 'dehumanise' and 'demonise' all Muslims.[39]

Haddad wants Islam throughout 'the whole world', with the enforcing under sharia legal conditions of *hudood* punishments. These would include stoning for adultery and the judicial murder of apostates.[40] The *deen* (religion/belief) of Allah would be 'superior above any other *deen*... superior to any other system... any law other than the law of Allah is invalid'. He repeated this message to students at a Queen Mary University Islamic Society dinner in 2010.[41]

At a press conference in Norway in 2012, when asked about stoning as a punishment, he said it made perfect sense to him from an orthodox Islamic perspective but was obviously not a reality now in Europe. 'I have never said that the adulterers or adulteresses have to be stoned in the UK or in Britain or in Norway or in any European country.'[42]

But a female journalist asked if it was true he was striving to have sharia law in Europe, at which time stoning could then be carried out. Haddad replied that 'once we apply Islam within the correct framework, it works perfectly', adding that some elements of Islam may look odd in isolation to non-believers but, as with pieces in a mosaic, once they were added the appearance of the whole was beautiful.

In an interview on Huda TV – a channel 'promoting the message of Islam'[43] – Haddad called for 'Islamisation of the whole globe'. He was then pressed by the interviewer on whether support for multiculturalism was really about a takeover by Islam: 'Really it's not about multiculturalism,' suggested the interviewer, 'it's about getting Islam into the door.' Haddad could not have made his ultimate goal clearer – it certainly had nothing to do with building a pluralist society:

> *Even if we say that, what's wrong with that? Because this is our aim at the end of the day... Our ultimate aim is not a matter of "taking over" using this terminology, our ultimate aim as Muslims is to have, to see Islam spreading all over the world and to see the word of Allah dominant on the whole globe, because justice will never be achieved unless the word of Allah is dominant.*[44]

And on the precise detail of how Britain will be integrated into the caliphate:

> *But we still have a long way to be the Islamic Republic of Britain. Even if it becomes the Islamic Republic of Britain... khilafah will not just happen all of a sudden. We have to prepare for it... let us imagine an Islamic state, Britain will become an Islamic state, let us imagine this. How is it going to become an Islamic state? Means the Prime Minister will be a Muslim. So how will he be Muslim? So at one point you will say Muslims should be MPs and PM... in*

*European countries the change takes place through so-called
democratic process whether we like it or we don't like it, we
hate it.*[45]

2. Abdur Raheem Green

Another leading Salafist preacher at the November 2013 Waterlily
event was Abdur Raheem Green, head of the *da'wa* (proselytising)
organisation iERA. Usama Hasan says the new convergence of
Islamists and Salafists has given this organisation a particular boost
(140,000 followers on Facebook in April 2016). Its distinctive flavour
derives from the fact that iERA was set up in 2009 by three Muslim
converts: Abdur Raheem Green, Yusuf Chambers and Hamza
Tzortzis. Tzortzis was a former member of Hizb ut-Tahrir, while
Green was once a colleague of Abu Muntasir, sitting on the ruling
body or *shura* of JIMAS. iERA places a particular emphasis on taking
the Salafi-Islamist message to a wider public.

This tactic has been described as 'soft Islamism', whereby Islamist
values and norms are promoted through dialogue. The Council of Ex-
Muslims of Britain has called iERA the 'Islamist movement's public
relations arm'.[46] Soft Islamism uses the language of diversity and inter-
faith outreach and of appearing to endorse multiculturalism.

Throughout 2015 iERA organised a series of debates under a
campaign title 'Don't Hate/Debate'. One event was titled 'Is Islam the
Cause or Solution to Extremism?'[47] The panel included the human
rights campaigner Peter Tatchell, who decided to test the limits of
what could actually be discussed. He invited the iERA representative
and others on the panel to specifically condemn capital punishment
for adultery, homosexuality and apostasy.[48] The resulting uproar from
members of the panel and audience made it clear that the debate was
to be contained within a narrow framing.

Abdur Raheem Green, or Anthony Vatswaf Galvin Green as he
was once known before his conversion, was born in Dar es Salaam,
Tanzania in 1964 to a Polish mother and a father he once described as
a 'colonial administrator in the British Empire'. Green was educated
at a Catholic private school, Ampleforth College, which was run by

Benedictine monks. His father lived in Cairo for a while and it was during a visit to his house that the young Green saw one of the servants praying – an image that left a mark. In the late 1980s he converted to Islam, and he is now a leading voice in UK Salafism.

He has advocated a Muslim state where Jews and Christians will be able to practise their faith but will have to pay a tax called the *jizya* 'to make the Jew and the Christian know that they are inferior and subjugated to Islam'. He has called on Muslims as individuals and as nations not to ally with non-believers and said that anybody talking about a 'unity of religions', let alone getting on with Jews and Christians, has made 'a statement of *kuffar*', i.e. expressed the words of an unbeliever.[49]

Not mixing with the non-believers is another theme of Green's. On one occasion he told an audience, he had been in a school in Sri Lanka when a child had asked if they could be friends with non-believers. And though some of the teachers were non-Muslim, Green explained to the child that, even if a non-Muslim loves you very much, you may one day turn to them for advice and what they tell you will not be based on the book of Allah. 'They will not fail to corrupt you.'[50]

Islam, he argues, is not a private faith. The word '*deen*' is different from religion in that it is all-encompassing. That means that every Muslim should be striving for a sharia-governed world and not serving the interests of secular nation states. This logically discourages Muslims from engagement in secular civic society.

On *hudood* punishments, Green has been filmed taking a strong line:

> *Adultery is punishable by death, and a slow and painful death by stoning. It is indicative of just how harmful this crime is to society.*[51]

He goes on to explain its wider societal benefits.

> *There is another direction from which the wisdom of such a punishment can be understood, and that is the death of*

> *two criminals can prevent the death and agony of many*
> *innocents.*[52]

It is clear that iERA does not support ISIS. In the autumn of 2014, it emerged that a group of six young men from Portsmouth who previously helped run a *da'wa* stall in the city centre and worn iERA T-shirts had gone to Syria and most had been killed in action.[53] [54] In response to media coverage, iERA published a statement on the group's website acknowledging that the group had been seen with iERA 'What's Your Goal' T-shirts. They explained that, while activists might use iERA material, the group was not accountable for how they interpreted it.

> *iERA supports local community teams and individuals by*
> *providing basic literature and T-shirts to help in creating*
> *Islamic awareness and in supporting local community*
> *engagement. iERA is not responsible for the acts of any*
> *teams or individuals that order our material on-line.*[55]

3. MEND – Sufyan Gulam Ismail

The event at the Waterlily in November 2013 was organised by Engage, which claims to work for greater civic participation of British Muslims through increased awareness of how Islam is portrayed in the media. Its declared aim is to encourage voter registration and it claims to strive for more active citizenship 'to create a more inclusive and tolerant Britain'.[56] The group was established in 2005 as Engage, sometimes called iENGAGE, but rebranded as MEND (Muslim Engagement and Development) in 2014.

MEND has built a regional network and positioned itself as a campaigning organisation against Islamophobia, while it has developed a quasi-representative function on behalf of Muslim communities in local areas. In this regard, it has organised hustings linked to the London mayoral elections as well as elections for the regional Police and Crime Commissioners. MEND also campaigned to get out the Muslim vote in the 2010 and 2015 general elections through a series of events around the country.

It has produced its own manifestos for elections that place demands for better hate-crime monitoring alongside criticism of the Government's counter-terrorist strategy, Prevent. This has included claims that children are being referred to Prevent for 'innocent mix ups in spelling or speech' and that Prevent is 'one of the most troubled areas of police relationships with Muslim communities'.[57]

In 2015 it organised a series of local events titled 'The Five Pillars of Islamophobia', purporting to be 'an evidence based exposé of the manufacturers of Islamophobia and the interests behind them'. The group also offers free masterclasses and workshops on the media looking at its reach and influence, the way Muslims are portrayed, and how to challenge content. Its 'media toolkit' offers advice on how to tackle the portrayal of Muslims in the press and on TV.[58]

In 2011, when it was called Engage, the group put itself forward to provide the secretariat function for the All Party Parliamentary Group (APPG) on Islamophobia. The APPG had been set up following concerns from the Muslim Council of Britain the year before over a rise in anti-Muslim hate crime. Engage pledged to 'travel to all parts of the UK to take evidence and record experiences to ensure members hear the voices of the Muslim community'. Shortly afterwards, the *Daily Telegraph* newspaper published an article: 'Islamists establish a bridgehead in Parliament'.

Paul Goodman, an MP at the time who had been vocal in raising the issue of anti-Muslim hate crime, wondered how Engage had ever been allowed to be in the position of running an All-Party Parliamentary Group. It could give evidence but, in his view, the group was not a representative body of the Muslim community.

> *It's essentially a monitoring website or an attack website (depending on one's point of view) which targets non-Islamist Muslims in particular.*[59]

The group claimed that, if it lost the secretariat, 'anti-Muslim prejudice will go unchallenged' and that it was under attack from 'right-wing bloggers and the pro-Zionist lobby'.[60] Parliamentarians begged to differ and Engage was removed.

In spite of its opposition to Islamophobia, it has clashed with the anti-Muslim-hatred-monitoring group Tell MAMA over its decision to invite Richard Benson and Peter Tatchell to become patrons. Benson was formerly chief executive of the Community Security Trust, a Jewish group, while Tatchell is a veteran LGBT human rights campaigner. MEND's founder, Sufyan Gulam Ismail, objected to having a 'pro-Zionist' recording Islamophobia.[61] He later apologised for his comments.[62]

Ismail 'retired' at thirty-nine, according to his own online biography, after a career at the accountancy firm Deloitte, in order to pursue 'philanthropic endeavours'.[63] MEND was one of these projects. Ismail was filmed in October 2014 at the Zakariyya Masjid (mosque) in Bolton,[64] where he claimed there was a 300-year-old Israeli lobby (*sic* – Israel was founded in 1948) operating in the UK, that society hated Muslims, and made the subsequently contested insinuation that when a mosque was burned down in Muswell Hill, north London – 'did you hear one politician condemn it?'.[65]

The claim about Muswell Hill mosque does not stand up to scrutiny. Home Office security minister James Brokenshire visited two days later, saying his visit showed the Government was 'standing against any forms of extremism or any forms of aggression or violence'.[66] The Mayor of London, Boris Johnson, added there was no place for prejudice or violence. The local MP Theresa Villiers called it 'an attack on all of us and our values'. As for the '300-year-old Israeli lobby', the Islamic Society of Britain gave an award to the Muswell Hill Synagogue for its help and support after the arson attack.[67]

4. CAGE – Moazzam Begg

The current Salafi-Islamist line-up, which has become a familiar feature of the British Muslim activist circuit, was almost complete. What this group needed was a charismatic figure, which it got with former Guantanamo detainee Moazzam Begg. The Birmingham-born British citizen was detained by the US at Bagram and Guantanamo for two years between 2003 and 2005. His organisation has taken up the cases of several Islamist prisoners around the world and opposed practices such as rendition and torture.

Begg is CAGE's outreach director; he has been engaging with mosques and local Muslim communities, speaking at numerous university Islamic societies and partnering with the National Union of Students (NUS) calling for civil disobedience to boycott Prevent. He has also been a regular fixture on the anti-war circuit, addressing meetings of the Stop the War Coalition.

Begg is opposed to ISIS but argues that 'the most credible voices against IS have been Islamic clerics traditionally associated with al-Qa'ida'.[68] He has named the Jordanian preachers Abu Muhammad al-Maqdisi and Abu Qatada as two people who should be listened to. Al-Maqdisi was the spiritual mentor to Abu Musab al-Zarqawi, a petty criminal turned al-Qa'ida jihadist who brought filmed beheadings to online audiences from the theatre of war in Iraq in the early 2000s. Zarqawi personally executed Nicholas Berg, an engineer from Pennsylvania who was shown dressed in an orange jumpsuit – the execution aesthetic now copied by ISIS.[69] Though Maqdisi fell out with Zarqawi, he was an ideological pioneer for Salafi-jihadism in its current form.[70] The Jordanian government released him from prison in 2014, possibly because he has spoken out against ISIS, but he remains a staunch supporter of al-Qa'ida's insurgency in the region.[71]

On 10 February 2015 Begg used his Twitter page to share with his 16,000 followers a Jordanian web channel's interview with Abu Muhammad al-Maqdisi. In the first sentence, the interviewer rightly described Maqdisi as a theorist of the Salafist-Jihadist movement. Maqdisi, condemning ISIS and the burning of the Jordanian pilot Muath al-Kasasbeh, was concerned about how the actions of ISIS were damaging the reputation of the jihadist movement. The article Begg shared was from a website called Al Muwahideen Media, an anti-ISIS but pro al-Qa'ida website. One article, for example, praised Osama bin Laden in heroic terms: 'This is a nation in a man. He is a man who is a nation by himself.'

Abu Qatada was deported from the UK to Jordan in 2014 where he was detained though subsequently cleared of multiple terrorism charges. Along with Maqdisi, he has earned lavish praise from al-Qa'ida leader Ayman al-Zawahiri:

> We in Al-Qa'idah place our trust in the shaykhs and ulema of jihad whose sincerity, fondness, and compassion for jihad and mujahideen has been proven by the [past] days, such as our beloved Shaykh Abu-Muhammad al-Maqdisi, Shaykh Abu-Qatadah al-Filastini, may God protect them.[72]

CAGE held a live video link with Abu Qatada in June 2015 at a Ramadan dinner attended by Gareth Peirce QC, who spoke about Qatada's legal history in the UK.[73] Begg then interviewed Abu Qatada. They discussed the subsequently released detainees Talha Ahsan and Babar Ahmad.[74] Begg has argued that, if Qatada had been allowed to remain in the UK, fewer young Britons might have joined ISIS.

Changing positions

An early critic of CAGE was Gita Sahgal, head of gender at Amnesty International, who back in 2008 had a very public falling out with her employer as she believed Amnesty had 'become too closely linked to' CAGE, which she described as a 'pro-jihadi group'.[75] Moazzam Begg, she wrote, was 'Britain's most famous supporter of the Taliban' and, while he could be given a platform to share his experience of unlawful detention and torture as a former inmate at Guantánamo Bay, she, as a gender activist, took exception to his support for 'hate preachers' who did not respect women's rights.

When the whole affair went public, Amnesty responded by suspending Sahgal in February 2010. Amnesty argued that Begg's experience in detention meant that his views on the Taliban could be put to one side.

> *At the time that Gita Sahgal left Amnesty International,*
> *we commissioned an independent external review into our*
> *work with CAGE and Moazzam Begg which concluded*
> *that it was reasonable for Amnesty to campaign with*
> *CAGE and Moazzam Begg in his capacity as a former*
> *detainee at Guantanamo Bay.*[76]

It took five years – and a BBC interview in which Asim Qureshi from CAGE was asked to condemn Haitham al-Haddad's views on FGM, homosexuality and stoning – for the Amnesty position to change. Qureshi said he was not going to respond to Haddad's views on camera as he was 'not a theologian'.[77] That interview and the fallout from the 'Jihadi John' episode – where Qureshi referred to the ISIS executioner as a 'beautiful young man'[78] after his death – forced Amnesty to break its links with CAGE. Amnesty's UK director Kate Allen announced the U-turn:

> *Recent comments made by CAGE representatives have*
> *been completely unacceptable, at odds with human rights*
> *principles and serve to undermine the work of NGOs,*
> *including Amnesty International.*[79]

Begg joined the growing conglomerate of Salafists and Islamists at a January 2014 event in Manchester titled 'Is Islam being Criminalised?' Several hundred people crammed into the Eastern Pearl Banqueting Hall and, according to the organisers, another 2,000 watched online.[80] Hizb ut-Tahrir, FOSIS, MRDF and iERA were together once more to 'counter the attacks against Islam in Britain'. Seating was segregated, by choice according to the *Asian Image* newspaper,[81] which called the event a 'cross-party' show of unity. 'Rarely do we see scholars and leaders come together to share a platform.'[82]

What the speakers were calling for in Manchester was the dismantling of the Government's counter-terror and anti-radicalisation strategies (particularly Prevent). This has become a leading theme for Salafi-Islamist events galvanising support, particularly among younger Muslims and students. Prevent is conflated with growing anti-Muslim hatred in society and wars in the Middle East to depict a generalised onslaught against Islam, very much in keeping with traditional Islamist narratives concerning the West's perceived desire to destroy the faith.

Completing the team

On Friday 13 November 2015, the Bedford Corn Exchange in the British Midlands hosted an event called 'Quiz a Muslim', bringing together a now familiar all-male platform of high-profile Islamists and Salafists. It once again evidenced the new spirit of cooperation between Islamists and Salafists, with Haitham al-Haddad and Abdur Raheem Green seated alongside Moazzam Begg and Taji Mustafa from Hizb ut-Tahrir.

In the chair that evening was the last piece of the Salafi-Islamist jigsaw. Dilly Hussain is deputy editor of 5Pillars, a news site launched in 2013, which is often regarded as the media arm of this convergence of Salafists and Islamists (168,000 likes on Facebook). Its editorial line is relentlessly positive towards the groups and individuals involved, while pouring scorn on the same Muslims the ideologues detest.

With a certificate in print journalism from the NCTJ (National Council for the Training of Journalists), Hussain began his writing career at *Bedfordshire on Sunday* before freelancing for the Iranian-backed Press TV and contributing to Islam21c.[83] Hussain once wrote that in his first news-writing class studying for the NCTJ he had been told that there was no such thing as 'impartial news'.[84] He went on to say this helped him see the bias in mainstream media; but it might help explain the very partial editorial line of 5Pillars.

Contributors to the 5Pillars 'Speakers Corner' section make up a familiar roll-call from the Salafi-Islamist bigwigs. This includes Abdur Raheem Green, Moazzam Begg, Sufyan Ismail and Hamza Tzortzis. Much of the website's coverage is devoted to deriding the Government's Prevent counter-terrorism agenda and adopting a critical tone towards those British Muslim civil society groups that work with it.

Hussain is very visible on the Salafi-Islamist circuit, but the head of the news team at 5Pillars is its editor, Roshan Muhammed Salih. He also started off in local newspapers, then London Weekend Television and on to the Al Jazeera English language service. Salih subsequently held the post of head of news at the Islam Channel between 2005 and 2007 before taking on the same position at Press TV.

Before the Bedford event, the *Bedfordshire on Sunday* newspaper reported that 'radical Muslims are descending on sleepy Bedford to give a talk and answer'.[85] The camera panning the audience that evening revealed that the seating was segregated, voluntarily or not.[86] Dilly Hussein later wrote on 5Pillars that this was the audience sticking to their 'normative Islamic practices'. He argued that segregation is a liberating choice.

> *Of course this isn't good enough for muscular liberals and pseudo-feminists who pay mere lip service to gender equality and freedoms.*[87]

That same evening, terrorists killed 128 people in a series of attacks at different venues in the French capital, Paris.[88] Four days later, MPs at the Home Affairs Select Committee upbraided CAGE for not having put out a statement on the tragedy on its website when it had previously rushed to comment on the death of ISIS terrorist Mohammed 'Jihadi John' Emwazi.[89] CAGE had referred to the death of this ISIS executioner in sympathetic terms at a press conference, which had led to a furore. The group replied that it was too busy dealing with Emwazi-related queries to say anything about Paris.

Coordinated strategy

The coordinated way in which this relatively new conglomerate of Salafists and Islamists operates on social media and through various online portals does sweep up many British Muslims, particularly the youth, in support of key Islamist issues. It might be segregated seating at university meetings or new counter-extremism measures from the Government. In October 2014, it was a reaction to the arrest of an individual called Tarik Hassane, accused of being involved in an ISIS terror plot.

He was suspected to be in the early stages of a 'significant' attack on UK soil. The *Daily Telegraph* reported that, months before on the ask.fm social media site, he had been asked whether Allah really wanted people to fight and kill in his name.

> *Yes. Not only does Allah want it, but he rewards those who do it with paradise.*[90]

On 9 October, CAGE put up a statement announcing it had spoken to friends and relatives of Hassane and that excessive force had been used in the raid. It was presented as another example of Muslims being victimised by the police and the authorities. The group referred to a 'mass hysteria' around the arrest and said that 'these young men become criminalised and their lives tarnished with the broad brush stroke of 'terrorism'.

A tweet written by Hassane with the words 'oi lads I smell war' had been part of a bigger conversation, according to CAGE, and was now presented stripped of all its context. In contrast, the group quoted one of Hassane's friends saying he was 'a very laid back and funny guy'.[91]

5Pillars took up the baton, damning 'a politically motivated arrest by a police state', repeating CAGE's claims that the tweet was out of context and too much violence had been involved in the arrest. Muslims, the article declared, were being 'victimised, abused and subjugated by the government'.[92] The author of this piece was Amar Alam, a research assistant at MEND and listed as a contributor to Islam21c.[93]

Alam then took a swipe at secular Muslims:

> *While some from the Muslim community are happy to embrace secular values, and follow a government set agenda by condemning anything they feel does not follow their interpretation of 'Britishness', those who follow an orthodox interpretation of Islam must make a stand by campaigning and defending their fellow Muslims.*[94]

Islam21c chimed in, reporting that, after the 'false arrest' of Tarik Hassane, there had been a 'major outcry' followed by a social media campaign on Twitter and Facebook. The hashtag #JusticeforTarik was attached to tweets saying 'a politically motivated arrest by a police state' and 'Mr Hassane, arrested for a tweet taken out of context'.[95]

However, the facts are always a stubborn thing. On 12 February 2016, Hassane pleaded guilty and admitted to planning an Islamic State-inspired plot to kill civilians in London during a series of drive-by shootings on a moped. Hassane planned to kill soldiers, police officers and civilians on the streets of the capital where, between 8 July 2014 and 7 October 2014, he had researched, planned and sourced a weapon and ammunition with a 'view to committing an attack or attacks on a person or persons within the United Kingdom'.[96]

The trial judge, Mr Justice Wilkie, instructed the jury to formally find Hassane guilty.[97] 5Pillars quietly removed its article from its website within twenty-four hours of the news breaking. CAGE did not. In April, 2016, Tarik Hassane was given a life sentence for plotting to kill soldiers, police officers and civilians.[98]

The by-now familiar line-up of Salafists and Islamists increasingly advanced a claim to speak for all British Muslims. On 20 January 2015 a letter was sent to the House of Lords complaining about the proposed Counter-Terrorism and Security Bill. It condemned the new law as 'manufacturing a witch-hunt against Islam and Muslims'. The letter was co-signed by Moazzam Begg, Asim Qureshi and Saghir Hussain, a pro-CAGE lawyer; Jamal Harwood and Abdul Wahid from Hizb ut-Tahrir; Abdur Raheem Green and others from iERA; Shakeel Begg from the Lewisham Islamic Centre; and Jamil

Rashid from the MRDF – one of Haitham al-Haddad's organisations. The HT website reproduced the letter with the headline: 'Muslim Community Writes to the House of Lords over the new CTS Bill'.[99]

Countering counter-terrorism: 'Prevent-a-Muslim'

At a Manchester event in January 2014, called 'Is Islam being Criminalised', the victimhood status of British Muslims was emphasised with comparisons to the American civil rights movement.[100] Nasir Hafezi, a lawyer, told the audience that Muslims had become 'the new second-class citizens and the new untouchables'.[101] He articulated a familiar view on these platforms: that Muslims were being persecuted because they wanted to practise their faith; were subject to unfair stop-and-search at airports; and were being spied on and approached to be informants. Judges who knew nothing about Islam were deciding who was an 'extremist' and unfairly curbing their liberties or right to work.

Another lawyer, Jahangir Mohammed from the Centre for Muslim Affairs,[102] claimed that the Government's counter-terror Prevent strategy was specifically designed to regulate all areas of Muslim belief in order to 'eliminate Islamism'. He described this as a kind of Orwellian thought crime aimed only at the Muslim population. He constructed an imaginary tale of a boy called Abdullah growing up in Britain and apparently harassed at all turns by the Islamophobic British state.

First, Abdullah goes to the madrasa aged eight or nine. Mohammed claimed that the teaching at the madrasa would these days be something funded by Prevent to encourage little Abdullah not to become an extremist and giving him the correct idea of what jihad means. Then he goes to school, 'where they have something called the Channel programme'. The fictional Abdullah is at home watching the news about Aleppo in Syria being bombed, then he goes to school and says how awful it is. Next thing, he is taken to see the Channel programme people, part of Prevent, as a consequence of his airing these views. This has even happened to individuals just for growing a beard, Mohammed claimed.

Abdullah then gets a place at university and becomes involved in the Islamic student society. He decides to book his favourite speaker, maybe Moazzam Begg or Haitham al-Haddad. But the university insists that men and women have to sit together and then the event is cancelled because 'Sheikh Haitham is a declared hate preacher and so is Moazzam Begg.'

Poor Abdullah can't hear any of his favourite speakers.

The adult Abdullah joins a mosque, gets involved in *da'wa* work with a charity and invites an 'overseas speaker'. The Charities Commission intervenes and writes to the mosque asking why an extremist has been invited to speak. At this point, Mohammed jabbed his finger at the audience telling them that, if their mosque was registered with the Charities Commission, then it answered to that body and not Allah.

Abdullah applies for jobs but, 'because he is on the Channel list', he cannot get work and becomes depressed. So now he visits a doctor where he unburdens himself about the 'nasty political ideas' that are forming in his head.

I have a false sense of grievance about this British foreign policy. There's something wrong with me. I'm not right in the head.

The doctor tells him not to worry because the Home Office is working on a cure called 'Prevent-a-Muslim'. But, in the meantime, the doctor gives him a prescription for the Channel programme because it has been extended to the health sector. Even more upset, Abdullah decides to go on holiday, but the security services are listening in. "Going on holiday" to the security services is code for "I'm going on jihad.""[103] He goes out of the country but then his passport is removed.

Abdullah comes back and returns home to his wife, but she has been on the Shanaz[104] programme – an initiative to help women spot the signs of radicalisation in their families and communities. Jahangir Mohammed mocks this programme in his fictional story, saying his hero is 'still not safe'. So then Abdullah sets up a *da'wa* stall that includes some terrorist material and he is arrested. Thinking he is safe in prison, he is then put through the Contest programme to deradicalise him.

Jahangir Mohammed has denied being an activist in Moazzam Begg's organisation CAGE,[105] but he co-authored an attack on the Government's counter-terrorism programme published by CAGE that chimed with his fictional character Abdullah's life experience: 'The Prevent Strategy. A Cradle to Grave Police State'.[106]

> *This policy encompasses almost all aspects of Muslim life, and targets all generations, in essence a cradle to grave surveillance state.*[107]

CAGE's view of radicalisation

1. 'Jihadi John'

CAGE's attitude to several high-profile terrorist cases reveals a pattern. The claims of proven or convicted terrorists to have been harassed by the state or motivated by western foreign policy are taken at face value. Their own accounts are accepted as true. The role of the British state is placed front of stage as the main factor in their radicalisation. Islamist ideology is never regarded as a factor – indeed the role of ideology is regarded as irrelevant.

Writing about Seifeddine Rezgui, who murdered thirty-eight tourists on a beach in Tunisia in June 2015, Moazzam Begg had this to say about his motives:

> *Warped as his ideas must have been, he saw the tourists as representatives of Britain. Britain that had wanted to destroy the caliphate past and, the caliphate present.*[108]

The similarities between CAGE's presentation of the cases of Mohammed 'Jihadi John' Emwazi and Michael Adebolajo are very striking. Emwazi, a University of Westminster graduate, gained notoriety over his executions of US journalists James Foley and Steven Sotloff as well as British aid workers David Haines and Alan Henning. He was also filmed standing over the head of Peter Kassig, and led a group of ISIS operatives in the killing of twenty-one captured Syrian soldiers.

CAGE hit international headlines in February 2015 when it held a press conference claiming to have had two years' worth of communication with twenty-seven-year-old Mohammad Emwazi, who had just been revealed by the *Washington Post* as being the true identity behind the infamous masked figure of Jihadi John. Asim Qureshi, CAGE's research director, told reporters:

> *You might be surprised to know that the Mohammed that I knew was extremely kind, extremely gentle, extremely soft spoken, was the most humble young person that I knew.*[109]

In a statement released by CAGE on 26 February 2015, the group claimed Emwazi had been radicalised as a result of harassment by the British security services.[110] The first two sentences of the statement spelt out the CAGE view:

> *Since 2001, the British authorities have systematically shifted the spotlight away from its foreign policy and its security agencies by placing blame for violence at home and abroad solely on Muslims. British security services have systematically engaged in the harassment of young Muslims, rendering their lives impossible and leaving them with no legal avenue to redress their situation.*[111]

Qureshi related a story of a young man trying to return to his birthplace of Kuwait but being confounded by the UK security agencies. Comparing him to the killer of Lee Rigby, Michael Adebolajo, he said that Emwazi had been exposed to 'suffocating domestic policies aimed at turning a person into an informant'. He had been abused by the UK, a country where 'individuals are prevented from travelling, placed under house arrest and in the worst cases tortured, rendered or killed seemingly on the whim of security agents'.[112]

Qureshi was challenged in a BBC interview in March 2015 to back up these claims.

> *Interviewer: On your website, you've claimed that UK individuals in Britain are tortured, rendered and killed on the whim of British security agents. Give me one person who has been killed on the whim of a British security agent?*
> *Qureshi: I don't know about that language in particular.*
> *Interviewer: It's what CAGE has said. You've claimed that people in Britain are jailed without due process. Who is in jail today in Britain without due process?*
> *Qureshi: Well, we would say a number of people were...*
> *(Asked the question again)*
> *Qureshi: Currently we would say no one...*[113]

CAGE argued[114] that Emwazi in August 2009 had planned a summer holiday to go on safari in Tanzania but was detained at the airport on arrival and eventually deported. CAGE claimed there was an attempt by MI5 to recruit him, but Emwazi wanted nothing to do with them. After getting back to the UK, Emwazi left for Kuwait to find work. On a trip back to London in 2010, Emwazi claimed he was taken into a room at Heathrow airport and abused by a police officer 'wearing an Indian turban'.[115] CAGE asserted that Emwazi had been 'harassed' by the UK intelligence services over a four-year period, which they believed led to Emwazi's gradual radicalisation and transformation into Jihadi John.

Yet the reality was that Emwazi had been on the UK intelligence services radar since his graduation year in 2009. The *Daily Telegraph* reported that he had been radicalised in Kuwait in 2007 by Khalid al-Dossary, a Saudi national now in US prison for terrorism, and

Muhsin al-Fadhli, a senior al-Qaʻida member.[116] MI5's view was that, rather than going on safari, Emwazi had become an associate of a number of high-profile suspected jihadists whom they were tracking across the world and who sought to travel to Somalia for terrorism-related activities.

The BBC obtained court papers[117] from 2011 suggesting that Emwazi and others sought to travel to Somalia as they had been involved in the 'provision of funds and equipment to Somalia for terrorism-related purposes and the facilitation of individuals' travel from the United Kingdom to Somalia to undertake terrorism-related activity'.

Emwazi had been brought to the attention of the authorities as a result of their monitoring suspected extremists with regards to recruitment to al-Shabaab in Somalia. Using the false name Muhammad ibn Muazzam,[118] Emwazi travelled to Tanzania in 2009 with another Briton calling himself Abu Talib and a German convert styled 'Omar'. Rather than going on 'safari', the security services believed his intention in going to Tanzania was to become involved in terrorism in the Horn of Africa.

CAGE's account of Emwazi's radicalisation, presenting him as a victimised Muslim, no longer looked credible. Emwazi had been radicalised years earlier in Kuwait. He had been on MI5's radar for good reason. His safari to Tanzania was in fact a journey to jihad, and the Tanzanian authorities reported that the reason for his being put back on a flight to the UK was that he had arrived at the airport drunk and rowdy.[119]

But the final nail in the CAGE account came from ISIS itself. The terrorist group wrote an obituary for Abu Muharib, as they referred to Emwazi, in the thirteenth edition of the ISIS online magazine *Dabiq*, published in January 2016 after he was killed in a drone strike in November 2015. Eulogising its fallen jihadi comrade, ISIS traced the start of Emwazi's 'jihad-related work' and radicalisation even further back than 2007 to 2005 after 'the blessed raids that rocked London and its transport system'.

Abu Muharib began to embark upon the path of hijrah and jihad. He would busy his days with jihad-related work together... None of this went unnoticed by MI5 (British intelligence), which started vigorously targeting Abu Muharib and those with him.[120]

As for his unfair detention at Heathrow, being unable to get back to Kuwait, *Dabiq* painted a very different picture, removing the victimhood narrative entirely and suggesting that he knew exactly what he was doing and was playing the officers who were interrogating him.

Despite the efforts of MI5, Abu Muharib never ceased in his struggle to make hijrah for the sake of Allah. On his last attempt to leave the UK for his homeland of Kuwait, Abu Muharib was stopped at the airport and kept for questioning by MI5, the result of which was their refusal to allow him to travel. During the interrogation, Abu Muharib would present himself as unintelligent, as was his method when dealing with intelligence agencies.

Arriving in Syria in 2012, Emwazi had a brief spell fighting with Jabhat al-Nusra before his unit defected to ISIS. After he joined, *Dabiq* made it clear that he was an active fighter and utterly committed. There is therefore a complete divergence between CAGE's portrayal of a victim of the British state, hounded into the arms of ISIS, and the description given in *Dabiq*. ISIS portrays a man dedicated to violent jihad and thoroughly radicalised over several years – an ideal candidate for the post of chief executioner.

2. The Lee Rigby murder

Many factors in the Emwazi story and CAGE's version of events arose with another case the group took a stand on – the murder of Fusilier Lee Rigby. On 22 May 2013, Michael Adebolajo and Michael Adebowale ran Lee Rigby down with a car as he walked near the

Royal Wootton Bassett in Woolwich. They then used knives and a cleaver to hack him to death.[121] Having committed the deed, they then stood their ground, spouting their motives to horrified onlookers who filmed them on their mobile phone cameras. Holding a weapon dripping with blood, one of them stated:

> *The only reason we have done this is because Muslims are dying every day... This British soldier is an eye for an eye, a tooth for a tooth. We apologise that women had to see this today but in our lands women have to see the same.*[122]

Adebolajo had been flashing on and off the security services radar between 2008 and 2013. In fact he had featured in five investigations by MI5 and, far from being an isolated lone wolf, Adebolajo had already established contact with jihadists in other countries. He was therefore not a self-radicalised assassin but somebody firmly plugged into the global terror network.[123]

In 2006 Adebolajo was arrested with an associate called Ibrahim Hassan during a protest against cartoons in a Danish newspaper that were perceived as insulting to the Prophet. The protest had been organised by a subsequently banned front organisation of the proscribed group al-Muhajiroun called Al Ghurabaa. Inflammatory placards at the protest read 'Butcher those who mock Islam' and 'Europe you will pay, your 9/11 is on the way'.[124]

Four years later in November 2010, Adebolajo was taken into custody along with five youths in Kenya, accused of travelling to Somalia to join the terror group al-Shabaab.[125] He was not convicted and instead was deported back to the UK. Back on British soil, Adebolajo claimed to have been beaten and threatened with electrocution and rape by the Kenyan authorities.

By now, MI5 had come into contact with him on several occasions, but levels of surveillance had varied considerably. In November 2014, after the murder, the report from the Intelligence and Security Committee to Parliament concluded there was a failure of different agencies to co-ordinate effectively, as well as insufficient backing for the Prevent programme.

CAGE took a different view, publishing a blog post by Adebolajo's brother, Jeremiah. In it he argued that, as no evidence had been provided of relevant social media interactions before Woolwich involving Adebolajo, there was no justification for an increase in online surveillance:

> ... *this report is nothing more than a distraction from the motives behind the attack and a way to put a particular segment of British society under further pressure and surveillance.*[126]

Another blog post on the CAGE site talked about criminalising the 'innocent'. It compared counter-terrorism measures in the UK to policies implemented under the apartheid regime in South Africa against the ANC. 'Those who supported the apartheid government and called for Mandela to be hanged yesterday, hail him a hero today.'[127]

In the same way that CAGE believed Emwazi ('Jihadi John') had been radicalised as a result of 'harassment' by the UK security services, the UK must have been complicit in the mistreatment of Michael Adebolajo in Kenya in 2010.[128] The real reason for radicalisation, CAGE concluded, is not extremist ideology or recruitment by terror groups but 'persecutory measures' by the UK Government that alienate British Muslims into acts of violence.

However, as with Emwazi, the trail from initial extremist activity to terrorism stretched further back. This came to light when BBC current affairs programme *Newsnight* interviewed the aforementioned Ibrahim Hassan on 24 May 2013 – under his assumed name of Abu Nusaybah.[129] He detailed knowing Adebolajo back in 2004 when they had converted to Islam and became involved with Omar Bakri Muhammad, founder of the banned al-Muhajiroun, which he admitted on air.[130]

When asked by the BBC interviewer about the murder of Lee Rigby, Hassan said he thought the reports were a 'joke' and did not believe them. As far as he was concerned Adebolajo had wanted to go and live in 'Muslim lands' because he was being 'bugged' by MI5. On leaving the BBC studio, Hassan was immediately arrested on charges of disseminating terrorist material, to which he pleaded guilty and was jailed.[131]

CAGE claimed in a 2012 article after the Adebolajo trial that the Government has yet to provide any empirical evidence that extremist ideology leads to terrorism. In the same article it states that Adebolajo himself saw his sense of Britishness being associated with violence committed around the world. So much so, one has to assume, that he felt compelled to hack a British soldier to death:

> *In the trial of Michael Adebolajo... he specifically stated during his testimony that he did not see any shame in referring to himself as a British Muslim, and indeed that he described himself as being one. The shame he felt was that the British part of his identity was being associated with murder, pillage and the rape of innocent people around the world.*[132]

The challenge

The challenge of posing an alternative to the view of Britain offered by the Salafi-Islamists is regarded by many Muslim groups as a poisoned chalice. They know that taking on this formidable force will simply earn them a heap of online abuse. Reconciled British Muslim voices challenging Islamist extremism are significantly smaller and have less influence, whether in communities, on campus or on social media. This may change as the Government's counter-extremism strategy, launched in 2015, gathers pace. One of its declared intentions is to 'actively support mainstream voices, especially in our faith communities and civil society'.[133]

Government, however, can be a blunt instrument in the fight against extremism. Proposed legislation in this area has resulted in ideas like Extremism Disruption Orders that would ban people from social media or speaking in public. This presents an obvious human rights issue. The Independent Reviewer of Terrorist Legislation, David Anderson QC, has already flagged up a warning to Whitehall.

> *If it becomes a function of the state to identify individuals who are engaged in, or are exposed to, non-violent extremist activity, it will become legitimate for the state to scrutinise, and for the citizen to inform upon, the exercise of core democratic freedoms by large numbers of law-abiding people.*[134]

He added that getting counter-extremism wrong in the UK would make it harder for people to integrate into British society and more pertinently play 'into the hands of those who, by peddling a grievance agenda, seek to drive people further towards extremism and terrorism'.[135]

More effective than legislation in the longer term would be a strong British civil society speaking out, making the point that Islamist ideology stands in stark contrast to human rights. Not only could it counter the joint Salafi-Islamist line in the area of extremism but also on an issue where it is making dangerous headway: counter-terrorism and, more specifically, Prevent.

THREE

THE ISLAMIST-LED ASSAULT ON PREVENT

Eco-Terrorism

Muslim mother Ifhat Smith claimed that her fourteen-year-old son was interrogated by Prevent officers at his school, the Central Foundation in Islington, London for using the word 'eco-terrorism' in class.[1] This had been in relation to environmental activists spiking trees with nails to stop chainsaws from chopping them down. Her son, she claimed, had been taken to an 'inclusion hut' and subjected to questioning about his views.

On 14 December 2015 she was interviewed by Sky News.[2] She said:

Prevent is allowing state sanctioned abuse of Muslim children.

The story was a front-page lead in *The Guardian*.[3] On the surface, it appeared to be a devastating account of the arbitrary injustice allegedly meted out to children by the Government's Prevent programme. The story was trotted out time and again, in community events, on campuses and shared widely on social media including the anti-Prevent website Prevent Watch,[4] which aggregates this kind of material. Yet the story, like many others, was not all it seemed.

The incident occurred in May 2015 but gained prominence as an exposé of Prevent when reported in *The Guardian* that September.

The parents of the fourteen-year-old told the newspaper they were taking legal action as a result of their son being removed from class and interrogated for ten minutes, during which time he had allegedly been asked if he had an affiliation with ISIS.

Ifhat Smith told the newspaper her son 'was presumed guilty because he was Muslim. As parents we are doing the right thing but still our son is accused. There was nothing in what he said that warranted him being taken out of class and treated as a criminal.'[5] However, in her December appearance on Sky News, she neglected to mention that a High Court judge had thrown out a judicial review she had applied for in October that year and ordered Smith to pay £1,000 for wasting court time.[6]

The Guardian reported that a child protection officer had been one of two people speaking to the boy. Smith claimed her son had been interrogated as part of the Prevent strategy in schools. But the school said it had not referred her son to Prevent, as did an Islington Council source.

The school argued that it had taken 'a reasonable and proportionate response'[7]: instead of being 'treated as a criminal' the child was spoken to, rather than interrogated, for a mere ten minutes from a safeguarding perspective, something that schools often do. The boy was immediately sent back to class with no action taken.

Mr Justice Blake in the High Court ruled that the judicial review demanded by Smith was 'considered to be totally without merit'.[8] He dismissed the claimant's argument that the Government's Prevent counter-terrorism strategy which 'seeks to protect schoolchildren from terrorist propaganda and ideology is unlawful because it is more likely that concern may be directed to children of Muslim faith'. This was, Justice Blake pointed out, because of 'the propaganda activity of extremists who are purportedly Islamic in faith'.[9]

The pattern of the eco-terrorist case is familiar to Prevent coordinators, police and other front-line agencies working to safeguard and prevent people from being drawn into terrorism. An allegation is made that a child or adult has been 'interrogated' over something that appears incredibly minor – something said in class, or wearing a particular item. However, in many cases, a referral that has been made about a child had had little to do with Prevent and has often involved other safeguarding issues.

This has not stopped the anti-Prevent activists from sharing these stories widely. For example Prevent Watch, an initiative that describes itself as 'Supporting Communities Impacted by Prevent', continues to feature the 'eco-terrorism' story on its site.[10] When many of these stories are contested and unverified, listing them does not give a clear picture of facts or truth. Yet questionable and unverified 'cases' from Prevent Watch continue to be quoted by other institutions, despite the organisation's clear anti-Prevent stance.[11]

Why Prevent was set up

Prevent emerged in 2003, in the aftermath of the 9/11 attacks on the World Trade Center in New York, as part of a new UK counter-terror strategy called Contest. The aim of Contest is 'to reduce the risk to the UK and its interests overseas from international terrorism, so that people can go about their lives freely and with confidence'.[12]

Contest was to encompass four elements: 'Pursue', to stop terrorist attacks; 'Prevent', to stop people becoming terrorists or supporting violent extremism; 'Protect', to strengthen protection against terrorist attack; and 'Prepare', to mitigate the impact of an attack that cannot be stopped. Pursue and Prevent were intended to reduce the threat from terrorism, while Protect and Prepare are there to reduce the UK's vulnerability to attack.

Prevent operates in what is termed a 'pre-criminal space'; it is not involved in actively pursuing terrorists but, instead, working with vulnerable people identified as being at risk of radicalisation. As we saw with Muneera in Chapter One, individuals referred to Prevent do not end up in the courts or in prison. The idea is to provide tailored professional support that will stop that happening.

Britons were implicated more and more as perpetrators in Islamist-inspired attacks from the 1990s and into the 2000s. London experienced a nightmarish multiple attack on 7 July 2005 when fifty-two people were killed on the city's transport network as a result of suicide bombings. If anybody had doubted the arrival of Islamist terrorism on British soil, then that day silenced the doubters. These were the first suicide attacks in the UK and some of those involved had been trained in terrorist camps abroad.

As of 2015, Prevent operates across forty-six 'priority areas' in the UK, with a local coordinator network. It works with over 2,790 different public institutions including schools, universities and faith bodies, and it engaged with nearly 50,000 individuals over the course of 2015.[13]

Until 2015, the Prevent programme was largely a voluntary undertaking. But it is now on a very solid statutory footing. One key reason given for the change is that young people in the UK continue 'to make up a disproportionately high number of those arrested in this country for terrorist-related offences and of those who are travelling to join terrorist organisations in Syria and Iraq'.[14]

Channel, and how it works within Prevent

Channel is part of the Prevent programme, but is widely misunderstood and deliberately misinterpreted by those opposed to Prevent. It was piloted in 2007 and rolled out across the UK in 2012. When somebody – a school student for example – is referred to Prevent because they have shown worrying behaviour that suggests a risk of radicalisation, the case can be referred to a Channel panel. This multi-agency panel brings together professionals from the health and social services and other professionals who will assess the relevant needs and advise some solutions. These ways forward might include mentoring on countering extremist ideology – but the same case might also include assistance with regard to mental health if there are other vulnerabilities present. That help might be offered to the individual alone. But parental consent is required if children are deemed to require Channel intervention.

Local authorities have a statutory duty to safeguard children and young people in relation to their social services functions as designated under the Children's Act 2004. The panel functions in a similar way to other local authority multi-agency structures dealing with gang violence or child sexual exploitation. It is, however, entirely voluntary, so those referred can refuse to cooperate and go their own way. Channel cannot work with or provide support to individuals who are already the subject of a criminal investigation as its remit is pre-criminal.

Channel draws in professionals from the NHS, social services, youth offending services, chairs of Local Safeguarding Children Boards and local authority safeguarding managers, among others. These specialists will review cases where somebody has exhibited signs of radicalisation because of online influence, bullying, family tensions, race or hate crime, lack of self-esteem and political grievances. Understanding how vulnerabilities overlap and interact is at the centre of Channel's approach.

Proving the point that Channel is voluntary, Will Baldet, a Prevent officer working in the Midlands, told us that parents often refer their own children to the programme because they are concerned that their youngsters may have been drawn to Islamist or far-Right views. During his eight years as a Prevent coordinator, he 'can count on the fingers of one hand the number of people who have turned down Channel'[15] when it has been offered to them. While the anti-Prevent campaigners claim it criminalises children, Channel is actually a means of stopping young people crossing over to the criminal legal space.

The community projects that are funded by Prevent are intended to prevent radicalisation of those people who are being targeted by either far-Right or Islamist extremists. It mirrors safeguarding processes used by other Government agencies in areas like gang activity, sexual abuse and bullying.

Talking to people who work in Prevent, it is clear that the threat of ISIS is of paramount concern; but Channel also deals with far-Right extremist referrals. The ratio of referrals for far-Right and Islamist extremism varies from city to city. According to the Hampshire

Prevent team who deal with all forms of extremism, most referrals to Channel in Hampshire and the Isle of Wight are for far Right extremism. Yet one cannot ignore the departure of hundreds of British citizens to join ISIS in Syria and Iraq, or those who have plotted to commit terrorist attacks in the UK.

However, it is not possible or desirable for the state to arrest and prosecute people at risk of being drawn into terrorism. Individuals can be radicalised, after all, without actually committing a criminal act. So Prevent fills a much needed gap – creating an opportunity to halt the radicalisation process in its tracks and to protect individuals from going down the criminal path.

Islamist-inspired groups put forward the idea that Prevent is creating a state-sponsored Islam that is safe and compliant. This simply bears no relation to what Prevent coordinators do in their everyday life, let alone to the approach of the Government. Pre-2011, Prevent had been criticised for its inclusion of community cohesion work, which was perceived as securitising British Muslims. The 2011 Prevent review narrowed the focus of Prevent to three key areas: working with sectors and institutions, providing advice and support in preventing people from being drawn into terrorism, and responding to the ideological challenge.

I believe that, in order to combat radicalisation, partnership work is vital, whether with statutory agencies, police or Government. Civil society groups have a unique and important role to play in reaching communities, working directly with those who have been radicalised, their families or local networks; and governments have a duty to work with and support such organisations.

In this spirit, Inspire, the organisation I run, has engaged with women to protect families from extremism, through its #Makingastand campaign. Our anti-ISIS work has been achieved with the support of Prevent. Recognising the value of #Makingastand, the Home Office helped fund our campaign to deliver its message to nine cities across Britain. It also provided technical assistance for Inspire's social media videos – short films of young Muslims dissuading other young Muslims from travelling to Syria, and highlighting the brutality of ISIS. These are examples of the important collaborative work that can be done between non-governmental civil society groups and the Government for the common purpose of protecting people from terrorism.

Truth versus fiction

What do real-life Prevent interventions look like, as opposed to the scare stories? Kamran from the West Midlands was aged fourteen when social care picked up on comments he made in support of Osama bin Laden and joining ISIS. He had recognised communication and behavioural difficulties, including autism, and had been on the internet unsupervised. His mother was in poor health and his father was absent on account of work. Through the Channel programme he was provided with a mentor to talk through the ideological and political issues he had become fixated on.[16]

Luckily for Kamran, his relationship with family and behaviour at school improved. The mentor reported that the teenager had matured, rejecting terrorist ideology. Kamran developed a broader range of interests and, most gratifyingly, now regards himself as a role model to others.

Another recorded incident was where Prevent intervened successfully with a fifteen-year-old who told school staff he supported al-Qa'ida and wanted to attend a terrorist training camp. He also admitted to watching extremist material online and said he had spoken to radicalisers on the web. He was referred to Channel, part of Prevent, and it transpired that he had learning difficulties, Asperger's Syndrome and exposure to domestic violence.[17] A multi-agency plan was agreed which provided support to his parents and resources for his school. Crucially, however, the support of additional agencies was identified and referrals were made to Children and Mental Health Services (CAMHS), among others.

One thirteen-year-old was drawing swastikas in his exercise books and on desks and walls, and using racist language. No referral was made at first until a youth worker at a club spotted the same behaviour. It emerged that the youth's father was in prison for racist views and the police were aware that his mother was a drug user. The boy had already made contact with a white supremacist group that was radicalising him. A multi-agency plan was put in place to support him and his parents.[18] The teenager was also exposed to positive role models and a strong counter-narrative against far Right extremism.

Schools themselves recognise the important role they have to play. At training seminars run for head teachers by the Association of School and College Leaders in the summer of 2015, teachers shared their concerns. One head teacher talked about how the father of a five-year-old was making his son watch videos inciting anti-Muslim hatred, while a Muslim father of a girl of the same age was getting her to view beheading videos.[19]

Prevent does not publicise these cases, as the aim is to enable these individuals to resume their lives without any stigma or punishment. However, the anti-Prevent activists are less reticent about naming those they claim have been victims of the system and putting these people on public platforms. For example, there was the so-called 'terraced house' incident.

In December 2015, it was claimed that a ten-year-old boy had been referred to Prevent over a spelling mistake. The BBC reported that, instead of writing that he lived in a terraced house, the child used the words a 'terrorist house'.[20] His family, based in Accrington, Lancashire, demanded the police and school apologise for the boy being interrogated.

This story of an alleged 'interrogation' by Prevent, as opposed to an exploratory chat over a minor infraction, turned out once again to have no basis in fact. Clive Grunshaw, the Lancashire Police and Crime Commissioner, took to his official website to castigate the BBC over its reporting and denied that a spelling error was at the centre of the police action. He said of the BBC report:

> *It pays very little attention to the truth of the issue and the fact that concerns were raised by the school about the boy's safety.*[21]

Grunshaw painted a very different picture. The boy had disclosed a 'worrying issue' in his schoolwork, including writing that 'I hate it when my uncle beats me',[22] not just making the reference to a 'terrorist house'. As part of its obligation to safeguard children in its care, the school had raised the issue through the appropriate channels leading to a visit by a neighbourhood police officer and social worker. It was never regarded as a terrorist-related incident; as Grunshaw pointed out, 'the reporter was fully aware of this before she wrote her story'.

Incidents of this kind put teachers and other professionals working with children on the defensive and could lead to failures to intervene where radicalisation of children or abuse is actually taking place. Schools find themselves damned by the anti-Prevent campaigners for intervening, then damned for not intervening by the media and sometimes even by the anti-Prevent lobby itself when something goes undetected. Yet everybody looking after children in a professional capacity has been required since 2015 to implement the 'Prevent Duty' – in other words, to have due regard to the need to prevent people from being drawn into terrorism.[23]

When nurseries were also expected to comply with the Prevent Duty, there was uproar that the Government believed we had 'toddler terrorists'. Yet the Duty recognised that young children may be exposed to such violence online or even from their own parents. One particularly bizarre example of this involved a Muslim convert convicted of 'inviting support for Islamic State' who photographed his children dressed as jihadists, complete with swords, posing in front of Islamic black flags.[24]

One infant and nursery school rang Inspire, the human rights organisation of which I am a director, for advice because a four-year-old girl in class kept repeating to her teacher that 'my mummy says we're going on holiday to Syria tomorrow'. This could have been a genuine holiday to Syria, it could also have been a mother seeking to take her daughter to join ISIS. Either way, the Prevent Duty places an expectation on nurseries and schools to act in order to safeguard the child concerned.

Nevertheless, ill-advised referrals, even if they do not lead to any further action being taken by Channel – as most do not – will give the anti-Prevent brigade rich pickings. Already, one case in Luton involving a four-year-old drawing a 'cooker bomb' that turned out to be a cucumber earned unwelcome media coverage and led to the local council intervening. Cases like this will arise, raising questions of what constitutes a sign of radicalisation. Better training will improve the performance of front-line staff, and thus reduce the occurrence of such unfortunate incidents.

The questions to ask those criticising safeguarding are: what do you want to put in place of Prevent, or do you seriously believe there is no problem at all? Has the Government invented a problem to criminalise Muslim kids, or is there a real threat of children being radicalised online and offline by terrorist and extremist far-Right groups?

Hostility and suspicion

In February 2016, unfazed by the High Court's judgment against her 'eco-terrorism' complaint, Ifhat Smith shared a platform at an anti-Prevent rally in north-east London with Jahangir Mohammed, the lawyer who wrote CAGE's review of its handling of the 'Jihadi John' affair.[25] Also on the platform was Haras Ahmed of Prevent Watch. Ifhat Smith was interviewed by the *Socialist Worker* newspaper and declared that Prevent was 'so draconian' that 'the best thing is to scrap it'.[26] Many of the anti-Prevent rallies held around the UK in 2015 and 2016 made a point of featuring individuals like Ifhat Smith at the centre of Prevent-related stories.

The 'eco-terrorism' story was the latest in a string of claims alleging that children from toddlers to teens were being referred to Prevent counter-terrorism officers. The overwhelming majority of these stories either turn out to have nothing to do with Prevent – they involve other youth safeguarding issues – or a referral has not resulted in an intervention.

These stories are the weapons used by a powerful anti-Prevent campaign, led and driven by Salafi-Islamists, that seeks to overturn the Government's counter-terrorism strategy. This campaign extends to education trade unions, sections of the political Left and some ordinary Muslims. Largely due to the Government's own reticence to defend its own counter-terrorism strategy, an uncontested space has opened up, allowing the activists to promote false information about Prevent. Civil society groups that work with Prevent are often accused of being Islamophobes and Government stooges.

When the Conservative-Liberal Democrat Government, elected in 2010, embarked on a relaunch of Prevent in 2011, it was met with a concerted backlash from Islamist groups. Terrorism analyst Jack Barclay believed Islamists tried to exploit suspicions that Prevent was a cover for domestic intelligence collection and a cover strategy to corrupt the Islamic identity of Muslim youth by spreading liberal and secular ideas. [27]

As Barclay states, some of those hostile to Prevent were ex-members of al-Muhajiroun (ALM), who saw in Prevent a direct challenge to their mission of promoting a militant Islamist awakening, or *sahwah*, among British Muslim youth. They viewed it as an ideological offensive running alongside military offensives in Afghanistan and other Muslim-majority countries. Whereas guns and drone strikes were used in those theatres of combat, the Government was supposedly employing secular ideas to 'divert the youth from developing a complete understanding of their religion'. [28]

Islamists in 2011, Barclay argued, felt that the newly revamped Prevent was stopping them from exercising their right to propagate their form of Islam, to engage in *da'wa*. It was an 'ideological raid' to stop them radicalising Muslim youth.

> *The re-launch of the Prevent strategy by the UK government is therefore seen by the extremists as a serious challenge to what they consider to be their duty as catalysts of a militant Islamist awakening.* [29]

In order to derail Prevent, the anti-Prevent Islamists have used unprecedented and shrewd tactics, reaching out and forming alliances on the political ultra-Left, academics and even civil liberty groups, while also managing to get their views aired in the liberal media and of course within Muslim communities. This has created an influential movement against a strategy whose focus is to prevent individuals from being drawn into terrorism, in the interests of our national security.

The CAGE view

The 'advocacy group' CAGE has taken a consistently hostile line towards both the 2011 relaunch of Prevent and the increased emphasis on rooting out extremist ideology. In its 2013 document 'The Prevent Strategy: A Cradle to Grave Police State' it outlined its main objections.[30] Terrorism and political violence were not grounded in ideology; Prevent is based on a neoconservative worldview bent on confrontation with Islam; people convicted in UK courts 'have been part of British society and embraced its values'; western government policies 'provoke violent action' and convicted terrorists have 'made this repeatedly clear in their public statements'; front-line professionals like teachers and doctors are being trained to be part of a surveillance state; and Prevent is a way to silence Muslims and 'pacify/ depoliticise their faith'. These claims have influenced wider discourse across the political spectrum.

In the above-mentioned 2013 document, CAGE advances the rather contradictory argument that terrorists have an ideology but acts of terrorism are not caused by ideology: 'All terrorists and acts of political violence have an ideology or goal. However, terrorism and political violence is not caused by ideology.' Instead, CAGE claims that terror acts are always a response by Muslims to 'unrepresentative regimes, often aided by Western policy and occupations'. The logic of this would mean that even groups like ISIS and al-Qa'ida are not motivated by a faith-based ideology but solely through grievance.

In his 2015 report, David Anderson QC, the independent reviewer of terrorism legislation, rebuffed the idea that terrorism is solely grievance-based and ideology-free:

> *Many people nurse grievances, with diverse origins in family circumstances, childhood experiences or the frustrations of adult life. Some are even motivated by those grievances to commit acts of violence. But they will not be terrorists unless they seek to justify their violent acts by reference to ideological factors. Ideologies which are invoked to justify acts of violence may fairly be described as extreme, or extremist.*[31]

In July 2015 the *Independent* published a letter condemning Prevent, co-signed by the newly allied leading lights among British Salafists and Islamists, together with a long list of academics, preachers, students and ordinary Muslims. As tweeted by CAGE, the letter was essentially the CAGE position,[32] conceding that ideology was a factor but that 'social, economic and political grievances give it legitimacy'. In effect, the CAGE view is that grievance cancels out ideology.

The letter continued with a textbook Islamist claim that Prevent was engaged in a Government-directed policy of attacking Islam in its totality:

> *Prevent remains fixated on ideology as the primary driver of terrorism. Inevitably, this has meant a focus on religious interaction and Islamic symbolism to assess radicalisation. For example, growing a beard, wearing a hijab or mixing with those who believe Islam has a comprehensive political philosophy are key markers to identify "potential" terrorism.*[33]

The Home Office dismissed the letter as scaremongering, simplistic and inaccurate.[34] It pointed out that dress code has nothing to do with the Prevent Duty whereas the threat of terrorist indoctrination does.

Channel guidance, for example, states that:

> *There is no single way of identifying who is likely to be vulnerable to being drawn into terrorism. Factors that may have a bearing on someone becoming vulnerable may include: peer pressure, influence from other people or via the internet, bullying, crime against them or their involvement in crime, anti social behaviour, family tensions, race/hate crime, lack of self esteem or identity and personal or political grievances.*[35]

CAGE claims that Prevent is based on the so-called 'conveyor belt' theory of radicalisation. Individuals who become non-violent extremists automatically evolve into terrorists. But in one article it quotes a 'leaked government memo' that states the exact opposite, with the Government saying it does not believe people are radicalised by means of a 'linear conveyor belt' from non-violent extremism through to terrorism.[36] The truth is, there is no mention of the conveyor-belt theory in the Prevent strategy.

Those working in Prevent recognise a range of factors that lead people to become radicalised. It is a subject that divides academic opinion. What is certain is that there is no one single route from extremism to terrorism. However, there are factors and influences, as the intervention providers interviewed earlier evidenced. Prevent has to plug into the many scenarios that can emerge from the interplay of these factors, and it does not possess or profess to be a predictive model. There also needs to be support from family or friends or other sources for any intervention to be successful.

Terrorists who claim their acts were provoked by western foreign policy are taken at their word by the Salafists and Islamists. Every terror act is framed as a by-product of US and UK intervention in Muslim countries. 'The West' is portrayed as a monolithic entity and the sworn enemy of Islam. This is rooted in the ideology of Salafi-Islamist movements. They create the notion of a global western-led conspiracy to destroy Islam. Prevent is then framed in this context as yet another weapon in the western armoury to achieve this objective.

The Prevent Duty on public sector front-line staff to safeguard at-risk individuals is described by CAGE as the politicisation of these workers based on a 'limited understanding of Islam and politics of the Muslim world'.[37] It is claimed that they are being trained by people who have only become experts 'due to government funding'. And behind them are 'hostile anti-Muslim websites and activists' putting pressure on public institutions to ban events and 'hate preachers'.

In April 2015 CAGE unleashed a high-profile campaign across the UK, speaking to Muslim communities in a number of cities. Its speakers claimed that Prevent would now be able to remove children from their parents without consent, using health and social services in order to implement a process of deradicalisation.[38]

In Bradford, Asim Qureshi of CAGE claimed the Government would consider taking away children as young as seven if they attended demonstrations by the Stop The War group or their parents did not consent to deradicalisation programmes.[39] Nazir Afzal, the former chief Crown prosecutor for North-West England, criticised Qureshi's comments, labelling them 'scaremongering, pure and simple... taking a child away from their parents is the last thing the State wants to do.'[40]

Bradford was at the centre of a media storm when it transpired that three sisters and their nine children had left the city bound for Syria.[41] In a June 2015 BBC TV *Newsnight* report, journalist Secunder Kermani asked local people for their reaction. He reported one comment that showed how anti-Prevent propaganda was infiltrating Muslim communities:

> *One youth worker in the area told me that some British Muslim women had expressed concerns to him that new government counter-terrorism legislation meant that their children could be taken away from them just for being deeply practising Muslims.*[42]

The Muslim Council of Britain

CAGE is not the only focus of opposition to Prevent. The Muslim Council of Britain (MCB) has been broadly hostile towards Prevent, describing it as a 'broken strategy' in a 2015 parliamentary briefing.[43] While it welcomed Prevent tackling all forms of extremism, it then went on to claim that the entire Muslim community was viewed as a threat to national security. It repeated the claim, also made by CAGE, that the Government adhered to a 'conveyor belt' theory of radicalisation.

The MCB has baulked at Prevent being put on a statutory basis, meaning it is now a legal requirement to safeguard young people in schools and universities. It complained that 'young children's futures may be impacted by incidents which previously would have been dealt with as a disciplinary issue.'[44]

In June 2015 the MCB argued[45] that it was the Government that was hampering anti-ISIS counter radicalisation efforts by not talking or engaging with the organisation. Yet in an interview for *The Guardian*[46] in January 2015, as British Muslims were leaving the UK to fight in Syria and to join ISIS, Dr Shuja Shafi, the head of the MCB, admitted he had 'no idea' why some young people were becoming radicalised.

The MCB has even argued that Prevent is driving Muslims towards the arms of extremists. The organisation has claimed that the Government only wants to talk to Muslims whose views match its own.[47] It is certainly true that the MCB and Whitehall have not been on speaking terms since 2009, when one of MCB's officials signed a declaration in Istanbul in support of providing arms to Gaza and the use of military action to defend the Hamas run territory if necessary.[48] But, since then, the net of consultation with British Muslims has widened to include Muslim civil society groups, charities, mosques and faith-based organisations.

Spying on society

Prevent stands accused by Islamists of introducing a spy network monitoring Muslim communities across the UK. What the Prevent legislation actually lays out is a programme to ensure that teachers in schools, for example, can spot the early signs of radicalisation. But it does not ask teachers to carry out spying activities, nor does it stop children discussing controversial issues.

However, in a post-Wikileaks climate of suspicion about state surveillance it is easy to arouse fears that Prevent is a tool of mass surveillance. Because it works with people who have not committed a criminal act but have been identified as being at risk, Prevent has been easily characterised as spying on the 'innocent'.[49] But its remit and funding clearly define Prevent as targeted safeguarding and nothing more.

Islam21c (the Muslim Research and Development Foundation's former online news service) reinforced the surveillance narrative against Prevent in schools by claiming that it causes young people to be more alienated and isolated from society and therefore easier to radicalise by terrorists. It called Prevent 'a byword for spying in many sections of society' and maintained that children were told by 'fearful parents' at home to keep silent on controversial issues. 'Self-censorship is rampant. Reassurance is little use.'[50] The article's headline asserted that Muslim teachers were fearful of objecting to the Prevent strategy.

This is all part of a 'cradle to grave surveillance' state that, in the view of CAGE and its associates, is being created to regulate all aspects of Muslim life in Britain. People are being 'prosecuted for their ideas and beliefs'[51] and there are no safeguards for Muslims to challenge decisions.

The reality, however, is that safeguarding is not spying, as Leicester Prevent coordinator Will Baldet explains. Nobody is being made to spy, but they are under a legal duty now to have due regard to the need to prevent those people who are being radicalised from being drawn into terrorism in the same way professionals working with vulnerable people would previously have looked out for other forms of abuse.[52]

Anti-Prevent in the universities

One of the most contentious arenas for the implementation of the 2015 Counter-Terrorism and Security Act (CTSA) is the new statutory backing for Prevent in the university sector. The CTSA has put Prevent on a statutory basis obligating public bodies like schools and colleges to carry out the Prevent Duty, compelling them to safeguard against the risk of radicalisation of those in their care. Both the student movement and lecturers have rounded on Prevent, hooking up with CAGE and other pressure groups to mount a strenuous campaign against its implementation on campus. Executive members of the National Union of Students have toured with Moazzam Begg of CAGE under the banner 'Students not Suspects' to galvanise opposition to the 2015 CTSA.

This roadshow hit Birmingham University in October 2015. Posters were put up around the campus with three headlines summing up the roadshow's aims:

> *Preventing Prevent. Cops Off Campus. Black Deaths in Custody.*

At the bottom were the logos of the supporting organisations: FOSIS (the Federation of Student Islamic Societies); UCU (the college lecturers' union); a pressure group called Defend the Right to Protest; the National Union of Students (NUS); and the NUS Black Students' Campaign. Absent from this list of logos was its most controversial participant – the 'independent advocacy organisation working to empower communities impacted by the war on terror', CAGE. NUS began associating with CAGE in early 2015.

At the 2015 NUS conference, Motion 517 called on delegates to reject the UK Government's Counter-Terrorism and Security Act. The legislation had received the Royal Assent just two months before in February. The NUS argued that the new Act was potentially racist. 'Muslims and Black people and communities are systematically targeted by this state surveillance' creating a 'political climate of intense paranoia and scrutiny'.[53]

Motion 517 made the bold claim that the UK Government was using the conflicts in Syria and Iraq and the general threat of terrorism to deliberately attack Muslim and 'Muslim-background' people. The legislation was an attempt to monitor, 'criminalise' and control Muslim students, curbing their freedom of speech and ability to organise on campus.

The NUS solution was to roundly reject any involvement with the Prevent counter-terrorism programme. Instead it would 'educate students on the dangers' of the Act. It urged student unions round the country to work with campus trade unions to make Prevent unworkable. And, topping the list of recommendations to conference, Motion 517 called on the NUS to work 'alongside civil liberties [groups] including CAGE' to repeal the Act and condemn Prevent.[54] The NUS waved through Motion 517 without a vote due to lack of time at the end of the conference.

A similar motion was passed in May 2015 at the Congress of the University and College Union (UCU), representing lecturers, which has come out resolutely against Prevent. 'The Prevent Agenda will force our members to spy on our learners, is discriminatory towards Muslims, and legitimises Islamophobia and xenophobia, encouraging racist views to be publicised and normalised within society.'[55]

This has resulted in a very potent coupling of an Islamist pressure group with Britain's students and lecturers to advance an anti-Prevent agenda. Not everybody in NUS was delighted with this turn of events, and the NUS website carried a statement in May 2015 saying the union would not work with CAGE:

> *CAGE is a deeply problematic organisation. It is clear that its leaders have sympathised with violent extremism and violence against women, and people associated with the group have sympathised with anti-Semitism. In the past they have aligned with both Hizb-ut Tahrir and the Muslim Public Affairs Committee (MPAC), which are subject to NUS's formal No Platform policy.*[56]

However, the NUS logo has appeared repeatedly on posters for 'Students not Suspects' events at which Moazzam Begg has spoken.

At a packed-out 'Students not Suspects' event at Birmingham University on 15 October 2015, Moazzem Begg sat next to the main NUS voice supporting the alliance with CAGE. This was the NUS Black Students' Officer Malia Bouattia (now President of the NUS).[57]

Bouattia said that opposition to Prevent in future should not centre on free speech. She claimed that there had been a 'disproportionate focus' on freedom of speech 'which as a concept has long been divested of any real political motivation'. What would really galvanise opposition was to put forward the proposition that the Government was trying to fundamentally change the nature of Islam. It wanted to turn this faith into a tame poodle.

> *The Prevent initiative is an attempt to reconfigure and engineer the entire foundation of Islamic faith in Britain to a state sponsored, un-threatening version in line with so-called British values*[58]

Bouattia talked about Prevent being a 'classic British tradition of divide and conquer, planting informants in Muslim communities, pitting Muslims against each other and policing the boundaries of the acceptable Muslim'.[59] Her view was echoed around the table in the speeches that followed, with the speaker from Defend the Right to Protest referring to the 'fantasy of British values'.

Begg's speech, which followed Bouattia's, centred on a series of anecdotes to prove that Prevent was a complete failure. The gist was that, over the past fourteen years, a series of ever-more draconian laws had been passed. The counter-terrorism dragnet was now catching people of all ages guilty of no crime at all – including toddlers. The picture painted was a mixture of cruelty and incompetence.

With the debate on counter-extremism and counter-terrorism on British campuses dominated by CAGE and its supporters within the NUS, student union officers up and down the country have made the most strident claims about Prevent, including this from an officer at the University of Strathclyde:

> *Part of the Prevent duty guidance explains certain symptoms that a university would have to look out for. The symptoms say that if you are not white, you are more likely to be a terrorist.*[60]

Anti-Prevent activists in the leadership of NUS clearly believe the momentum is with them. In one guide to resisting Prevent, they write about dismantling the Government's counter-terrorism strategy.[61] They also claimed that Prevent is 'rooted in a hard-right wing/ neoconservative perception of the world and Islam'. Prevent is said to share the same ideology as the English Defence League, strengthening the 'Islamophobic notion that Muslims are a suspect community in Britain'. Prevent has apparently launched a new 'Cold War' against Islam and Muslims; and the battle against 'Islamist extremism' parallels that against communism and the Soviet Union, which gave rise to McCarthyite hysteria.

The Prime Minister responds

The defiant stance of many in academia towards Prevent provoked a response from the Government on 20 July 2015. On that date David Cameron responded to the criticisms being made by the NUS and others in a speech delivered at Ninestiles School in Birmingham – a school attended by Moazzam Begg's son. The venue allowed Cameron to showcase an educational institution that promoted a 'commitment to British values as well as outstanding academic success'.[62] He pointed to the shared community around the school bringing together children from many faiths and backgrounds. It went, he said, 'to the heart' of what he wanted to talk about.

Cameron flatly denied that the Government was trying to demonise anybody. The urgent task was to tackle Islamist extremism, but not Islam the religion. Most Muslims were capable of holding down a reconciled identity that embraced both Islam and being British. And his call to oppose extremism was because those fostering it were dividing Muslim communities and causing damage.

He went through a litany of conspiracy theories that have been used to support the notion that the Government's counter-extremism push is all about oppressing Muslims: that 9/11 was inspired by Mossad and that British security services knew about 7/7 but let it happen to provoke an anti-Muslim backlash.

The Prime Minister rounded on the NUS, asking why student leaders would oppose Holocaust deniers and yet allow Islamists a free rein on campus:

> *When David Irving goes to a university to deny the Holocaust – university leaders rightly come out and condemn him. They don't deny his right to speak but they do challenge what he says. But when an Islamist extremist goes there to promote their poisonous ideology, too often university leaders look the other way through a mixture of misguided liberalism and cultural sensitivity. As I said, this is not about clamping down on free speech. It's about applying our shared values uniformly.*[63]

He asked the NUS why it was giving prominent support to an organisation like CAGE that had referred to the notorious IS operative Jihadi John as a 'beautiful young man'. He told the student body that working with CAGE could only 'shame your organisation and your noble history of campaigning for justice'.[64]

'Not making anyone safer'

The list of UK students who have engaged in terror predates the formation of the so-called Islamic State, and includes:[65]

- Amer Mirza – a student at the University of Humberside convicted in 1999 for a petrol bomb attack on a Territorial Army base in West London
- Mohammed Naveed Bhatti – convicted in 2007 of conspiracy to cause explosions; studying at Brunel University when arrested. Also arrested in connection with this plot was Omar Abdur Rehman, a student at the University of Westminster
- Waseem Mughal – in July 2007 he admitted inciting murder for terrorist purposes. A student at the University of Leicester.

However, while most Muslims studying in British universities are peaceful and law-abiding and do not subscribe to Islamist politics, a small minority clearly find the emergence of a self-proclaimed 'caliphate' in Syria and Iraq – and Libya – to be very seductive. It validates their worldview and identity. Lecturers are not being asked to spy on Muslim students but to be aware of this numerically small group, some of whom may go down a terrorist path.

Students themselves have reported fellow undergraduates whose behaviour has been worrying.[66] In December 2014, students at Birkbeck College in London reported their concerns about twenty-year-old David Souaan, from Serbia, who had pictures of himself posing with guns in Syria and clearly held an extreme interpretation of Islam. In May that year he was arrested at Heathrow airport on his way to Syria. He had previously been in that war-torn country in December 2013. During his trial, it was revealed that one video clip on his phone showed a man's throat being cut. He was found guilty of planning to join terrorist forces in Syria and jailed for three-and-a-half years.

A year after the Prevent Duty came into effect, many of CAGE's allies and others wrote a joint letter to *The Guardian* airing the now-familiar concerns that the strategy was forcing doctors, teachers and front-line staff to monitor 'people's religious and political views'. The letter managed to conflate a 70 per cent increase in hate crimes against

Muslims reported to the Metropolitan Police with Prevent, which it alleged was 'encouraging ethnic profiling'.[67]

Signatories including lawyers, academics and anti-Prevent Islamists called 'on the government to take urgent action to repeal this legislation'. For the full list of signatories, a click-through button took the online user to the 'Students not Suspects' website, the campaign organised by the National Union of Students with support from CAGE and FOSIS.[68]

They argued that Prevent 'is not making anyone safer'. While calling for the end of Prevent, they offered no practical alternative to prevent people from being drawn into terrorism. Meanwhile, ISIS continues to pump out powerful propaganda films encouraging British Muslims to commit terrorist atrocities in the UK and join its so-called caliphate.

Free speech in the classroom

Two education unions have been particularly prominent critics of Prevent: the National Union of Teachers (NUT) and the University and College Union (UCU). The NUT conference in 2016 reaffirmed its opposition to Prevent, stating that it was worried the strategy was stopping teachers and pupils discussing global issues and would 'smother the legitimate expression of political opinion'.[69]

The conference voted that the Government should entirely withdraw Prevent from schools and develop a totally new strategy. But, while Prevent persisted, the union wanted to ensure that equality rights were upheld, students were not 'racially profiled' or victimised 'for reason of faith, culture or legitimate political expression'.

NUT officials have claimed that Prevent is stopping classroom debate. Prominent NUT activist Rob Ferguson went much further, telling the Marxism 2015 conference that Prevent was a 'bridgehead into schools to attack whole Muslim communities'. He told the same meeting that the legislation was about identifying vulnerable individuals at risk of both violent and non-violent extremism. Then

Ferguson quoted the Prevent Duty for schools, saying that 'non-violent extremists purport to identify grievances to which terrorist organisations then claim to have a solution'.[70]

> *That one clause wipes out any pretence or claim at a commitment to free discussion and debate in the university lecture hall or the classroom.*[71]

The University and College Union activists assert that Prevent will force its members to 'spy on our learners'. It also claims that Prevent will 'help racist parties such as UKIP to flourish', and encourage discrimination against Muslim staff and students as well as normalising racist views in society.[72] The union's conference condemned Prevent as a dangerous strategy; the organisation provides downloadable posters on its website with the slogan: 'I dissent from Prevent'.[73] However, the vote on Prevent was held in closed session without the media present and it was reported that the motion, urging non-compliance, was so close it required a recount.[74]

As repeatedly emphasised by the schools inspectorate Ofsted, schools have not been asked to draft new procedures for radicalisation, nor are they being asked to 'spy' on children. Children at risk of radicalisation should be dealt with through existing safeguarding policies and referred through the same safeguarding pathways that schools already have in place.

Nor is the Duty seeking to close down discussion in class; in fact it is encouraging the very opposite. Geraint Evans, Ofsted's National Lead for Extremism, has made it quite clear:

> *If I was to hear about a school shutting down debate because of fears about referral, that would be of great concern to me... Let me make it absolutely clear the expectation from Ofsted – good practice is where schools and college look for opportunities for young people to have discussions about controversial issues.*[75]

This is also the advice coming from the Department for Education. Rather than closing down debate, authorities want views discussed and challenged. Only then can extreme views be addressed – by openly discussing them, a practice schools should be adopting in class. This is of paramount importance because schools may be the only place where a child's views are challenged, especially if intolerant and extreme views are being promoted at home, as identified by a head teacher who had the dual problem of parents subscribing to far-Right and Islamist extreme views.

Since the introduction of the Prevent Duty in July 2015, the Home Office claims that 400,000 front-line staff in schools, colleges and local authorities have received Government-produced training to raise their awareness of radicalisation.[76] In the early days, it was clear that some teachers struggled to know exactly what was expected of them. An increasing amount of information is now being made available and includes a useful website produced by the Department for Education called Educate Against Hate.

One repeated concern expressed by teachers, however, is the lack of confidence about the distinction between Islam and Islamist extreme ideologies in the context of radicalisation. Theology, for obvious reasons, is not an area the Government has chosen to step into. The task of providing this training has often fallen into the lap of Muslim civil society organisations, many of whom are not fully equipped to meet the demands from numerous frontline agencies across the country.

Prevent, it needs to be stressed, is not about addressing conservative Islam, nor is it an attempt to socially engineer a secular Islam.[77] It simply seeks to deter people from supporting both Islamist and far-Right terrorism. Partnering with civil society groups who are able to talk to teaching staff about the distinction between Islam and Islamist extremism is important. Teachers may not always understand the difference between conservative practices of Islam and extremist beliefs. As a result, some may wrongly suspect pupils are being radicalised.

Engaging with the community

Since February 2015 the Home Office has engaged through Prevent with 372 mosques, 385 community organisations and 156 faith organisations.[78] Prevent local coordinators are in contact with Muslim groups and individuals on a daily basis. The Home Office reports that this network engaged with nearly 50,000 individuals in 2015 – from within and outside the UK's Muslim communities.

The Home Office also reported that 130 community-based projects were delivered in 2015 under Prevent, reaching over 25,300 participants. A total of 58,000 pieces of illegal material were removed online in the same year. This includes ultra-violent material from ISIS cynically modelled on video games and shared by school children. Counter-narrative products developed in partnership with civil society groups generated over 15 million online viewings in 2015 compared with 3 million in 2014.

Inevitably, those numerous civil society groups who have sought to deliver Prevent at a local level have clashed with the Islamists. Many of these groups have been unfairly and vociferously attacked and repeatedly denigrated by the Islamist anti-Prevent lobby for supporting a much-needed counter-radicalisation strategy.

This has resulted in many Muslim groups who are prepared to work with and support the Government's Prevent strategy not disclosing their support, in fear of being characterised as apostates or accused of being 'native informants' paid to spy on Muslim communities. This very negative atmosphere has been fostered by the anti-Prevent Islamists, leaving Muslim civil society groups feeling isolated and embattled.

The media's response to Prevent has also often been damaging. Journalists, without the full facts, have parroted stories of children being rounded up by Prevent when closer scrutiny would show that many of these stories had no foundation. The 'chilling impact' of the media's reporting on Prevent was noted in an article in *The Observer* on radicalisation in the UK:

Media coverage has not always helped inform a reasoned debate. The media have a duty to report how policies are being implemented locally, but accusing schools of over-reacting in cases where facts are not yet established risks having a chilling impact on local perceptions of the police and schools. Journalists quick to decry nanny-statism need to avoid sensationalism and recognise the impact their reporting can have on professionals' willingness to intervene.[79]

Other concerns about the application of Prevent have focused on the different approaches of local authority Prevent coordinators responsible for the delivery of Prevent across the UK in communities and the public sector. Activities vary in each city; some coordinators have worked hard engaging the trust of local communities, bringing mosques and others on side. Others have concentrated more on schools and universities. They all have a key role to play in clarifying misconceptions regarding Prevent.

Regardless of what its opponents think, some kind of strategy is required that intervenes between terrorist radicalisers, who are a reality, and their vulnerable targets. At present that is Prevent – it may be something different in the future. In evidence to the Home Affairs Select Committee, the Independent Reviewer of Terrorist Legislation David Anderson QC wrote in February 2016 that it was undeniable Prevent had become toxic to many British Muslims.

However, Anderson also noted, 'It is quite possible that some of those attacking Prevent (not of course all) are motivated by a wish not to promote harmony but to sow grievance and division.'[80] He added that it was 'perverse' to undermine the safeguarding role of schools, citing the case of the Muslim convert who had photographed his children holding a sword in front of an ISIS flag.

Prevent had become a source of rumour and mistrust, Anderson noted, as opposed to the powers that the police can exercise under Pursue: extended arrest, detention powers, port powers, passport removal and relocation. Everything that impacts communities under counter-terrorist legislation seems to be bracketed under 'Prevent'. And the sorry truth is that Prevent has become a lightning rod for all kinds of unrelated issues, where many Muslims who may hold grievances about the media or other policies have often unfairly pointed the finger towards Prevent.

But in order to instil confidence, to root out 'unverified cases' and to demonstrate the achievements of Prevent, always ignored by the anti-Prevent critics, an independent review of the strategy, as has been argued for by David Anderson, could help address many of the concerns raised.[81] Others have argued an independent review is not required, just greater transparency in the implementation of Prevent.

Under attack

Prevent has suffered sustained criticism and castigation from the Salafi-Islamists in a concerted attempt to destroy the brand. This campaign has met with some success. Yet no alternative strategy has been mapped out at a time when the country's terrorist threat level is ranked at severe and European cities have come under attack.

Faced with this onslaught against Prevent, the Government has taken its time in coming out to defend its own counter-terrorism policy. It sometimes seems to have been stung by the criticism to the point where it is incapable of reacting. Civil society groups that have defended Prevent publicly have then been left to fend for themselves.

There are on-going issues with Prevent that need resolving. Training of front-line staff is still an issue if needless referrals to Channel are to be minimised. Prevent is simply an additional layer of safeguarding concerned with a single issue of terrorism. The bodies that now have a statutory duty to implement Prevent – schools and colleges for example – are already safeguarding their young charges. But Prevent has been presented as an instrument for silencing anti-Government dissent; this is an unfounded view, but the situation is not helped by high-profile unfortunate referrals.

The Government also needs to tackle the misinformation

circulated about referrals. When some British Muslims have come to believe that praying five times a day or wearing the hijab will lead to a Prevent referral, then there has clearly been a breakdown in communication between Government and the public. The freedom of worship and religious expression could not be compromised by Prevent even if that was the aim, which it is not, as this freedom is protected by both UK law and Article 9 of the European Convention on Human Rights.

The threat that Prevent was set up to handle – terrorist radicalisation – is not imaginary or some kind of McCarthyite witch hunt as detractors claim.[82] In January 2016, ISIS promised a 'Doomsday attack' on the UK that would eclipse the November 2015 Paris killings and turn 'children's hair white'. An ISIS video warning of the terror to come on British streets featured London landmarks like Big Ben, Buckingham Palace and Trafalgar Square.[83]

After the 2015 Paris attacks, British intelligence services declared that they had foiled seven terror attacks in the past year, including one in the previous month.[84] ISIS and al-Qa'ida have put a renewed emphasis on Muslims perpetrating random attacks with knives, guns and even rocks on non-Muslims – so-called 'lone wolf' attacks in their home countries. At the same time, some Britons continue to pack their bags for Syria in the belief they are fighting for a caliphate.

The director general of MI5, Andrew Parker, told a City of London dinner in 2015 that, since the 7/7 London bombings in 2005, his organisation had doubled in size. Two thirds of its work was now focused on counter-terrorism. He admitted that MI5 could not have predicted how the ISIS threat would grow.

> We are seeing plots against the UK directed by terrorists in Syria; enabled through contacts with terrorists in Syria; and inspired by ISIL's sophisticated exploitation of technology.[85]

Prevent plays a central role in the UK's counter-terrorism strategy, stopping people crossing the line into criminality. What is clear, however, is that Salafi-Islamists, for clear ideological reasons, have sought to misinform Muslims and the wider public about Prevent, particularly at a time when the security threat level to the UK from ISIS and al-Qa'ida affiliates remains at 'severe'. Prevent was, and always has been, an ideological battle for Britain's Salafi-Islamists.

FOUR

IDENTITY POLITICS: ISLAMISM AND THE ULTRA LEFT, THE FAR RIGHT AND FEMINISTS

In March 2016 a group of demonstrators stood outside the headquarters of the National Union of Students and protested about so-called safe spaces and no-platform policies on UK campuses. These have been used to prevent the human rights activist Peter Tatchell, the ex-Muslim Maryam Namazie and two prominent feminists, Germaine Greer and Julie Bindel, from speaking to students in British universities.[1] The gathering was described in one report as a 'grand coalition of humanists, atheists, liberal Muslims and human rights activists'.[2]

The demonstration was in reaction to a climate of clampdown on free speech in universities.[3] Contrary to the Islamists' claim, this curbing of democracy is not the fault of Prevent co-ordinators or counter-terrorism policies. It is emanating from those sections of the student movement that have allied with Islamists to form possibly the most powerful voting bloc within the National Union of Students. This faction is excluding non-Islamist Muslims and secularists from campuses on the grounds of 'Islamophobia'. And its influence has extended into the education trade unions and even sympathetic sections of the media and academia.

The concept of 'identity politics' has become ever more prevalent and powerful since it was coined in the late twentieth century. It concerns political movements or positions motivated by particular groups of society, defined by (e.g.) race, gender or sexual orientation. As employed by Salafists and Islamists, identity politics has sucked in feminists and LGBT (lesbian, gay, bisexual and transgender) activists who are prepared to defend people adhering to an ideology, Islamism, that is misogynist and homophobic. They will even defend it against 'Islamophobic' secular and ex-Muslims.

The demonstration proved that the emergence of identity politics, particularly in the student movement but also on the political Left and Right, has redrawn the battle lines on issues like free speech, secularism and democracy. Libertarian right-wingers stood next to traditional socialists, and secular Muslims rubbed shoulders with atheists. Peter Tatchell looked a little startled as he took to the megaphone.

> *We're here to defend free speech against those who want to restrict legitimate debate. Some of us have political disagreements with each other on various issues. I am critical of some of the people and organisations at this protest and some of them disagree with me. But that's fine. We are all united in our agreement that free speech should be defended and intolerant ideas should be challenged.*[4]

Sixty-four-year-old Tatchell, an LGBT activist for five decades, had intended to speak in early 2016 at Canterbury Christ Church University on the subject of 're-radicalising queers'.[5] But then an email from the NUS LGBT officer Fran Cowling declared she would not share a stage with a man who was racist and transphobic, an accusation utterly rejected by Tatchell. It was based on a letter Tatchell had co-signed demanding freedom of speech after the feminist Germaine Greer was barred over her views on transsexuals.[6]

The whole affair brings into sharp focus a crisis across the political spectrum, fed by the rise of identity politics, that is working to the benefit of Islamist extremists – as well as the far Right. It has split the Left and Right, leaving some, like Tatchell, a little bemused to discover with whom they now have to stand as allies. As an illustration of the impact of identity politics, showing how some on the Left, feminists and even other LGBT activists are prepared to side with the Salafi-Islamists, the example of Maryam Namazie is very instructive.

Legitimate questioning or Islamophobia?

Maryam Namazie is an ex-Muslim, therefore an apostate to Islamists. Her views on Islamist ideology are very much from an atheist and old-style secular Left-wing point of view. The Iranian-born activist is the spokesperson for One Law for All – a group campaigning against sharia councils in the UK – and she also represents the Council of Ex-Muslims of Britain. Her style on social media is combative, but equally she receives a high level of very spiteful abuse over her departure from Islam.

In late 2015 she found herself being turned away from colleges over the accusation she was Islamophobic and inciting hatred. What she actually does is critique Islamism and questions the 'culture of offence'[7] that makes challenging such ideas increasingly impossible. A speech to be delivered at Trinity College, Dublin was delayed by six months after a student society pulled out from supporting the event.[8] She was then barred from speaking at the Warwick Atheists, Secularists and Humanists Society.[9]

The reason given by Warwick was that she was in contravention of their 'safe space' policy, which includes not inciting hatred. The 'safe space' idea was pioneered by the gay and women's movements in the US in the 1960s and 1970s and is now a familiar feature of campus politics worldwide.[10] The original concept was that social groups whose ideas were at risk of being shouted down by 'mainstream' opinion should have a safe space in which they could discuss and develop their thoughts without being challenged. In its modern form it is often characterised as a policy of 'no tolerance' to hostile views being expressed by parties deemed to be racist, homophobic or otherwise unacceptable.

Three months after banning Maryam Namazie, staff at the University of Warwick voted to condemn the Government's Prevent strategy on the grounds that it introduced a culture of surveillance and paranoia.[11] The same, apparently, does not apply to a culture of 'safe spaces' where veteran civil rights activists can be barred from university campuses because they might upset Islamists.

Warwick eventually rescinded its earlier ban, and Namazie spoke on the subject 'Apostasy, Blasphemy and Free Expression in the age of ISIS'.[12] Addressing a packed lecture theatre, she argued that it was wrong for university campuses to conflate Islam with Islamism and said that the latter needed to be challenged. While the Warwick event eventually passed without incident, the same was not the case at Goldsmiths College in London. Things there turned very nasty. It would prove to be a highly instructive episode in the light of the situation now developing in British universities.

Goldsmiths' Atheist, Secularist and Humanist Society asked Namazie to speak on the same topic. In November 2015 the society received an email from the Islamic student society at Goldsmiths warning that their invited speaker was 'renowned for being Islamophobic and very controversial'.[13]

> *Just a few examples of her Islamophobic statements, she labelled the niqab [cloth covering the lower face] – a religious symbol for Muslim women, 'a flag for far-right Islamism'. Also she went onto tweet, they are 'body bags' for women. This is just 2 examples of how mindless she is, and presents her lack of understanding and knowledge about Islam.*[14]

The tone of this complaint – as with similar incidents with other speakers at other colleges – implied that, if she were to set foot on campus, then the very safety of the minority being discussed would be compromised. In order to maintain a safe space, opinions that threaten ('challenge' would once have been the word) must be excluded.

Namazie got to speak; but, throughout the one-hour meeting in a packed lecture theatre, there was a constant hum of low-level disruption from a group of men who objected to her speech. They walked in front of Namazie and grumbled disapproval in the front row.

When Namazie showed some stills from the 'Jesus and Mo' cartoons (a satirical series of conversations between an imaginary Jesus and the Prophet Muhammad), one of the men stood up and pulled the plug out of her projector. As she talked about her views on the UK's sharia courts, the same men at the front hissed two words repeatedly:

Safe space! Safe space! Safe space!

All of this was captured on film and can be viewed online. After several minutes of disruption and the calling in of a security guard, Namazie told the audience – very calmly – that she was offended when Muslims called for the death of apostates and that, in thirteen countries, this punishment was actually on the statute book. She said that Islamists with guns and gallows arbitrarily define in these states what is correct Islam, and they have killed both atheists and Muslims as a consequence.

> *When we immediately say that anybody who criticises is offensive, we are trying to shut down debate.*

This led to escalating pandemonium, with a lone security guard called in to try to calm things down.[15]

Free speech versus safe space

In its reporting of the hour-long event, the Islamist news website 5Pillars homed in on Namazie's thirty-second irritated confrontation with the young male student who had pulled the plug out of her projector.[16] That reportage was predictable enough, but more unexpected was the reaction of other societies at Goldsmiths to the events of that evening. Far from rushing to the defence of free speech, they defended the student union's safe space policy instead.[17]

One might have assumed, for example, that the Goldsmith Feminist Society would rally to the support of a woman being barracked by a group of men. Instead, the society posted a statement online declaring:

> *Goldsmiths Feminist Society stands in solidarity with Goldsmiths Islamic Society. We support them in condemning the actions of the Atheist, Secularist and Humanist Society and agree that hosting known islamophobes at our university creates a climate of hatred.*[18]

Shortly afterwards, in spite of the national media interest that was generated by the Feminist Society comment, the Goldsmiths LGBTQ+ Society waded in on its Facebook page in support of the Islamic student society. It referred to 'solidarity with the sisters and brothers of our Goldsmiths ISOC' and accused those who had invited Namazie of 'Islamophobic remarks, attitudes and harassment'. It urged respect for the 'necessary privacy of safer spaces'.

> *We find that personal and social harm enacted in the name of 'free speech' is foul, and detrimental to the wellbeing of students and staff on campus.*[19]

There is a certain irony that those claiming that the Government's Prevent strategy is clamping down on dissent and destroying free speech are far more culpable in this regard by using 'safe spaces'. One explanation for feminists and LGBT activists defending safe spaces is that these movements invented the concept four or five decades ago – but in a different context. The subsequent move to 'weaponise' safe space has turned it into a tool for removing university administrators who offend students and banning speakers deemed to incite hatred or discord.[20]

The solution to this censorious development of safe spaces is, as Namazie suggested in an interview with the BBC after her experience at Goldsmiths, to take the concept back to being about protecting people but not giving ideas a protective wall to hide behind. Criticism of religion, she argued, is an intrinsic part of the democratic debate. People do not have to listen but equally they cannot ban it. The same BBC report featured a young student called Charlie Parker who was setting up a Free Speech Society at the London School of Economics.[21]

With no sense of irony, the student union was already threatening to ban it.[22]

So untenable has the National Union of Students' position become on banning feminists, secularists and veteran Left-wing activists that it is now a subject of media ridicule. One article suggested that the NUS should publish a regular 'League Table of Oppression'.[23] If we are ever to achieve social justice on Earth, then the NUS needs to decree 'the precise privilege of every person' on the planet, commented the *Daily Telegraph*'s sketchwriter. This followed an NUS motion announcing that gay men are 'no longer oppressed within the LGBT+ community', should lose their LGBT representation within the union, and are often guilty of 'misogyny, transphobia, racism and biphobia'.[24]

Feminists, Islamists and the stoning of 'adultresses'

Further evidence of the warming relations between sections of feminism and Islamism was the decision by the Exeter University Feminist Society to support an event with CAGE's Moazzam Begg in March 2016. The society agreed to lend its name to a 'Students not Suspects' rally with Begg headlining and Shelly Asquith on the same platform representing the National Union of Students.

On Twitter, the Exeter feminists made their position crystal clear: 'Prevent is a harmful, Islamophobic piece of legislation, and it's a shame that what was meant to be an event to combat this has been derailed and hijacked.'[25] In a subsequent statement, the Exeter FemSoc said that, as claims against the speakers had 'not been confirmed by any reliable source', they would support the event 'despite the fear-mongering and questionable tactics of some who disagree with the event's premise'. There was also some uproar about the event on Twitter, given the opinions of CAGE's Asim Qureshi on the stoning to death of apostates and adulterers under sharia conditions, as expressed in a 2012 interview with Wikileaks founder Julian Assange (see Chapter 2).[26]

An audience member on the evening of the Exeter event asked why the far Right and fascists were banned and yet CAGE was allowed on campus when its director of research supported such draconian punishments against women and non-believers. Begg responded curtly that 'your question is a red herring', to majority applause and laughter. Sidestepping the question very skilfully, he continued that he was at the meeting in the context of what had been done to him at Guantanamo 'and the effects of anti-terror legislation'. Qureshi could account for his personal opinion, but Begg was not going to offer a view.

> I don't know anybody who has been stoned to death in the UK. I don't know anybody who has been tried as an adulteress [Begg's word] in the UK. I don't know anybody who is applying those rules in the UK.

After Begg refused to answer the stoning issue head on, the NUS's Shelly Asquith waded in to define fascism as racist and genocidal but also applicable to the Henry Jackson Society (a conservative-leaning think tank) and its equality-promoting offshoot Student Rights. She defended working with CAGE on the basis that, while some individuals in CAGE might have views she did not agree with, the organisation in its entirety was not objectionable.

To segregate or not to segregate

Deciding who should and should not speak on campus has vexed many university leaders as well as student unions. The question of external speakers demanding certain measures as a condition for speaking on campus has proved to be particularly problematic. An example would be an Islamist speaker who insists on seating being segregated at meetings before agreeing to appear. This dilemma led Universities UK (UUK) – the body representing the country's vice-chancellors – to publish some controversial guidance in 2013. In effect, it agreed with Islamists that refusing to concede to the demand of external speakers for gender segregation was denying students access to their views, thereby undermining free speech.[27]

One paragraph in the guidance from Universities UK caused a media storm:

> *Assuming the side-by-side segregated seating arrangement is adopted, there does not appear to be any discrimination on gender grounds merely by imposing segregated seating. Both men and women are being treated equally, as they are both being segregated in the same way.*[28]

FOSIS, the Federation of Student Islamic Societies, characterised the ensuing debate on segregation as 'vilifying Islamic societies and Muslim students.'[29] FOSIS's head of communications, Camilla Khan, wrote that it was incorrect to think that segregation implied hierarchy. She argued, in contradiction of many Muslim theologians and commentators, that 'male and female seating is a simple religious manifestation that has been established for multiple millennia' and to remove it would 'alienate Muslim students from social engagement by denying their right to religious freedom'. Segregation was presented in this article as 'Muslim female empowerment'.

The underlying assumption was that all Muslim students would demand segregation. One example that negates that was a gala dinner held by the Islamic student society at the London School of Economics in March 2016. A seven-foot screen was erected across the function room at the Grand Connaught Rooms, a central London venue, dividing men and women. This was given the thumbs-up by the college's student union, but Muslim students who attended told a journalist that they felt 'intimidated' and did not feel it was a necessary expression of their faith.[30]

Secularists, the mainstream media and many Muslim commentators greeted the Universities UK report with horror. Islamists, however, were delighted. Islam21c accused critics of the report of taking 'a step in the direction of fascism' and being part of the 'Islamophobia machine'.[31] The site went on to conjure up some new insults for the enemies of Islamism. Those claiming segregation amounted to gender apartheid were 'Useful Idiots and Malicious Agents of Hate'. Islam21c described the subsequent intervention by Prime Minister David Cameron to get Universities UK to reconsider its position as 'tyrannical'.

iERA (Islamic Education and Research Academy) presented segregation as a normal Islamic practice and something that men and women would naturally choose to do. With a tortuous piece of logic, it claimed that the freedom of speech of a religious group could be 'curtailed unlawfully' if an unsegregated area were to be imposed, making it impossible for the event to go ahead.[32] Abdur Raheem Green of iERA claimed that, with a global 'revival in adherence to normative Islamic practices', British universities might be damaged economically if they made Muslim students 'sit with people of the opposite sex'.[33]

The group felt that the UUK report vindicated iERA in the wake of an earlier decision by University College London to bar the group from speaking on its campus after men and women had been seated separately at a debate between American cosmologist Professor Lawrence Krauss and iERA's Hamza Tzortzis, titled 'Islam or Atheism: Which Makes More Sense?'[34] Krauss protested in the strongest terms and threatened to walk out over what he perceived as segregation.[35]

Saleem Chagtai of iERA, on BBC Radio 4's *Today* programme, argued that segregation was no different from Eton and other colleges in this country, which were sex segregated. Some Muslims went even further, comparing the everyday normality of gender-segregated toilets to segregated seating at a university event.

Promoting liberal concepts to defend their illiberalism, iERA argued[36] that gender segregation was in line with the Equalities Act and that the UUK report had given them the thumbs up. However, the Equalities and Human Right Commission did not concur with iERA; on the contrary, it stated that gender segregation outside of religious worship was indeed unlawful.[37]

Which direction is Left?

Since the 1990s, identity politics have overwhelmed traditional socialist ideology. Working-class politics have been replaced by 'a rising tide of fractious racial, ethnic, religious and gender conflict'.[38] Class has given way to an emphasis on culture and the Left now often bolsters group identities it would once have challenged. This clearly seems to apply to Islamism.

Embracing multiculturalism and cultural relativism, the pro-Islamist Left has conflated Islamism with Islam, assuming that Islamist leaders speak for all Muslims and that their ideology is normative Islam. The logic then proceeds that any criticism must be Islamophobic, even if it comes from other Muslims. Those Muslims who criticise Islamism are not being true to their own identity and so the Left pours equal scorn on their heads alongside their Islamist allies.

> *In fact, this politics doesn't merely ignore dissent, in many ways it forbids it. The likes of Stop the War Coalition, Socialist Workers Party, Unite Against Fascism... are there as prefects to silence dissenters and defend Islamism as a defence of 'Muslims'.*[39]

Identity politics and multiculturalism have led some on the Left into a de facto merger with Islamism, in turn marginalising secular voices within Islam. The logic of their position leads socialists to attack Muslims campaigning for gender equality and community cohesion. It is, as the American activist Meredith Tax puts it, an alliance of the Muslim Right and the Anglo-American Left.[40]

Stop the War

The current mindset of this section of the political Left was demonstrated at a Stop the War Coalition (StWC) meeting in March 2016.[41] This group was founded in September 2001, in the weeks that followed the 9/11 attack on the World Trade Center in New York.[42] Its most significant moment was under the Tony Blair administration, the vast demonstration against the Iraq War on 15 February 2003 in London.

Stop the War's patrons and officers span the Labour Party, Green Party, Respect, National Union of Students, trade unions and far-Left groups. Jeremy Corbyn, the Labour leader elected in 2015, was Chair from 2011. Other long-term supporters are prominent Left-wing politicians like George Galloway and Diane Abbott (both patrons).[43] British Muslim political figures involved include The Cordoba Foundation's Anas Altikriti and Salma Yaqoob as patrons and Shamiul Joarder from Friends of Al-Aqsa on the steering committee.

The group expounds the view that there is a clear linkage between wars in the Middle East, the rise of Islamophobia, and the UK Government's Prevent counter-terrorism programme. What the group's analysis does not allow any room for is the influence of Islamism as an ideology in the UK and among many Muslims around the world.

Back in 2001, two Left-wing Iraqi activists pulled away from StWC when it refused to condemn Islamist-inspired terrorism. Moayed Ahmad was a member of the Politburo of the Worker-communist Party of Iraq. He and his political comrade Dashti Jamal resigned from the steering committee of StWC over concerns that instead of backing the 'on-going struggle for freedom, equality and well-being by the working class, the communists, the women, the socialists, the radical and secular people and freedom lovers in those countries', StWC had gone for 'lining up with the savage Talibans and the likes of Political Islam'.[44]

The two Iraqis wrote these words, which were remarkably prescient, summing up the situation today with utmost clarity:

> *The left tells us that adopting a radical view towards Islamism enhances racism in the west, but this is a backward view of the worst kind. It advocates enslaving generations in Asian and Middle Eastern communities under the yoke*

of Islam and denies them the right to have secularism and
universal human values and rights.

At the March 2016 meeting of StWC, the group's cordial relationship with CAGE was very evident. Proceedings were paused to allow for a video message to the audience from Moazzam Begg. He was introduced as a heroic figure who had 'campaigned against the War on Terror and the racism associated with it'.

His narrative fitted the Left's worldview like a glove. Muslims were oppressed and demonised, 'targeted by the right wing media and the politicians who are unscrupulous in creating an atmosphere that targets Muslims'.[45] The UK, France and Russia were on the same side, bombing Syria and creating an unprecedented refugee situation. Islamophobia was on the rise as a result of not just war and refugees but a deliberate policy by the UK Government, under its Prevent programme, to target all Muslims simply because of their faith. Begg claimed people had been rounded up for writing poetry or reading books or just saying the word 'terrorist'. He closed his video address with a 'first they came for the Muslims' warning to his audience – echoing the famous Holocaust poem of Martin Niemoller[46] – that Prevent would not stop at its 'Cold War against Muslim' but come for non-Muslim radicals too.

The StWC's speakers, including the group's convenor Lindsey German, a former member of the central committee of the Socialist Workers Party (SWP), echoed most of this. The message was this: Muslims are facing what happened to the Jews in the 1930s, supervised by an Islamophobic state machine. The Middle East wars, the refugee crisis, terrorist attacks in Europe – these are all excuses to turn the screw on the entire Muslim population. Democratic debate is being shut down by Prevent, and Islamophobia is a 'weapon of mass distraction', turning attention from the Government's domestic and foreign policy failures.

The scorpion dance

As early as 1994, the editor of *Socialist Worker* – Chris Harman – wrote an influential pamphlet urging Marxists to enter a kind of scorpion dance with Islamism and not reject it outright as a form of fascism. In spite of appearances and its hatred of the Left, women's rights and secularism, Islamism (argued Harman) was not akin to Nazism but more like Argentinian Peronism.

Harman rejected those on the Left who characterised Islamism as Islam with a fascist face. Conversely, he also warned against blindly accepting Islamism as a progressive and anti-imperialist movement of the oppressed. Instead, he urged a 'careful course through the contradictions of Islamism'.[47] It discriminated against women, let local ruling classes off the hook by only attacking western imperialism and attacked secularists. But it also destabilised the hold of capitalism over the Muslim world and was an expression of the exploitation of millions of people.

So the solution for Marxists was to operate alongside the Islamists when they were in opposition to the same enemy: 'with the state never, with the Islamists sometimes'.[48] Over time, the secular socialists of the SWP and others could influence the 'Islamist youth' and 'create secret doubts in the minds of at least some of them'.

> *Socialists can take advantage of these contradictions to begin to make some of the more radical Islamists question their allegiance to its ideas and organisations.*[49]

Many Marxists have argued for the existence of something called 'false consciousness', where an exploited group of people view their oppression through the prism of an ideology that in fact acts against their own interests.[50] Harman's advice to his fellow comrades is along these lines. Yes, Islamism can do some frighteningly reactionary things but it would be wrong to leave these Muslims without our guidance. We can offer them critical support, working on their prejudices as we go along. Islamists will be defended when they are fighting the state, but socialists 'will also be involved in defending women, gays, Berbers or Copts against some Islamists'.[51]

However, something has gone amiss with this scorpion dance. The underlying assumption seems to have been that Marxists would ultimately be the dominant intellectual and political partner. In an almost patronising way, it was assumed that the poor, oppressed Muslims could be steered by degrees from Islamism to socialism. In fact, it seems to be the socialists who have been steered towards Islamism. The bitter truth about this scorpion dance is that the Islamists saw the Marxists coming.

'Working with them to change them'

The former mayor of London Ken Livingstone's appearances alongside the Egyptian cleric Yusuf al-Qaradawi in 2004 were early examples of the extent to which the Left has been prepared to work with Islamists. In 2001, Qaradawi had unreservedly condemned the 9/11 attacks and stated in a *fatwa* that it was acceptable for 'Muslim American military personnel to partake in the fighting in the upcoming battles' against whomever the US decided to target as the perpetrators of terrorism.[52]

But he had also given his blessing to suicide bombings by those 'forced to defend themselves by turning themselves into bombs'.[53] He had stated that apostates should be killed and homosexuals judicially executed.[54] He also opined that Adolf Hitler had been sent by Allah to deal with the Jews and that the Holocaust was 'a divine punishment for them'.[55] Peter Tatchell called Qaradawi 'a reactionary fundamentalist cleric',[56] while the Muslim Association of Britain (which organised the 2004 visit) claimed that attempts to ban Qaradawi constituted an attack on all Muslims.[57]

Livingstone decided to share a platform with Qaradawi. And he was unrepentant at a mayoral hustings in 2008 when he claimed the preacher had told him in person that he was opposed to killing homosexuals and striking women, and believed that Jews were 'children of the book'.[58] Livingstone said that he could not believe the criticism of Qaradawi because most of it was in the Right-wing press. Livingstone added that one had to work with people within Islam in order to change it.[59] The answer from many secularists was – yes, but did it have to be Qaradawi?[60]

The language trap

In the weeks after the November 2015 Paris terrorist attacks, anti-Muslim hate crime tripled in London, according to the Metropolitan Police.[61] Women in particular have suffered horrific and unprovoked assaults by thugs, simply because of their appearance. There are fears among many ordinary Muslims that the tide of hatred and bigotry is rising.

It is the duty of the Left, as it was with racial attacks against Blacks and Asians in the 1970s, to take a firm stand against racism in all its forms. But the Left has fallen into a trap laid by the Islamists over 'Islamophobia'. Instead of just condemning violent attacks on individual Muslims or campaigning over issues like discrimination in employment, the term has been broadened to cover any criticism of religious theology or Islamist ideology. Some commentators question whether the word 'Islamophobia' has caused more problems than it has solved in this regard.

> *Islamist use of the term 'Islamophobia' is a major reason to avoid using the word when describing discriminatory acts or hate speech. Anti-Muslim actions or speech are directed at individuals or institutions and they have remedy in the law. But what is the remedy for 'Islamophobia' when framed as a prejudice against sacred texts or a whole religion?*[62]

The end result of this is censorship. As we will see with feminism below, the consequences are so bizarre as to be almost Kafka-esque, and certainly not what the Left could originally have intended. This censorship has led to veteran human rights activists being accused by

Left-wingers of Islamophobia because they have challenged Islamist ideology or simply called for free speech. In effect, sections of the British Left have ended up policing national discourse on Islam on behalf of Islamism.

Two terms that should definitely be purged from the public discourse are 'house Muslim' and 'native informant'. They are used to vilify Muslims who openly reject and counter the Salafi-Islamist narrative and engage with the establishment.

'House Muslim' derives from the Black Power and anti-slavery movement in the United States. To get an idea of how offensive it is to British Muslims working in collaboration with Government to prevent radicalisation, one should listen to Malcolm X's use of it. The 'house Negro' in his terminology, was a slave who 'loved his master more than his master loved himself', talked like his master, ate like his master and enforced his laws against the slaves in the fields.[63] However, the manipulation of Malcolm X's term extended to include Muslims who campaign for human rights and oppose Salafi-Islamism is a mark of disrespect to the man himself.

The term 'native informant' rests on the notion that Islamist ideology is synonymous with normative Islam – what most Muslims are deemed to believe. Under this scenario, Muslims who challenge that ideology are deemed to be betraying the majority of their fellow Muslims, effectively rejecting their own identity, and helping the perceived enemy.

'Imperialist feminists'

The fact that many feminists have found common cause with political Islam may seem initially shocking, let alone surprising. But identity politics has a lot to answer for. One term that has become very questionable in this regard is the label of 'imperialist feminist'. It started out well enough by critiquing the US's concern for the plight of Afghan women while it was at the same time mounting a military operation in the country in 2001.[64] Feminists were entitled to ask whether this war really was about women's rights at all, even if the Taliban had crushed and disenfranchised the female population of that country.[65]

Those who appeared to be justifying imperialist wars with recourse to gender were labelled 'imperialist feminists'. But then something went wrong with this argument. It was not just western feminists who were at fault speaking out about the condition of Muslim women in Muslim majority countries. But now it could also be Muslim women themselves in war zones who might knowingly or not be supporting imperialism by objecting to their treatment by Muslim men. Deepa Kumar, a proponent of the theory of imperialist feminism, made this statement:

> This is not to suggest that Afghan women who speak of the atrocities faced by the Taliban are automatically 'native informants' or collaborators with empire. Women have a right to speak out about their oppression no matter where they are located. However, there are those who either consciously or inadvertently enable empire. ... In short, the ideology of Imperialist Feminism doesn't only emerge from elites and their institutions in the West but from people in and from the Global South as well.[66]

So Muslim women raising issues about their own oppression had allowed themselves to become tools of the US. Academic and author Meredith Tax is bitterly critical of this theory. Kumar and Tax have clashed online over imperialist feminism. Tax argues it is almost impossible now to stand alongside Muslim women without being accused of the sin of Orientalism (i.e., exaggerating the 'exotic' and 'different' nature of Eastern cultures). Neither feminists in the West nor campaigners in Muslim countries can win:

> If she is white, she will be told she is colonialist; if she is a woman of colour or feminist from the Global South, she will be considered to lack authenticity.[67]

(The concept of 'Global North' and 'Global South' is the current academic terminology for the economic and social divide between rich 'developed' and poorer 'developing' countries.)

Meredith Tax counters that plenty of feminists were aware that the rights of Afghan women were being invoked cynically by the US administration for propaganda purposes. They were neither compliant nor blind to the facts. She argues that, not only has Kumar brushed aside the opposition of western feminists to the war, but she 'ignores the struggles of feminist movements in Muslim-majority countries, where empire and government are often closely aligned'.[68]

Kumar is not the only feminist who regards criticism of gender inequality and discrimination in Muslim societies as a western imperialist construct. Professor Saadia Toor believes that 'the new imperial project' poses as a saviour of women and LGBT people in Muslim societies 'as an ideological cover for racist wars abroad and xenophobia at home'.[69] This imperialist narrative is then given legitimacy by 'certain key neo-conservative Muslim intellectuals'.[70]

Secular feminists like Gita Sahgal and Karima Bennoune have come under fire for framing Muslim women's issues within the framework of human rights. For such actions, they are accused of stigmatising Muslim men while turning all Muslim women into victims.

Karima Bennoune, a law professor who describes herself as a 'secular person of Muslim heritage',[71] is another secular feminist who endures the ire of the believers in imperialist feminism. In her book *Your Fatwa Does Not Apply Here*,[72] she catalogued the testimonies of Muslim women in a struggle standing up to Islamist groups in Muslim majority and minority societies around the world. These stories, far from being welcomed by feminist commentators, were seen as tools to reinforce western imperialist war aims:

> *Both the victims and violators are assumed to inhabit illiberal, anti-democratic societies in the global South, whereas the saviours come from the liberal democratic global North.*[73]

Indian feminist scholar Gayatri Spivak coined a mocking phrase damning what she felt were colonial-minded reformers: 'White-men-saving-brown-women-from-brown-men'.[74] The classic example of this from the era of empire would be Lord Cromer, the British consul general in Egypt from 1883 to 1907, who believed Islam was inferior and that its treatment of women was abominable. However, his concern for the veiling of women in Egypt was somehow paired with a refusal to allow women the vote back in Britain. Back in the home country, Cromer founded the Men's League for Opposing Women's Suffrage.[75]

Nobody is suggesting that Muslim women today require a Victorian hypocrite like Cromer to 'save' them. Nor for that matter should western feminists believe they have to 'save' anybody.[76] What they need to do is support Muslim women fighting gender inequality in the UK and around the world. Simply because gender has been deployed to legitimise imperialism does not mean all struggles by Muslim women against patriarchy and ideologically justified oppression are a cover for Western war aims or Islamophobia.

Such arguments have severely hampered Muslim women activists who find themselves being squeezed in the middle ground. Fighting sexism emanating from Muslims, they have been accused of helping to promote anti-Muslim prejudice. Although they oppose the actions of bigots who co-opt the language of Muslim women's rights in order to feed anti-Muslim prejudice, Muslim misogyny remains a lived and painful reality for some Muslim women. This appears to be an inconvenience in the ideological discourse for some feminists. So maybe it is time to modify Spivak's phrase to: Feminists-supporting-Muslim-women-fighting-Islamist-ideology.

Feminists must turn to those Muslim women who are looking to achieve gender equality by reclaiming Islam and the Qur'an from the Islamists. Far from being tools of imperialism or Eurocentric cultural supremacists, these are women who believe their faith is being distorted to drive a misogynist agenda.[77] They see the rewriting of the Prophet's own life with the airbrushing out of the roles of powerful women in the early history of Islam. And they hear medieval jurisprudence being used to attack women's rights in a deliberate attempt to silence women and confine them to the private sphere.

The gender jihad

Today many Muslim men and women true to their faith are engaging in a 'gender jihad',[78] a struggle for reclaiming women's rights guaranteed by Islam. Using the egalitarian teachings of Islam, a number of individuals and organisations across the world from as far and wide as Morocco to Indonesia, Egypt to Pakistan, as well as here in the UK, are working to reclaim Islam's spirit of justice for all, regardless of gender.

Writers like the legal anthropologist Ziba Mir-Hosseini[79] distinguish between the spirit and teachings of the Qur'an and the opinions of later jurists or *fiqh*. The true divine sharia, she argues, is in the former and not the latter and contains the basis for an egalitarian Muslim family law.[80] Arguing this means of course crossing swords with those within Islamism who support patriarchy as God-given. Feminists, it would seem logically, should support writers like Mir-Hosseini. Or for that matter, organisations like Musawah – founded by women from Egypt, Turkey, Gambia and Pakistan – applying feminist and a rights-based approach to 'search for equality and justice with Muslim legal traditions'.[81]

Feminists need to recalibrate their approach to Muslim women. Supporting gender equality within Islam is not about legitimising imperialism or western foreign policy – even if it has been used in that way. The idea that a Muslim woman should not speak out on oppressive behaviour or policies in Muslim majority countries or communities as it may feed 'Islamophobia' does little to resolve long-standing issues facing Muslim women. This has created a hierarchy of oppression in the minds of some within academia, and among liberal and Left-wing commentators, in which women's rights (Muslim in particular) are placed on a lower rung to Islamophobia.

What is incredibly depressing about the debate around so-called imperialist feminism is that, while campaigners for gender equality are informed that they are tools of the western war machine, Muslim women and girls face a range of very real problems that urgently need to be addressed. These seem a million miles removed from the arcane discussions that some feminists are having in the ivory towers of academia.

In the UK, Muslim women continue to find difficulties getting jobs, with a markedly higher unemployment rate among these women than is the case with their Hindu and Christian counterparts.[82] Abhorrent cultural practices continue to be experienced by Muslim women, including forced marriages, honour-based violence and FGM, though these are not restricted to Muslim societies alone. Many mosques continue to deny women access or provide poor facilities, access and representation.

There has also been a rise in recorded hate crime directed at British Muslim women where racists have pulled at their clothing or inflicted acts of horrific violence.[83] In fact, women seem to have taken the brunt of the racist backlash resulting from terrorist action.

The answer to these issues is not to vex about whether these problems are just a front for western policy aims. It is not to accuse those who take up these issues of 'gendered orientalism'. The real answer is to defend the universally applicable human right to equality of opportunity regardless of gender. It is to extend to Muslim women exactly the same standards that apply to non-Muslim women. Equality under the law should be the guiding principle of feminism.

The Law Society and sharia law

Yet equality for Britain's Muslim women is not always afforded. Incredibly, some of those advocating discriminatory guidelines that would impact negatively on Muslim women were from bodies like the Law Society. In March 2015, the society issued a practice note on guidance on sharia wills which they described as 'good practice' in assisting solicitors with sharia probate matters.[84] 'Good practice' included

> *... illegitimate and adopted children are not Shari'ah heirs*
> *... The male heirs in most cases receive double the amount*
> *inherited by a female heir ...*[85]

Rather than promoting the egalitarian sharia interpretations advocated by women like Ziba Mir-Hosseini and Muslim groups like Musawah, the Law Society chose to promote a particular interpretation of sharia law that endorsed the distribution of estates in a way that discriminated against Britain's Muslim women.

In issuing such guidelines the Law Society, campaigners argued, had not acted in accordance with its own Equality and Diversity Framework or with international law, in particular with the Convention on the Elimination of All Forms of Discrimination against Women (CEDAW). A small handful of seventy protestors made up of humanists, Muslims, atheists, ex-Muslims, human rights campaigners and others challenged the Law Society, demonstrating outside its offices on 28 April 2014.[86]

It took eight months for the Law Society to withdraw the practice note and apologise; but not everyone was thrilled with the news. MEND (Muslim Engagement and Development), while claiming to challenge 'Islamophobia and anti-Muslim discrimination', instead saw the removal of the practice note as 'the latest casualty of excitable Islamophobic groups'.[87] Guidelines that would have resulted in discriminatory practices against Muslim women were not perceived by MEND to be a form of anti-Muslim discrimination.

The far Right and the Muslim 'threat'

While the Left and feminism have entered what looks like a prolonged period of identity politics navel gazing, the same phenomenon has been a huge shot in the arm to the far Right. The so-called

Counter-Jihad Movement, made up of many groups across Europe, has tapped into identity politics to foster a narrative that Europe is a continent with a distinct cultural history and traditions that are now threatened by a growing Muslim population. The movement poses as comprising defenders of free speech and equality before the law, with the clear implication that these liberties are under threat from Islam in its entirety.

This is mirrored in the Islamist contention that Muslim and European values are irreconcilable. This ignores the historical interactions between the Muslim and Christian worlds across all branches of knowledge. But it is also increasingly being analysed as more of a crisis within European liberalism than between Muslims and Christians. As one academic has put it, this is a playing-out of intra-European tensions more than a seismic clash between Islam and Christianity.[88]

The populist nature of this movement and its libertarian streak (defence of free speech) has thrown some people off guard, wondering if it can really be classified as far Right. But one influential academic study insists that its underlying ideology of anti-Muslim hatred is enough to place the movement in that political bracket.[89] This ideology is almost a mirror image of Islamism. The latter depicts a centuries-old crusade by the West against Islam that is a fight to the death. The cultural nationalists of the Counter-Jihad Movement see a jihad in the opposite direction bent on destroying Europe.

> *The European Counter Jihad movement's activism is inspired by an ideology which presents the current jihadist terrorist threat to the West as part of a centuries-long effort by Muslims to dominate Western civilisation. The ideology also insists on the existence of a conspiracy to "Islamise" Europe through the stealthy implement of Islamic Shari'ah...*[90]

As opposed to seeing Islamism as a loud but minority strand within Islam – and a political ideology – the movement instead views all Muslims as de facto Islamists. Emergency measures are seen as necessary to stem Islam, and some individuals influenced by this ideology have resorted to murderous violence. The Norwegian far-Right terrorist Anders Breivik, who killed seventy-seven people in July 2011, published a rambling manifesto on YouTube, 'A European Declaration of Independence', that was full of references to the Knights Templar, 'the Rise of Cultural Marxism', 'Islamic Colonization', etc.[91]

The Counter-Jihad Movement is creating a climate in which the most extreme elements on the Right can promote views that would have been unacceptable in the post-war years. A variety of groups and personalities can be identified under this umbrella, but they are not necessarily linked and may even be antagonistic. They range from the English Defence League to populists like the Dutch politician Geert Wilders.

In order to bolster their Islamisation-of-Europe conspiracy theory, the Counter-Jihad Movement draws on the supremacist and triumphalist messaging of Islamist ideologues. Therefore the counter-jihad network Stop Islamisation of Europe (SIOE) states on its website that 'it is rapidly becoming a crime to criticise Mohammed and Islam' and 'Muslim leaders use our own virtues of tolerance and freedom against us to establish Islam's own intolerance and oppression'.[92] SIOE is part of a network that is headed by American counter-jihadist activists Pamela Geller and Robert Spencer.

The American author Robert Spencer is a right-wing anti-Islam ideologue who has written several books analysing what he believes is the true nature of Islam.[93] In the Spencer view, there is no distinction between a true peaceful Islam and the hijacked Islam of terrorist groups. In books like *Islam Unveiled*,[94] he claims that Islam has a fixation with violence that goes back to its roots. He questions whether Muslims can ever fit into the West's 'multicultural mosaic'.

Geller is a frenetic blogger running Atlas Shrugs, the American Freedom Defense Initiative and Stop Islamization of America. Her website describes Geller as 'a foremost defender of the freedom of speech against attempts to force the West to accept Sharia blasphemy laws, and against Sharia self-censorship by Western media outlets'.[95]

The sites aggregate stories about ISIS, Muslim countries, Syrian migrants and religious leaders with the editorial line that 'our Judeo-Christian culture is far superior to the Islamic one'.[96]

The American Freedom Defense Initiative, one of Geller's groups, organised a contest to draw cartoons of the Prophet Muhammad at a venue in Garland, Texas in 2015, just four months after the killing of journalists at the *Charlie Hebdo* magazine in Paris in reaction to such a cartoon. The Garland event came under terrorist attack ending in a shootout between security and two gunmen, Nadir Soofi and Elton Simpson, who were both killed.[97]

Muslim American leaders had told people before the event to ignore Geller's obvious provocation. Linda Sarsour, a New York City Muslim activist, told the far-Right blogger that free speech cuts both ways. Geller could 'draw any damn cartoon she wants and I defend her right to do so. I have always fought for her right to be a bigot and I have the right to counter her bigotry with my own speech.'[98]

Incredibly, a group of counter-jihad activists in the UK attempted to organise a similar 'Draw Mohamed' exhibition in London for September 2015 until counter-terrorism police warned that people might be killed if it went ahead. One of the main organisers of this cancelled event was Anne Marie Waters, a former UK Independence Party (UKIP) candidate who is also director of a website called Sharia Watch.[99] The English Defence League and Britain First, two far-Right groups in the UK, had been approached to get involved. The latter group backed away rapidly and on an associated blog accused the organisers of using the cartoons to spark 'massive violence from Muslim communities'. Even allowing for a degree of hyperbole, the warning from a far-Right group was chilling:

> *Those behind this insanely dangerous idea believe that heavily armed Muslim drugs gangs will be drawn into the clashes and that Jihadist sleeper cells will also seize the opportunity to come out as militant leaders of their community as part of a massive recruitment and radicalisation drive. With the same stunt to be pulled on*

the same day in countries including Sweden, Denmark, Holland, Germany and France, the people behind the whole plan believe that there is a real chance of kicking off a Europe-wide civil war.[100]

Far-Right activists in the UK

The far Right has developed its own brand of identity politics, latching on to fears over immigration, the perceived rise of Islam in Europe, and multiculturalism. An article in *The Economist* argued that the far Right has tapped into deep-seated anxieties over culture and identity that include anti-Muslim sentiment.[101] New forces have arisen strongly promoting anti-Muslim prejudice and even talking about a 'cultural civil war'.[102]

Tommy Robinson (pseudonym of Stephen Yaxley-Lennon), who co-founded the English Defence League (EDL), has been the UK's most visible far-Right figure in recent years. Claiming to have renounced the football hooligan approach of the EDL,[103] he has tried to launch a UK branch of the German counter-jihad group Pegida, telling one interviewer he wanted a five-year ban on building mosques and Muslim immigration to the UK. Pegida is a German acronym meaning Patriotic Europeans Against the Islamisation of the West.[104]

Pegida has not attracted the numbers Robinson had hoped for in the UK, but the reason is not so much an absence of sympathy for his views as reflecting where the organisation is positioned. HopeNotHate – a group that monitors the far Right – says Pegida is not violent enough to attract former English Defence League members, while people concerned about radical Islam may think Pegida is not moderate enough. For those who want a war against Islam on the streets, the most extreme end of the far-Right spectrum beckons – in particular, National Action. This takes us from the populist part of the far-Right spectrum towards neo-fascism.

National Action is widely regarded as the most dangerous of the extreme Right-wing factions operating in the UK at present. It is seeking to emulate the success of Golden Dawn in Greece and is avowedly National Socialist. Over the past couple of years it has tried to recruit on university campuses and produces the kind of overtly racist literature that groups like the EDL and Pegida have generally avoided. It has also teamed up with Polish far-Right activists in the UK – as was evident at a violent demonstration in Liverpool in early 2016.[105]

The group mocks other extreme Right-wing organisations for seeking respectability and focusing on victimisation. It glories in talking about itself as 'empowering, vibrant, social, masculine, aggressive'.[106] Words like 'Aryan' and anti-Semitic images of Jews can be found on its website. Its ultimate aim is as follows:

> *It is the uncontroversial [sic] and sincerely held belief of all National Action members that there will be a race war in Britain and the whites are going to win it. ... It is with glee that we will enact the final solution across Europe – that will be justice.*[107]

The internal report on National Action's Liverpool demonstration, where its members had a stand-off with anti-fascist demonstrators and a large police presence, was full of calls for discipline and less time spent drinking in the pub. The group calls its masked and balaclava-wearing operatives 'soldiers' and opponents are dismissed as 'pasty students and drug addicts'. On its website, it proudly published a quote from Liverpool's mayor Joe Anderson when he said of National Action: 'Their views are so extreme and utterly noxious that they make the BNP [British National Party] look like Amnesty International.'[108]

Sections of the media have in effect assisted the far-Right's anti-refugee and anti-Muslim messaging. Media headlines have included references to a 'Muslim rape crisis,'[109] or 'Muslim rape epidemic';[110] one Polish magazine depicted on its cover a Caucasian women draped in the European Union flag being torn at by brown-skinned hands, with the headline: 'The Islamic Rape of Europe'.[111] This is the largest-circulation conservative weekly journal in Poland – it claimed that the crisis had been masked because of 'tolerance and political correctness'.[112]

The Right and the UK media

As Muslims in the UK face increasing anti-Muslim attacks, there is a sense that the media are only too happy to report Muslims as perpetrators of violence but never as its victims.[113] There are also the ridiculous scare stories. The *Daily Express*, for example, once ran a front-page article claiming piggy banks were going to be outlawed because they might offend Muslims.[114] And a spoof video made by a Muslim prankster claiming that the children's TV character Peppa Pig was causing offence ended up being taken seriously by global media outlets.[115] When the prankster claimed his son wanted to be 'a pig instead of a doctor now' and that a campaign was going to be launched to promote a character called Abdullah the Cat, many journalists might have twigged this was a joke.[116]

Since the Salman Rushdie affair in 1989, British Muslims have become a regular subject for the media in different guises. Whether it is al-Muhajiroun demonstrating provocatively, or the arrest of terrorism suspects, the media has not captured the life experience of most ordinary Muslims who are not involved in these activities.

> *The concern has been vocalised by many Muslim advocacy groups, organisations, academics and activists who argue that representations of Muslims in the British media are persistently negative, unfair and discriminatory and have subsequently contributed to establishing a climate of fear or a 'moral panic' with the Muslim 'folk devil' at its heart.*[117]

British media outlets have inadvertently provided grist for the far-Right propaganda mill. Terror plots and the refugee crisis have not always been handled with sensitivity. A Cardiff University study found that reporting on refugees was more 'polarised and aggressive' in the UK than any other country in Europe.[118] While newspapers like *The Guardian* took a more liberal line, there was strong endorsement of a military solution to the refugee crisis in newspapers like the *Daily Telegraph*, *Daily Mail* and the *Sun*. Readers' comments on these papers' websites claimed that migrants wanted to 'get to England and then screw the taxpayers for every penny they can get'. Other reader solutions included sending back the migrants, then destroying their boats.

The far Right aggregates this kind of content to build up its anti-Muslim narratives. A reported sexual assault on a ten-year-old boy in Austria, where the suspect was an Iraqi migrant, was headlined on the website of the far-Right group Britain First as: 'Video! Migrants think it is normal to rape people if they need sex.'[119] The web article had two tags to drive views: 'Islam' and 'Migrants'.

Some newspapers have attempted remedial action. For example, the *Daily Mail* ran a story in July 2015 in which it wrote about 'Muslim gangs' in east London slashing the tyres of a Home Office Immigration Enforcement van. The vehicle was transporting officials who had gone to question suspected illegal Bangladeshi immigrants. Local community leaders condemned the attack. But, more significantly, the *Daily Mail* retracted its description of the vandals as a 'Muslim gang' and offered an apology, agreeing that the faith of those involved was irrelevant.[120]

The British journalist Mehdi Hasan has summed up his exasperation at careless stereotyping of Muslims:

> *I get pretty exhausted of having to constantly endure a barrage of lazy stereotypes, inflammatory headlines, disparaging generalisations and often inaccurate and baseless stories.*[121]

New Atheism

One final area where identity politics have impacted negatively on secular and progressive Muslims concerns the way in which Islam has been framed by some New Atheists. New Atheism emerged in the early 2000s as a movement of secularists, humanists and atheists who felt religion was being increasingly privileged and unchallenged in public spaces. Writers like the late Christopher Hitchens and Sam Harris were not just criticising Islam but also Christianity – particularly in the United States. They wanted a continued separation of Church (or Mosque) and State, the pushing back of religion into the private sphere, and a staunch defence of science and reason as a basis for human knowledge over divinely revealed truth.

What primarily concerned them was a perception that modern relativist attitudes were putting science on the same level as faith. For example, there were the demands in the US that 'intelligent design' should be taught alongside evolution.[122] They disliked the rise of the evangelical movement on the American Right and feared blasphemy laws were being re-introduced under the guise of protecting religious minorities – especially Muslims.

What irked New Atheists like Richard Dawkins, a renowned scientist and author, was the perception that Islam was violently hostile to any criticism, was backward in its social attitudes (particularly on women and LGBT), and provided an ideology that endorsed murderous terrorism. In the wake of 9/11, these views resonated.[123] However, Dawkins and other leading New Atheists have conflated Islamism with Islam and ended up creating a 'religion that amounts to a monstrous straw-man which they then burn at the stake'.[124]

After the *Charlie Hebdo* killings in January 2015, Richard Dawkins put all Muslims in the dock with one tweet:

> *No, all religions are NOT equally violent. Some have never been violent, some gave it up centuries ago. One religion conspicuously didn't.*[125]

What a New Atheist should be saying is that these acts are inspired by a faith-based ideology – Islamism – that feeds on grievance. This ideology does undoubtedly take some of the building blocks provided by Islam, but it builds a murderous structure that the overwhelming majority of Muslims would not recognise as their faith. If the majority of Muslims in history had adopted this kind of reading of sacred scripture, it is doubtful that Islam would have lasted.

Identity politics is killing free speech on campus, silencing Muslim women in struggle, boosting both Islamism and the far Right, and pushing reconciled Muslim voices to the fringes. It makes implicit assumptions about Islam – from an Islamist, Left or far-Right perspective – and insists all Muslims must adhere to that definition or be regarded as not truly Muslim. It ignores the fact that most ordinary Muslims are not in favour of a violent ideology and that in surveys and polls they support British values more than the general UK population.[126] Yet the myth persists that the ideology of Islamism is the true expression of what it means to be a Muslim.

FIVE

VOICES FROM THE FRONTLINE

After the 2005 London bombings, the realisation that UK citizens were prepared to carry out attacks in this country spurred a number of British Muslim activists into renewed action. Whether or not they understood that they were facing a steady rise in Salafi-Islamism, they realised there was a dire need to promote the idea of a British Muslim identity.

Some groups already occupied this space, such as the Islamic Society of Britain (after its split from Islamist influenced organisations), City Circle and the Association of British Muslims. They were now joined by new groups like Radical Middle Way, founded in 2005, which challenged literalist interpretations of Islam by recourse to the teachings of scholars. 2006 saw the emergence of British Muslims for Secular Democracy, and Faith Matters, asserting respectively that such concepts as human rights were compatible with Islam and that individuals could practise their religion as faithful Muslims in Britain.

Initially, this put the Salafists and Islamists on the defensive. But, over the past five years, the tables have very obviously turned. It is now the Salafi-Islamist ideologues who are in the ascendancy, with those advocating a reconciled British Islam being increasingly pushed to the margins. This reversal of fortune was achieved by the collaborative effort of the familiar Salafist and Islamist advocates relentlessly touring up and down the country, penetrating university campuses, using social media collaboratively and turning Prevent into a hot-button issue with Muslims, the ultra-Left and students.

In contrast, the situation with non-Islamist Muslim civil society has been disparate, less coordinated and made up of part-time activists. Some of these organisations are now shadows of their former selves. These groups have lacked the resources, manpower and funding that have been available to the Salafi-Islamist activists. They have also tended to be engaged in a range of activities of which countering extremism might be just one aspect. For example, there is a group in Birmingham that tackles radicalisation among young people but is also running programmes for substance abuse and alcohol dependency. Another group operates Prevent-funded workshops but also manages youth football teams and other sports activities for disadvantaged teenagers.

This chapter will take a closer look at the contributions of British Muslims who have opposed extremism, either by coming together or as individuals. They may have found it harder to grab the headlines, but they have made a vital, often very hopeful, contribution to the quality of life in Britain and to social cohesion.

Not In My Name

It requires courage to take on extremist narratives and face the social media backlash. Even launching an initiative to condemn ISIS brutality can earn a rebuke from the Salafi-Islamists, as one group discovered. During the autumn of 2014, ISIS filmed a series of executions of western hostages, releasing the videos on YouTube. These included kidnapped aid worker Alan Henning, a Rochdale taxi driver who had been so moved by the humanitarian plight of the Syrian people that he had gone to the region to offer his help, with fateful consequences. His executioner was another Briton, Mohammed Emwazi, otherwise known as 'Jihadi John'.

In the hours and days that followed Henning's death, Twitter witnessed the eruption of a sustained campaign led by understandably appalled Muslim youth in London, with the hashtag #notinmyname. A group of young people in Walthamstow, east London, organised this initiative, holding up placards on camera and posting the images to social media. They were young leaders in a group, funded in part by Prevent, called the Active Change Foundation. This was a unique response to a new type of terrorist outrage that dominated the media headlines at the time.

These passionate Walthamstow teenagers invited youngsters in every country to simply write the hashtag on a placard, take a photo and post it to Twitter. Non-Muslims were also asked to join in. The objective, they explained, was to distance the actions of ISIS from the teachings of the Islamic faith. In no time at all, hundreds of youngsters in different languages posted the slogan. There were eventually over 885,000 views on YouTube and 6.6m tweets using the hashtag. It reached more than 300 million people, 'all of them denouncing the violence and corruption of ISIS/Daesh'.[1]

On 24 September 2014, something happened that the group could never have expected. The President of the United States, Barack Obama, name-checked the Walthamstow teenagers in a speech to the UN General Assembly, mentioning their group and hashtag by name.[2]

> *Look at the young British Muslims who responded to terrorist propaganda by starting the Not In My Name campaign declaring ISIS is hiding behind a false Islam.*[3]

Then came the backlash. Dilly Hussein of the Islamist website 5Pillars described the hashtag Not In My Name as a 'vicious circus show' that had entrapped Muslims. It was smearing the whole of Islam with guilt by association with terrorist attacks. Muslims were being forced to apologise for crimes committed in their name.

> *The sight of prominent Muslim figures and organisations tripping over themselves when they race to condemn on national TV, you can't help but think, how different it is*

when let's say white Britons or Americans commit similar crimes.[4]

The Not In My Name campaign was characterised by critics as making all Muslims responsible for atrocities in Iraq and Syria unless they spoke out against these acts of violence. Instead of being seen as a statement of unity with the wider British public or as an attempt by these teenagers to reclaim their faith from ISIS, it was described as reinforcing the notion of Muslims as a homogenous block. Those who felt this tended also to buy into the idea of Muslims being yet again denigrated by western opinion. They emphasised the hypocrisy of western governments over foreign policy. This episode illustrated well how difficult it is for British Muslim groups to make a simple statement against terrorism without bringing a hail of criticism down on their heads.[5]

Fiyaz Mughal – Faith Matters, Tell MAMA

One man who has felt the heat from the Salafists and Islamists is Fiyaz Mughal. Based in central London, the larger-than-life Fiyaz is a ball of energy. He is a restless soul irritated by the seeming inability of his fellow civil society activists to push back the Salafi-Islamists. He would like to see a movement for Muslim engagement in British society as strong as the actions of those who, in his view, spread suspicion and fear.

Back in 2006 he set up Faith Matters to strengthen relationships between different religious communities, in order to build greater social cohesion. It also sought to address the specific needs of converts to Islam, giving them support in attempting to minimise exposure to extremist narratives. The group also produced a ground-breaking publication in 2010 examining the services provided by UK mosques to Muslim women, pinpointing areas that needed improvement to ensure inclusivity.

Four years ago he set up another organisation called Tell MAMA (the acronym standing for Measuring Anti-Muslim Attacks). The aim was to encourage the reporting of anti-Muslim hate crime and track trends round the country. Fiyaz wanted to tackle anti-Muslim prejudice in order to expose bigotry, not to bolster a sense of victimhood among Muslims.

> *We work on bringing faith communities together and on tackling extremist messages, both of the far right and of those groups influenced by al-Qaʻida or Daesh. This is done through helping victims of anti-Muslim prejudice and in directly tackling the narrative of far right groups and anti-Muslim bigots.*[6]

Fiyaz told us that, since 2012, his work has helped over 6,900 people, leading to the arrest of some 460 people who were promoting anti-Muslim hatred and breaking up some far-Right networks. He has worked alongside the Crown Prosecution Service and police forces in England and Wales to expose and disrupt the activities of anti-Muslim bigots.

When it comes to countering Islamist extremism, Fiyaz has been a pioneer in breaking down divisions between Muslims and Jewish people:

> *We were the first organisation to take Muslims to the Holy Land and the West Bank on interfaith activities in 2007 and we regularly break down the narratives of those groups who suggest that Muslims and Jews cannot get on together.*[7]

Fiyaz wanted Tell MAMA to be a bold statement of opposition to all forms of discrimination, including anti-Semitism and homophobia. This led him to invite the veteran LGBT and human rights activist Peter Tatchell to become a patron of Tell MAMA in April 2014. At the same time, he brought in Richard Benson, the former chief executive of the Community Security Trust, a Jewish hate-monitoring organisation.

If Fiyaz was wondering what the Salafi-Islamists would make of his move, he soon found out. 5Pillars reproduced an interview Fiyaz Mughal had given to *Gay Star News* on Tatchell's appointment, then added the following from unattributed sources:

> *Critics have accused Fiyaz Mughal of going against the normative teachings of Islam which considers homosexuality a sin and bans promotion of it. Others have said that he is undermining the good work his organisation has done in monitoring Islamophobia by conflating other agendas.*[8]

This developed into an increasingly bitter spat with 5Pillars, which would go on to call repeatedly for the winding up of the organisation. It later editorialised that Tatchell and Benson were 'very unpopular amongst many Muslims, which has made it difficult for Tell MAMA to gain the trust of the people they want to protect'. The same article claimed Fiyaz was viewed as being a tool of the establishment and demanded that he condemned Prevent.[9]

5Pillars damned Tell MAMA for working with the Government while it congratulated MEND (Muslim Engagement and Development) for securing a commitment from ten police forces in England and Wales to report Islamophobia more effectively. It then went on to detail the funding that Tell MAMA has received over the past four years (information which is in the public domain) and cited links to activists like Tehmina Kazi of British Muslims for Secular Democracy as proof of its unsuitability to continue receiving funding.

Fiyaz was of course aware that a united campaign against hatred that brought the Jewish and LGBT communities on board would be contentious to some. But the Jewish charity organisation Community Security Trust (CST) has a record of opposing attempts by the far Right to convince Jewish people to support anti-Islam projects. For example, in 2009, the CST advised the Jewish community to stay away from counter-jihad groups like Stop Islamisation of Europe (SIOE), which had called for 1,000 Jews to turn up with Israeli flags outside Harrow mosque.

> *A demonstration against Harrow mosque under the banner*
> *Stop the Islamisation of Europe is as stupid and offensive*
> *as a demonstration against Harrow synagogue under the*
> *banner Stop the Zionisation of Europe.*[10]

The CST made the point that, no matter what Jewish people thought about the situation in Palestine or the views of groups like al-Muhajiroun and Hizb ut-Tahrir, 'nobody should be fooled into supporting SIOE's incitement against all Muslims'.[11] It continued with the salient point that anti-Muslim bigotry feeds both the far Right and 'its Islamist extremist counterparts', ultimately fuelling terrorism. To get involved in something like the SIOE's action would ultimately blow back on the Jewish community.

The link-up between Fiyaz and the CST did not impress MEND. Its former chief executive Sufyan Islamil was scathing. He told a congregation at Cheadle Mosque in Greater Manchester in November 2014:

> *We don't want the government to fob us off with some phony*
> *thing called Tell Mama, which has got a made pro-Zionist*
> *pretty much heading it or in a very senior capacity and is*
> *making all sorts of comments we might not agree with when*
> *it comes to homosexuality, to be recording Islamophobia.*[12]

In a statement on his website, Ismail subsequently acknowledged he made these remarks, as they were filmed. He accused the Harry's Place blog, which put the video on the web, of being a 'notorious, pro-Zionist, Islamophobic website'. But he was forced to concede he had used the words spoken above.

> *I accept that my choice of words could have been better and*
> *clearer. In hindsight, I would have expressed my thoughts*
> *more clearly and more accurately.*[13]

These battles with the Salafi-Islamists have left Fiyaz somewhat deflated. He would like to see stronger leadership from bodies like the Muslim Council of Britain who are 'very good at issuing press releases' but not providing the direction for a reconciled British Islam that is so clearly lacking. If the MCB cannot up its game, then he predicts it will end up becoming obsolete. After that, the field will be left clear and uncontested to those pushing victimhood narratives and an unceasing hostility to all western values.

Looking at the younger generation, Fiyaz worries that not nearly enough has been done to engage youth in a way that would challenge the Islamist programme. These people may already have been lost to Salafi-Islamist ideology. That ideology has become so entrenched that even he has been upbraided by a twenty-year-old for not having a beard. Forty-four-year-old Fiyaz shook at the memory of that encounter. He is not minded to take lectures on his faith from people half his age.

Tehmina Kazi – British Muslims for Secular Democracy

Tehmina Kazi has advised Fiyaz in the past; her association with him raised eyebrows at 5Pillars because of her involvement with British Muslims for Secular Democracy (BMSD). If ever an organisation's name had been conceived to rile Salafi-Islamists, then this was the one. To those ideologues, it is almost a contradiction in terms. How can a Muslim – they ask – support man-made political constructs such as democracy, human rights and gender equality? However, BMSD also found that many non-Muslims struggled to understand how one could be a Muslim and support secular democracy at the same time.

Quite easily has been the response from BMSD. The organisation was the brainchild of Nasreen Rehman and Yasmin Alibhai-Brown. Back in 2006 they were concerned at the growth of anti-Muslim hatred, but also at a rejection of democracy and social inclusion within the UK's Muslim communities. Both problems fed each other and needed to be tackled. The two founders wanted to promote support for secular democracy and to impress on Muslims the importance of keeping faith and state separate. No one faith should exert an undue influence on others.

Tehmina throws herself fearlessly into challenging situations. When she joined in 2009, BMSD was wondering how to defuse the highly provocative demonstrations being held by al-Muhajiroun (ALM). Its media-savvy protestors would turn up in front of the cameras with placards in large print that they knew would be easily read on TV and in the press. Slogans like 'Sharia for the UK' and 'Democracy Go To Hell' presented an unhelpful image of Muslims. To puncture their protests, the BMSD showed up with placards in the same typeface: 'Laugh at those who insult Freedom – they are very silly people'; 'Liberal Democracy will rule the world'; and 'Pluralism: the true solution'.

Though this was all jocular on the surface, it belied a very serious intent. ALM was turning young minds towards a deeply hostile view of the UK and some of those under its influence went on to become terrorists.[14] This eventually led to ALM being proscribed by the Government.[15]

Islamists often depict democracy as part of a western assault on Islamic principles; and secularism is often perceived to be a dirty word, for a number of reasons. But Tehmina wants Muslims to realise that it brings huge benefits, not least a guarantee of religious freedom. She is not a huge fan of the French model of *Laïcité*, a more rigid form of secularism enshrined in a written constitution. What she likes about Britain and wants other Muslims to appreciate is found in the positive traditions of fair play and justice:

> *As British Muslims we are able, for the most part, to practise our faith in an atmosphere of respect and security, with recourse to established anti-discrimination provisions if this is not the case.*[16]

Secularist bloggers have come under increasing attack and even been murdered in Muslim majority countries like Bangladesh, while being punished by the legal system in Saudi Arabia. Back in 2012, Tehmina spoke up for Hamza Kashgari, a Jeddah-based columnist facing blasphemy charges in the Saudi courts for concocting an imaginary conversation with the Prophet Muhammad on Twitter. Writing for *The Guardian,* Tehmina noted sadly that, while 7,894 people had signed a petition in Hamza's support, over 26,000 liked a Facebook page calling for his execution.

Tehmina believes that these bellicose voices within Islam have forgotten the essence of what their faith means. 'It is not a sword or shield for the global political stage, nor is it a stick with which to beat minorities.'[17] In spite of her intervention and that of others around the world, Kashgari spent two years in a Saudi prison before being released in October 2013.[18]

Whether it is gender segregation on campus, LGBT rights within Islam or the creation of a parallel legal system based on an interpretation of sharia law, Tehmina Kazi bravely articulates the secularist position within a Muslim context. She has also joined forces with Peter Tatchell to challenge the use of safe spaces in universities to silence secular and progressive opinions while tolerating Islamism. In March 2016, she joined him at the protest outside the National Union of Students headquarters in London to defend free speech.

In 2011, Tehmina had to contact the police over threats of violence she received after a CNN interview where she defended the right of an academic and activist, Usama Hasan, to give a lecture on evolution.[19] His argument, originally made during the 2008 Darwin Bicentenary, was that evolution is compatible with the Qur'an and that many Muslims today have developed a 'childlike view of science' that needs to change.[20]

Usama Hasan – when theology leads to threats

Usama is both a religious scholar and a scientist. He has degrees in Physics and Artificial Intelligence from the Universities of Cambridge and London. He previously lectured at Middlesex University, is a fellow of the Royal Astronomical Society and was Planetarium Lecturer at the Royal Observatory in Greenwich. He was tutored by his father, the well-known Salafist scholar Sheikh Suhab Hasan, and he holds certificates of scholastic learning (Ijazas) in the Qur'an, Hadith and the traditions of the Prophet Muhammad. Usama memorised the entire Qur'an at the age of twelve.

Usama has used his theological knowledge to challenge Islamist and ultra-conservative claims about what the faith really stands for. He has put forward his views with a calm and rational demeanour. For example, in 2011 he wrote an academic paper on 'Islam and the Veil', arguing that the issue of women's dress had been blown out of all proportion in modern Muslim discourse.[21]

The reaction of his critics to his learned opinions has been vociferous and violent. When his three-year-old daughter was diagnosed with cancer, it was a judgement from Allah, according to some opponents. Usama's comments on both evolution and the right of Muslim women not to cover their hair led to death threats in 2011 and his own voluntary decision to suspend his role in taking Friday prayers at the Leyton Mosque in east London.[22]

This followed some ugly scenes that year, captured on video and put on YouTube, where his attempts to explain himself to the mosque congregation were constantly interrupted by heckling. A later statement from the mosque alleged that some had 'incited murder against Dr Usama'[23] and an anonymous leaflet attacking him was distributed. With attempts to remove him as a trustee of the mosque and a stream of online comment condemning his views on evolution, Usama made a statement retracting some of his views but condemning those who had threatened to kill him and others who had ignored those threats while engaging in 'mediaevalist hair splitting' over theology.[24]

So heated did the pressure become on Usama that fellow Muslims felt compelled to set up a 'Defend Usama Hasan' campaign group.[25] The hijab and evolution issues, as well as Usama's revised views on the centrality of jihad in Islam, support for secular democracy and robust opposition to extremism within Muslim communities, had triggered a wave of hostility towards him.

Originally a Salafist, Usama has moved by degrees to a position he refers to as post-Salafism, though in discussion it is clear he finds this kind of labelling part of the problem within British Islam today.[26] He is now at the Quilliam Foundation, a counter-extremism think tank. Association with Quilliam is automatically deemed to disqualify somebody from speaking on Muslim issues, in the view of the Salafi-Islamist ideologues. An article in 5Pillars asserted: 'Dr Hasan and the QF [Quilliam Foundation] for whom he works have absolutely no credibility within the Muslim community to speak on issues concerning them and their beliefs.'[27]

The same article took issue with Hasan over a claim he made in an interview that the concept of sharia law has been hijacked by extremists obsessed with taxing non-Muslims, beheading, crucifixion and enslavement. Hasan made the point that all of these practices had been abolished by the Ottoman Empire, which many Islamists regard as the last legitimate caliphate.[28] 5Pillars retorted that there was 'an ocean of facts, opinions and evidences from Muslim scholars' saying the opposite and Hasan's views were 'outlandish'.[29]

Usama has also found himself ostracised in the university sector. He was involved in an incident at the University of Plymouth in 2014 that foreshadowed what would happen to Maryam Namazie at Goldsmiths in late 2015. The announcement that he was to speak at the college triggered a template letter from the Islamic Society (ISoc) that students were encouraged to send to the vice-chancellor, Wendy Purcell.

As with similar letters from ISocs, this one claimed that Usama being at the university would undermine the 'peaceful and cohesive environment we enjoy on campus'.[30] The ISoc took issue with Usama not condemning his colleague at Quilliam, Maajid Nawaz, for tweeting the 'Jesus and Mo' cartoon that Namazie made a point of showing to students at Goldsmiths before one of them pulled the plug out of her projector. Usama was not talking about the Jesus and Mo cartoon but instead addressing the future of Islam and democracy in the wake of the Arab Spring.

Nevertheless, the ISoc mounted a counter-demonstration against the meeting attended by about thirty people, including Yusuf Chambers of the iERA (Islamic Education and Research Academy). His Facebook page (with just over quarter of a million followers in April 2016), hailed the ISoc protest as a 'real victory in social justice'.[31] As with Namazie, the ISoc's opposition was joined by feminist representatives. The local Fawcett Society (which campaigns for women's rights) alleged that Usama's recent retweeting of another cartoon condoned domestic violence. It had depicted a husband and his burqa-wife under a sign 'Taliban marriage counselling'. A speech bubble over the Taliban counsellor's head read, 'Have you tried throwing rocks at her?' The hashtag #lifeofaMuslimfeminist was added to the tweet and at one point it was trending on Twitter.

What was clearly intended to be a dig at the Taliban's well-documented acts against women was construed by the Fawcett Society in its letter to the vice-chancellor as making light of domestic violence by men and undermining the message that it was never acceptable. 'The University has a duty of care to its students and to ensure that it remains a safe place for its students irrespective of faith or gender.'[32] Depicting Usama as a threat to women was strangely inappropriate, as he has written a seventeen-page theological refutation of domestic violence in Islam.[33] His paper highlights how fundamentalist misinterpretations of the Qur'an have often been sanctioned by legal systems in some Muslim majority countries and argues that this violates the spirit and ethics of Islam. Often described as a male Muslim feminist, he has also worked with human rights groups such as the Iranian and Kurdish Women's Rights Organisation and Karma Nirvana to challenge forced marriages and so-called honour-based violence.

The Plymouth branch of the Fawcett Society found itself on the same side of the argument as the Salafists of iERA who have encouraged gender segregation at their meetings. In spite of the lobbying from the ISoc and Fawcett Society, the vice-chancellor did not prevent Usama from speaking. But this use of safe spaces to exclude non-Islamist Muslims from campus has since escalated, not diminished.

Mina Topia – misogynist abuse for speaking out

As the Namazie case at Goldsmiths evidenced, being a Muslim woman does not guarantee support from campus feminists. This is alarming, given the reality that Muslim women speaking out against Islamism can expect an especially hostile reception. Mina Topia is a young British Muslim activist who has studied Islamic history and takes issue with the Islamist interpretation of her faith's history and theology:

> Religion can accommodate varied type of interpretation including liberal and progressive interpretations but too often Muslims don't recognise the diversity of interpretations, in their minds there can only be one.[34]

Mina believes British Islam too often takes an ultra-conservative form. Her own family background is Deobandi, a Sunni revivalist movement. But it is not the same Deobandi Islam that was practised by her grandparents in India.

> Their interpretation sat quite comfortably with their Indian culture in a positive way so while being conservative as Deobandism is, they wore Indian clothes and embraced Indian culture, they didn't wear the Arab abbaya like you see many British Deobandis do today. Deobandism is also increasingly being influenced by Salafism and Wahhabism and all these ideologies all say the same thing. There is only one way of practising Islam and nor can you challenge that view.[35]

Unlike Tehmina Kazi, who has a public profile, Mina describes herself as 'just an ordinary Muslim', but one who is vocal about how her community and religion have been hijacked. In Birmingham, where she comes from, Mina has engaged with the council in providing insights about how best to respond to locally based Islamist activism.

She has become involved with Muslim women's groups, campaigning against polygamy as well as the abuse and discrimination faced by Muslim women.

She also writes for a women's blog challenging openly the narratives of Islamists in the UK. But she does this anonymously because of what has happened to her. As she puts it, 'Even regular Muslims like me who oppose Islamism are bullied into silence.'

In August 2014, the BBC brought together a group of young Muslims to discuss the so-called caliphate declared by ISIS.[36] Mina was among a group that included a thick-set man who was strap-lined on screen as 'Saif ul Islam'. This Hindu convert to Islam, born Siddhartha Dhar, more popularly known as Abu Rumaysah, lived in Walthamstow and was associated with the banned al-Muhajiroun. He owned a company renting out bouncy castles to children's parties.[37] He was the first to give his view of the 'caliphate' on the BBC programme, declaring it to be a state governed by the Qur'an and Sunnah (teachings, deeds and sayings of the Prophet Muhammad), with one leader who ruled Muslims and non-Muslims. The state's borders would expand, annexing one country after another until the entire world was under its control.[38]

Mina countered that the emerging ISIS territory was in fact a totalitarian state that should be condemned for curtailing other people's human rights. 'If somebody doesn't fit the right mould, they lose all their rights.'

Another Muslim woman on the panel invited Saif ul Islam to leave and join 'his' caliphate, goading him that he would not depart the UK for a hard life in ISIS territory. Yet this is exactly what he did a few weeks later. Soon he was posting a photo of himself online cradling his baby while holding an AK-47.[39]

Mina had been arguing on air with a soon-to-be terrorist, subsequently alleged to be the voice behind an English-speaking ISIS executioner succeeding the now-killed Mohammed Emwazi.[40] Yet even questioning the position of a figure like this made her a target for sexist abuse. Realising that Mina had been the anti-caliphate voice on the BBC round table, one angry Islamist tweeted:

*I unblocked you when I realised you were that stupid liberal
cow that had verbal diarrhoea on the round table. You're a
joke.*[41]

On her Twitter page Mina had photos of her hen night. These were
defaced and retweeted. This was no ordinary Twitter trolling. This
was 'Muslim slutshaming', an increasing phenomenon experienced by
some Muslim women on social media. One picture of a group hug was
annotated with the words 'Me and my girlies going out representing
Islam'. Another picture of Mina with her friends eating and drinking
was captioned: 'A roundtable discussion on the caliphate… with
a nice bottle of red.' She was called 'a pisshead', 'a fat cow', 'a liberal
bullshitter' and told:

Drunken liberal garbage doesn't count.

Mina admits feeling fearful about dissenting against extreme
ideologies openly. 'Where is the space within our own communities
to dissent against their views?' Nevertheless, Mina is determined to
play a role; as a new mother she recognises that, for the sake of future
generations, inaction is not an option.

Mustafa Field – Faiths Forum

Mustafa Field is an Iraqi-born Shiʻi who grew up in London and
strives for greater inter-faith dialogue. He has not only witnessed his
birthplace being ravaged by war and the activities of ISIS, but has also
seen young Britons leave the UK for the lure of a so-called caliphate.
His home country is ravaged by sectarianism and intra-Muslim hatred
and he is determined the same fate will not befall the UK.

In early 2016, he took a group of British Sunni imams to Iraq to
help strengthen their arguments against terrorist ideology when
they returned to this country. They were taken to areas only recently
liberated from ISIS control and met local people with harrowing

stories to tell.[42] For example, there was a woman in Tikrit who had sheltered Iraqi government troops who had been stranded and cut off when ISIS invaded the town. Other soldiers had been killed in a mass execution, but their lives were saved through her selfless bravery.

To build greater understanding between different religions and combat intra-Muslim hatred, Mustafa was involved in founding Faiths Forum for London in 2010, bringing together representatives from nine faiths. Recent initiatives have included a 'Prayer for the Nation', which was a solemn wording read out in mosques after the November 2015 Paris bombings. Over 1,500 imams and faith leaders agreed to read it at Friday prayers. One leading imam said it allowed 'British Muslims to express a national identity in their own way'.[43]

Mustafa did not sense a Sunni-Shi'i division when he was growing up in the British capital. It was never an issue at home and the idea of 'othering' different Muslims was completely alien. His first encounter with explicit sectarianism was when he attended Westminster University at the start of the millennium. As a Shi'i student he did not feel he was able to practise his faith or that there was a safe place for him at the ISoc, in the prayer room or other spaces taken over by the ISoc. When he asked the Islamic student society if he could be a representative on the student body, the answer was resoundingly negative.

> *I often heard derogatory comments about Shi'i Muslims on campus. Many Shi'i students did not feel welcome in ISocs. Despite being a fringe movement, it was the Salafi stroke Wahhabi stream which completely dominated, and they were not representative of the vast majority of Muslim students on campus.*[44]

In 2001, he took the decision to form the first Shi'i student society at Westminster, known as the Ahlul Bayt. There are now around thirty of these societies around the UK. From the outset, the focus was not only on theology but on broader societal issues. Mustafa was also determined to ensure that their outlook would not be insular or dogmatic and would engage with other religions. One society, for example, organised a Bar Mitzvah Day to reach out to Jewish students in 2015.

This was a marked and deliberate contrast with the Salafi-Islamists whose voices are the loudest on the ISoc scene. Mustafa recalls hearing a very prominent Salafist preacher compare Shi'i to dogs during a talk at Brunel University in 2001. Taken aback by this remark, Mustafa confronted the preacher afterwards, only to be told that if the Prophet were alive today, 'he would strike a spear through your head'.[45]

In 2003, a group of Salafists imbued with the teachings of Abu Qatada burst into one of Mustafa's Shi'i events, yelling abuse. Looking back, Mustafa blamed this kind of sectarian behaviour on an underlying extremism imported from Saudi Arabia:

> The overwhelming root of all anti-Shi'i rhetoric is from Saudi. The literalist interpretations come from Saudi. Young Shi'is are seeing killing of Shi'i Muslims for their beliefs – and no other reason.[46]

Unfortunately, tensions between Shi'i and Sunni Islam are growing on the world stage. The sectarian murders filmed by ISIS have had a greater impact than the geopolitical tensions between Sunni Saudi Arabia and Shi'i Iran. ISIS has shown Shi'i people put on trial for their beliefs and then beheaded and even truck drivers shot at the roadside for not adhering to the ISIS-approved version of Islam.[47]

In August 2014 ISIS was accused of slaughtering up to 670 Shi'i prisoners in Mosul after taking over the city.[48] The separation of Shi'i prisoners and summary executions are reported to have happened elsewhere in ISIS territory. The danger is that acts like these and the ideology that underpins them will cause sectarian tensions in Muslims communities around the world.

Already there have been isolated incidents in the UK that Mustafa believes are warning signs that must be heeded. In June 2015, for example, the words 'Shia Kafir' were daubed on the Hussania Islamic Centre in Bradford. Mustafa believes we need to examine where those who perpetrate such acts get their ideas from and why they believe such behaviour is in any way acceptable.

Both Shi'i and Ahmadis have been at the receiving end of campaigns urging boycotts of their businesses. Tell MAMA discovered a leafleting campaign in Leeds and Bradford that the organisation linked to increased bullying of Shi'i students at schools.[49] The social media messaging service Whatsapp was being used to circulate demands to boycott Shi'i takeaways because 'both are owned by shias who are supporters of Hezbollah and bashar assad do not give support to those who are killing sunni Muslims in syria'.[50]

Following the March 2016 sectarian killing of Ahmadi shopkeeper Asad Shah in Scotland by a Sunni Muslim, leaflets were distributed across London calling for more Ahmadis to be killed. A copy of one leaflet was obtained by a news organisation. It referred to the Ahmadis as apostates deserving the designated punishment for such an offence. The leaflet suggested giving each Ahmadi three days to 'get back into the Islamic fold. If he does not, he is to be awarded capital punishment.'[51]

Mustafa visits Sunni mosques to try to break down the barriers that are giving rise to these prejudices among a minority. It was galling to be thrown out of a Salafist mosque, where he once ventured in to pray, because he was recognised and 'we know what your beliefs are'. He has even been physically attacked in a Sunni mosque simply for being Shi'i. Even a mosque near his workplace is deemed to be out of bounds, so he prays in the office rather than risk any confrontation there. However, he refuses to allow his own negative experiences dent his efforts in working to build bridges between Britain's Shi'i and Sunni Muslims and with other faith groups.

Mohammed Ashfaq – Pathways to Recovery

Mohammed Ashfaq works in Birmingham with young people vulnerable to radicalisation because of their lack of life opportunities. He is a gentle giant with a welcoming smile and a deep scar running down the side of his face. Standing outside the Kikit Pathways to Recovery drugs and alcohol addiction drop-in centre, he will often see groups of kids shuffling by, unemployed and just killing time on the streets.

The centre is based on Stratford Road in the Sparkhill district of Birmingham – a working-class neighbourhood that has attracted unwanted media coverage in the past as the home of several terrorist suspects.[52] It is also where Guantanamo detainee Moazzam Begg hails from. Mohammed Ashfaq says:

> We're a drugs centre – encouraging people to get off the stuff. But sometimes when we open our doors in the morning, the smell of cannabis from the street is overpowering. It shoots into the office.[53]

He describes the youth in the area. These teenagers endure a constant refrain from their families that they are 'a no-good drug addict', 'can't get a job' or 'can't do anything decent'. Unsurprisingly, confidence is often rock bottom and depression is common. They feel that they've let everybody around them down. Instead of pinning their lack of life chances on broader socio-economic factors or Government policy, they carry the entire burden of failure on their own shoulders.

On either side of Kikit are shisha cafes and kebab shops with a mainly Somali or South-Asian clientele. The shop next door, a pharmacy, gave the premises to Mo Ashfaq because the landlord recognised only too well the problems rife in the area. Cannabis, Mo notes, isn't what it used to be. It is incredibly strong and packed with chemicals that can tip already-damaged minds over the brink. Added to that is the increasing availability of a synthetic 'weed' called Black Mamba, a perilous substance that results in so many hospital admissions that the emergency vehicle involved is often dubbed the 'mambulance'.[54]

It is not just drugs and alcohol that Kikit tackles but other overlapping vulnerabilities. This includes the risk of young people being radicalised into violent ideologies. All the Kikit practitioners are trained to not only wean youngsters off dope but also present counter-arguments to theologically based extremism. These vulnerabilities are so often combined that Kikit has developed a unique initiative titled the Muslim Recovery Network (MRN). It mixes the kind of approach pioneered by Alcoholics Anonymous with Islamic principles. As the Kikit's website explains:

> We look to Allah to guide us on the Path of Recovery. While recovering, we try hard to become rightly guided Muslims, submitting our will and services to Allah.

To find those lost souls affected by both addiction and extremism, Mo sets up an outreach stall outside different mosques in the Birmingham area every week. This always features the Kikit 'drugs box', comprising rows of old music cassette cases with different types of drugs paraphernalia in each one. This is to help Muslim parents tidying their children's bedrooms to spot the danger signs of addiction – getting an idea of what substance is being taken and then making a referral to the centre. The young people themselves may also turn up of their own accord as happened with two young men who were on the verge of leaving the UK to join the so-called Islamic State.

> What happened is that we built a relationship with these two individuals who kept coming to us asking questions about the different drugs samples in the box. They denied every having tried drugs themselves but wondered how we would help somebody who was. After some questions on cannabis and heroin, I put it to them – 'that wouldn't be you by any chance?' They then laughed and admitted it.

The two lads had been following Mo Ashfaq and his team from mosque to mosque, clearly reaching out for help. They were put on to the MRN. The first step was to resolve the drugs issue. When Mo is confronted with young people he suspects might be slipping into violent ideologies, he tackles the substances that are clouding their minds at the outset. Once these two were clean, he asked them for their views on ISIS. Like many young Muslims Mo has put the same question to, they tensed up. Then their feelings spilled out, tripping over each other to make their points:

> *'I'm not very happy about the way this country portrays Muslims on the news.'*
> *'In today's world – if you're a Muslim, you're evil.'*
> *'Everything is negative.'*
> *'To the average white person, we're somebody who chops people's heads off.'*

They exhibited an anguish Mo has witnessed many times. These are young people following the news media and upset by editorial angles they believe demonise their faith. They are conflicted. On the one hand, they still feel proud of their religion. On the other, they wonder if there is something wrong with Islam. This internal conflict mixed with their other vulnerabilities results in a rising anger. In their social group, passing a spliff round, the conversations were often heated and full of fury.

Mo told them to try and talk about Syria the next time with no drugs or alcohol and see what happened. A week later they reported back that the news from Syria, Iraq and Palestine still affected them deeply, but the rage had dissipated. Nevertheless, they had questions, some of them accompanied with quotes from the Qur'an. It became obvious to Mo that somebody in the group was pushing back against Kikit's counter-extremism messaging.

> *We couldn't answer some of the objections being raised so we referred them to the local Prevent [counter-terrorism] Co-Ordinator Waqar Ahmed and asked if he could get opinions from scholars. Whoever was talking to our two lads was manipulating them. I think it was a friend in their group. He was probably being brainwashed in turn.*

In fact, it often appeared that a kind of chain was operating from one group of youths to another. One person in the group would be more radicalised than everybody else and would be feeding tough questions along the chain for answers. Mo hopes that the MRN can tap into these informal networks to seed its arguments, which will hopefully spread virally using the same method of dissemination employed by the extremists. The radicalisers in these groups of dope-smoking youths are not necessarily members of any group, but they have absorbed the arguments of extremist ideologues from online and offline sources.

After a few weeks, the two young men dropped a bombshell announcement at an MRN meeting. The discussion at the Kikit centre had paused for a cigarette break when the youths opened their rucksacks in the small kitchen at the back of the building. One of them turned to Mo with a slight tremble in his voice:

> *We're so glad we met you guys because we were that close to going to Syria.*

Mo scoffed, thinking they were pulling his leg. But then the air tickets were pulled out. He examined them and sure enough, the boys had somehow got enough money together to make the trip. One of them then got his lighter, flicked the switch and set fire to the tickets. Mo's lower jaw dropped to the ground as he watched the flames envelop the two pieces of paper. If a single moment validated his approach, then this was it.

Antidotes to poison

The Salafists and Islamists have enjoyed considerable success over the past five years in dominating the discourse within the British Muslim activist scene and reaching out to the student movement and the identity-politics end of the Left. They have coordinated their activities and messaging to considerable effect.

For the activists we have met in this chapter it can seem as if the Hydra of Greek mythology confronts them. This monster had many heads and, as one was struck off, another grew in its place. So it is with the Salafi-Islamist monster – a multi-headed creature with one body and considerable strength. Those who take it on, tend to meet a grim fate. The poison comes from all angles, deterring anybody else from joining the fight. Heroically they fight on, but aware that, to win, the movement against Salafi-Islamism needs to be much stronger.

Isolated and under-supported, brave souls like Mustafa and Tehmina fight for community cohesion and an identity that sees no contradiction between being a Muslim and British. At present, such voices represent isolated figures with insufficient support from wider society. But these voices matter in defending human rights and equality. They play a major role in building cohesive communities and a pluralist future, who in the face of hostility, deserve our support.

WINNING THE BATTLE AGAINST EXTREMISM

Inclusive politics

In spite of the best efforts of Islamists, Britain continues to see signs of genuine hope. Among the most noticeable was the election in May 2016 of London's first Muslim mayor, Sadiq Khan. Here was a man clearly comfortable with several strands of identity: being British, Muslim and a Londoner.

This was a story of aspiration that challenged both the Islamist and far-Right narratives. 5Pillars had editorialised that Khan did not deserve Muslim support and that first preference votes should go to rival candidate George Galloway (who received barely 1 per cent of support on the day). The reason given was Khan's pledge to get tough on extremism and radicalisation as well as his alleged 'pro Israel rhetoric'.[1]

As for the far Right, the Britain First candidate Paul Golding turned his back on Khan during his victory speech.[2] During his campaign, Khan declared that as a British Muslim he would be best placed to tackle extremism and keep the city safe from terrorism. He reminded voters he had voted in favour of gay marriage and received a fatwa against him by extremists as a result. Yet in spite of this, Khan's political opponents repeatedly made his faith an issue and falsely insinuated links to extremists.[3]

Brought up in a working-class environment in south London,

Khan represents a growing trend in British Islam that sees Muslims desiring better education and higher-paid jobs and wanting to play full roles in society, whether through politics, business or the arts. The new mayor articulated a broad and inclusive view of an identity politics of the future in his first post-election interview:

> I am the West, I am a Londoner, I'm British, I'm of Islamic faith, Asian origin, Pakistani heritage so whether it's [ISIS] or these others who want to destroy our way of life and talk about the West, they're talking about me.[4]

British Muslims: the good news

While Sadiq Khan may be a British Muslim of exceptional prominence and achievement, he is not an atypical or isolated figure. The overwhelming majority of British Muslims remain patriotic, attached to Britain and hostile to the radicalisation activities of ISIS. Survey after survey finds that they are more loyal to the Union Jack than are the general population. A poll by Survation in 2015 found that three quarters value both their Muslim and their national identity, while only 3 per cent feel it 'is not important for British Muslims to integrate into British society'.[5]

This has given rise to what has been dubbed 'the Muslim Pound'. It is one way of expressing the estimated £31-billion contribution that British Muslims are making to the UK economy.[6] In the *Sunday Times* Rich List, there are now fifteen Muslim tycoons. England and Wales now have 114,548 Muslims in higher managerial, administrative and professional occupations. Just over a third of small and medium-sized enterprises in London are Muslim-owned, many in traditional business areas but increasingly in a wider range of sectors.[7] Historically there have been high unemployment rates among Britain's Muslims, but that is changing.

There is similar good news with regard to Muslims gaining degrees. In the ten years from 2001 to 2011, the number of Muslims with degrees rose from 20.6 per cent to 24 per cent. More aspirational Muslims are moving out of traditional clusters like Tower Hamlets in London, according to Manchester University's Centre on Dynamics of Ethnicity. Its 'index of dissimilarity', which measures integration, has revealed a slow but definite move towards more mixing, with Muslims ranked on this index above Sikhs but below Hindus.[8]

British Muslims: the bad news

But there also exists a negative trend among some Muslims who advocate extreme views, violence, and acceptance of the belief that the West clashes with Islam.

A BBC survey in 2015 found 20 per cent of British Muslims believed western liberal society could never be compatible with Islam. And in the year when the French satirical magazine *Charlie Hebdo* was attacked and several of its journalists were gunned down, about 11 per cent thought that organisations printing images of the Prophet deserved to be attacked.[9] This is nothing to do with being 'conservative' as a Muslim; it is an extremist interpretation of Islam.

At the most extreme end of the negative trend come ISIS and other Islamist extremists, and their call to reject western nationhood and democracy altogether in favour of a 'caliphate' governed by a supremacist interpretation of sharia law. They believe that Muslims must split themselves off from mainstream society in order to create sharply delineated battle lines for the war that lies ahead between a self-proclaimed caliphate and the non-believers.

ISIS believes that its declaration of a 'caliphate', combined with terror attacks in western cities, will force Muslims into a binary choice between leaving to live in the territory held by ISIS or residing in the West and becoming apostates to their faith. The 'grey zone' of coexistence, as ISIS puts it,[10] will finally be extinguished in an apocalyptic confrontation between Islam and the crusader infidels.

This binary view divides the world into Dar al-Islam, the land of Islam represented by ISIS and its supporters, and Dar al-Kufr, which is the West and its supporters. Those Muslims who reject ISIS are dubbed apostates and lumped in with the enemy. There can be no 'grey zone' of coexistence. In the words of the ISIS online magazine *Dabiq*:

> *Muslims in the crusader countries will find themselves driven to abandon their homes for a place to live in the Khilafah, as the crusaders increase persecution against Muslims living in Western lands so as to force them into a tolerable sect of apostasy in the name of Islam before forcing them into blatant Christianity and democracy.*[11]

Like many Muslims I believe that, at its core, Islam calls for justice, mercy and peaceful, compassionate coexistence. It is distressing therefore, to me as a Muslim, to see extremists from within the faith practise brutality and hatred against others. They provide ample material for anti-Muslim bigots who then seek to denigrate and dehumanise all Muslims – including those who are working to build bridges in our society and who are defending universal human rights. While Islamist terrorists seek out Muslim human rights activists in order to kill them, anti-Muslim bigots act as if we do not even exist. For the bigots, all Muslims and Islam are deemed to be the problem. Such an attitude does little to defend and protect the middle ground that Islamist extremists seek to destroy.

I am deeply concerned about the development of contemporary extremist ideologies within Islam. The damaging consequences of Salafi-Islamism affect ordinary people – both Muslim and non. It is imperative therefore that Muslims do all they can to reclaim their faith. Championing what Islam stands for, a huge responsibility in such a turbulent time, ultimately lies in the hands of Muslims who claim to live out the values of the faith.

As a Muslim, I care deeply about human rights and believe in, support and advocate a compassionate Islam that respects universal and fundamental human rights. How then do we win the battle against extremism, and for British Islam?

Women matter

In 2008 I co-founded the counter-extremism and women's rights organisation Inspire. The aim was to empower women to create positive social change, recognising that they have a key role to play in defending human rights, strengthening communities and helping to build resilience to extremist ideologies.

I believe that countering extremism helps to protect women's rights; equally, securing women's rights acts as a bulwark against extremism. There is no doubt that Salafi-Islamism views gender equality with much disdain; extremists regularly deny women their most basic rights. In my view, the recent rise of Salafi-Islamism, and political Islam more generally, has resulted in devastating consequences for women, not least because it has supported the codification of discriminatory and violent sharia laws in some countries.[12] When women's rights are advanced, it represents a blow against this kind of extremism. The struggle for women's rights is a key battleground for both violent and non-violent Salafi-Islamists.

In my twenty years of community activism, I have come to recognise the powerful role that women play in combating extremism. Often it is women who appreciate fully the threat posed by extremism to families and communities. Mothers, sisters and daughters have had direct experience that gives them a painful insight into the problem. But I have also seen how women as activists take direct action in dealing with problems, resolving conflicts and building peace.[13]

In September 2014 Inspire launched an anti-ISIS campaign called 'Making A Stand', directly engaging with hundreds of Muslim women across the UK. The core message was simple enough: at a time when ISIS sought to radicalise British children and was encouraging acts of terror in the UK, women must make a stand and take the lead. Approximately 100 Muslim women from Bristol to Bradford got on coaches and minibuses to take part in the launch event in London. The Home Secretary, Theresa May, joined us. Whatever political view attendees had, everybody endorsed the minister's comment that:

Women can play a unique and powerful role in combating the extremist threat here and abroad, taking the lead in stopping preachers of hate from preying on young people.[14]

In the weeks that followed, at the request of many Muslim women, I visited nine cities, taking the campaign to hundreds of women from Pakistani, Bangladeshi, Somali, Arab, English, Welsh and Kurdish backgrounds. Sectarian differences were not an issue for the Sunni, Shi'i and Ahmadi women who attended. Whether I was in Leeds, London, Bristol, Birmingham or Cardiff, the same message came loud and strong: women wanted to challenge extremism, hatred and the polarisation of British society. They wrote their own personal pledges of how they would be making a stand against extremism.

'I will be making a stand challenging extremist ideology within my college.'

'I will be making a stand by confronting the men who are promoting extreme views at the Islam stall in the town centre.'[15]

We ran our workshops equipping mothers with theological counter-narratives so that they could feel more confident about challenging their children's views within the home. There were lively discussions about whether enough was being done by local Muslim communities to challenge extremism when it arose. The women who spoke talked about the various barriers they faced with regard to their families and communities, and the lack of engagement from agencies that should be supporting them.

Sometimes, the ability of women to tackle the suspected radicalisation of their children was rooted in a language difference. A son or daughter's first language might be English, whereas the mother's native tongue was Arabic, Urdu or Punjabi. Raising teenage children is of course hard enough; but not being able to have the required level of discussion because of a linguistic limitation is particularly frustrating.

The women also spoke about generational divides opening up over culture, and ideological differences over religion. They found these gaps very hard to bridge.

But these women knew they had to do something. If they could not answer their children's searching questions, then their children would go online and find a plethora of extremist websites. The mothers who attended the 'Making A Stand' workshops were often distressed that their children did not view them as credible authorities on religion. Whereas the parents adhered to a cultural Islam inherited from their country of origin, their children were seeking a new globalised identity, and this search often led them to Salafi-Islamism. Mothers struggled to know how to intervene in these complex and nuanced discussions. The 'Making A Stand' workshops often provided these women with the first opportunity they had known to collectively share experiences and support.

Mothers told me that, while many mosques were doing good work, they had not done enough to teach counter-narratives or develop meaningful relationships with today's youth. When one local Muslim community challenged the local mosque to do more, its members were told that deconstructing ISIS propaganda was the job of parents.

As for madrasas, there are good examples of these religious schools performing a valuable service; but equally some teach a narrow and intolerant understanding of Islam. Too many of the women I met said that these bodies required some form of regulation.

There were concerted attempts to silence the voices of women during the campaign. In Cardiff, for example, a five-page pamphlet was distributed to local mosques ahead of my arrival, with pictures of myself and other organisers. We were accused of having removed some women from their ESOL (English for Speakers of Other Languages) classes in order to 'to exert [our] influence in mosques and communities'. Already disgruntled that women were learning English, the leaflet made clear its opposition to the empowerment of women. Husbands and fathers were encouraged not to allow women to attend the workshop.

Many Muslim women remain undaunted. One decided she did

not want her child exposed to Salafi-Islamist preachers. She met with some staunch disapproval from the local Muslim community as she insisted that a planned event be cancelled. Although she was dubbed a 'kafir' and apostate, the event did not go ahead. This was one small victory brought about by a single woman making a determined stand.

In another case a group of women had discovered that, in what they had thought was an Arabic and Islamic studies class, their daughters were being told to discontinue their education after the age of fifteen. The teacher, an imam at the mosque, told them that pursuing a secular education was pointless. One boy was informed that merely touching a musical instrument would send him directly to hell. Once the mothers found out about this, they marched down to the local mosque to confront the imam concerned. The stunned cleric stood before several furious women telling him that his views were not welcome and he should stick to teaching Arabic. He meekly complied.

These women recognised the importance of making a personal stand in the struggle against extremism. We may not hear about these unsung heroes, but they are quietly engaged in the battle for British Islam. Yet too often Muslim women activists face gender-discriminatory attitudes within their own communities, especially from self-appointed leaders. Empowering and investing in women should take place at every level of society, and especially in Muslim communities.

Equality and human rights in schools

Kamal Hanif is an award-winning head teacher. In 2005, at the age of thirty-three, he returned to Waverley School in the Bordesley Green area of Birmingham, where he had once been a pupil, to become its new head. It is larger than the average school, covering an age range from four to nineteen. Nearly all the students are from Pakistani, Bangladeshi, African or Somali backgrounds, with English often spoken as a second language.[16]

Kamal came to the school with a visionary outlook and enthusiasm for promoting human rights and equality. He wanted to equip students with the tools to help them become conscientious and compassionate members of society. Pupils are familiar with the school's values – Humanity, Equality, Aspiration and Respect (HEAR) – creating an environment that he believes allows all pupils to flourish. This is because mutual respect is encouraged alongside a strong desire to learn.

Stonewall, the lesbian, gay, bisexual and transgender (LGBT) rights pressure group, accorded Waverley 'champion' status for encouraging kids to respect different sexualities.[17] At school assemblies, Kamal has shown pupils images of those physically attacked because they are LGBT and the unacceptability of hatred towards members of that community. This can be challenging, given that many of the pupils come from very conservative Muslim families. Kamal, a Muslim himself, has to convince the parents that it is essential they buy into the ethos and values he has fostered at the school.

He has had to deal with religious requests regarding uniform, in particular for girls, and parents wanting to take their children out of music classes. Kamal stands firm against such requests. He stresses that Waverley is not a faith school, though parents are free to find one if they want. But, at his school, there is a strict adherence to the principles of human rights, equality and tolerance.

Kamal's approach stands in sharp contrast to the Muslim Council of Britain's advice to the education sector in 2007, in a document titled 'Meeting the needs of Muslim pupils in state schools'. It framed the needs of Muslim children in schools in very conservative terms. For example, girls should wear the hijab with only face and hands exposed, not engage in acts of collective worship, and be able to opt out of sex and relationship education.[18] Objections were raised to whole areas of art, music and drama on theological grounds. And there was a call for gender segregation in school visits and physical education activities.[19]

Adherence to the MCB document would socialise children into a conservative interpretation of Islam. Kamal's approach to teaching

Muslim children could not be more different. His school saw children of all faiths mixing comfortably and respecting diversity. No wall had to be built around their faith to protect it from the outside world, because it was strong enough to accept the views of others. This prepared his pupils for life in modern Britain.

By encouraging pluralist attitudes, Kamal Hanif believes he is making his pupils more resistant to radicalisation. This does not mean that he plays down the reality of anti-Muslim hatred. He has been at the receiving end of bigotry himself. But he wants the young people in his care to avoid falling into a victimhood trap and to see their future in British society in positive terms.

Schools can play a pivotal role in promoting respect, equality and human rights, the very values that undermine extremist narratives. Waverley School is an example of good practice that can be emulated by other schools in helping build a more cohesive society.

Deconstructing ideology

For the past eight years, as part of my role in Inspire, I have delivered numerous programmes in cities across the UK, teaching theological counter-narratives to extremist ideology to countless Muslim men, women and youth. With the help of British Muslim theologians, we have explained the religious and political ideology of extremists, both past and present. We have deconstructed those ideas showing, for instance, that militant jihad is not an obligation as al-Qa'ida and ISIS claim. Rather than representing the oft-held idea of holy war, jihad connotes striving and exertion against something, where the cause is goodness and justice. One of the earliest understandings of jihad concerned the protection of the rights of minorities. The call to jihad was used to preserve and defend their places of worship against aggressors.[20]

The term *ummah* was examined, showing how it has been used in a supremacist way to imply religious exclusiveness, when once it meant all our neighbours and wider humanity, regardless of faith. We challenged the dualism of Dar al-Islam (a place where a Muslim lives and practises) and Dar al-Kufr (the land of unbelief) promoted by Islamist groups. As early as the eighth to twelfth centuries, Muslim jurists were arguing that the real house of Islam was wherever justice could be found (Dar al-'Adl). Contemporary theologians state that Muslims in this country have a contractual obligation to the State, regarding Britain as Dar al-Islam, with its rule of law, justice and equality. Scholars have argued that faith-based territories such as Dar al-Islam and Dar al-Kufr are outdated concepts. Islamists advocating the idea of caliphates that discriminate against non-Muslims violate not only contemporary notions of citizenship-based nation states but also Islam's call for equality, justice and human dignity.

I have seen at first hand how such education is missing in British Muslim communities. Nearly all of the women participants I have worked with had never encountered such important theological counter-narratives. They would themselves suggest that many Muslim institutions and mosques fail to educate their congregation, both adults and youth, in theological counter-narratives to extremist propaganda. How can parents teach their children without this knowledge? It is not enough to utter the words 'Islam is a religion of peace' when the verses of the Qur'an are being twisted by terrorist radicalisers.

As one woman told me after having attended an Inspire programme:

> *If I had known this information ten years ago when my children were teenagers, I would have taught them about the issues raised in this course. This is the first time I've been educated on such a crucial and important topic.*[21]

Some leading religious thinkers are leading the way. Sheikh Abdallah bin Bayyah is a former professor of Islamic Studies at the King Abdul Aziz University in Jeddah and a hugely respected scholar on the global stage. He leads the Abu Dhabi-based Forum for Peace and spoke at the 2015 United Nations Countering Violent Extremism Summit. He argues that the values of equality, human rights, political participation, freedom and democracy are fully reconcilable with Islamic teachings. Bin Bayyah has called on Muslims and Muslim countries to build a human rights-based culture and to observe treaties like the Universal Declaration of Human Rights.[22]

Tearing into Islamist ideology, he asserts that caliphates are not the way forward and instead modern-day nation states that promote citizenship and equality should be embraced. The major values of 'neutral secularism are to be considered positive values'. These include respect for beliefs, neutrality or impartiality with regard to different religions, and recognition of individual and social human rights that the state protects.[23]

Muslim scholars and faith institutions have an important role to play in deconstructing Salafi-Islamist ideology, especially as the ideologues claim to hold a legitimacy based on Islam's religious scriptures. However, what is required is greater amplification of these teachings to push back against extremist ideology – in mosques, in Muslim institutions and on social media.

A breakdown in communication

The UK Government has a central role to play in fostering a climate of belonging. How it engages with British Muslims will either enhance British Islam or alienate Muslim citizens. Young Muslims from different heritages – South Asian, Somali, Middle Eastern – are too easily exposed to jihadist ideology online or in their local community. Yet the Government often fails to recognise that the way it communicates only serves to estrange them further. The right words, or the right channels, are simply not chosen.

Tone of voice has often been an obstacle to the Government in reaching Muslim voters with key messages. Take the aftermath of the attack on the satirical magazine *Charlie Hebdo* in Paris in January 2015 that left eleven people dead. A palpable sense of shock was felt across Europe (though few would have suspected that in November of the same year Paris would see a night of terrorist murder resulting in ten times more deaths). In the wake of *Charlie Hebdo* there was pressure on the UK Government to assure the public that a similar tragedy could not unfold in a British city.

In the days that followed, the Communities Secretary, Eric Pickles, wrote a letter to mosques throughout the UK calling on Muslim leaders to challenge extremism.[24] It described what had happened in Paris as 'an affront to Islam' and recognised that Muslims throughout the UK had spoken out to say that action like this was not in their name. The letter went on to state that faith leaders were in a unique position to 'demonstrate how belief in Islam can go hand in hand with British identity'. The Government called on mosques to proclaim that British values are also shared Muslim values.

The letter was co-signed by Lord Ahmad, the Home Office Minister for Countering Extremism, and himself a Muslim. He had just chaired a meeting of the Anti-Muslim Hatred Working Group in which community concerns had been heard, and in which he had reassured Muslim leaders of the Government's commitment to protect people from anti-Muslim attacks. Nevertheless, in spite of the letter's careful wording, the Muslim Council of Britain led the charge against Eric Pickles in particular. Dr Shuja Shafi, Secretary General of the MCB, resented the 'insinuation that extremism takes place in mosques' and what he saw as the implication that Muslims had not done enough to challenge terrorism.[25]

The MCB's reaction was clearly unhelpful and misguided. Other Muslim groups welcomed Pickles's letter. David Cameron suggested that the 'problem' lay with the MCB if that was their response to a 'reasonable, sensible, moderate letter'.[26] But it took *The Guardian* to point out that, while Pickles had the right idea in terms of content, sending a round-robin letter to mosques showed a certain high-handedness his critics could exploit.[27]

The Government could have delivered its message in a more constructive way. It would have been more fruitful to call a meeting with faith leaders, engage with them directly, and ask how Government could support them in promoting the idea that British values are Muslim values.

However, that letter paled into significance in terms of Government miscommunication by comparison with the announcement by the Prime Minister in January 2016 of a £20-million fund to help Muslim women with little or no command of English.[28] This should have been presented as an empowering measure, helping 200,000 Muslim women who are left isolated and disadvantaged in British society through having poor English skills.[29]

The Prime Minister made the link between mothers not being able to speak English and the risk to their children – brought up in the UK – of being radicalised. The language barrier can be a compelling reason why the dangers signs are either not spotted or dealt with effectively. The official announcement had plenty to commend it, advocating gender equality and real freedom of choice for both women and girls – all good progressive stuff. Yet when it came to launching this, the linking of the announcement to extremism was counter-productive and unnecessary. As one commentator put it: 'Their problem is not, of course, what they are saying but the way that they say it.'[30]

Most of the Government's engagement with British Muslims has either been through the counter-terrorism or counter-extremism strategies. Since 2010, it has lacked an effective integration and community cohesion strategy, which has resulted in non-terrorism-related issues being promoted under counter-terrorism policies. The Government does appear to be moving in a direction where it wants to boost integration and opportunities, however, with, for example, a review being led by Louise Casey – a Government official with a long record in social welfare.

In May 2016, the Queen's Speech announced a new counter-extremism bill. The legislation was presented as a measure to 'prevent radicalisation, tackle extremism in all its forms and promote community integration'.[31] The Government is heading in the direction of banning organisations deemed extremist, gagging individuals and empowering local authorities to shut down any venues where they believe extremist views are being expressed. There would also be increased restrictions on what can be broadcast, including online. As many commentators noted, this came at a time when the Government was talking about abolishing the 1998 Human Rights Act.

A wide range of voices have spoken out against the bill, including David Anderson QC (the independent reviewer of terrorism legislation), Sir Peter Fahy (the former policing lead for the Prevent programme), counter-extremism think tanks and human rights groups. I have also spoken out, as it is my view that human rights will be undermined by such a bill, when legally defining who is an 'extremist' remains highly problematic. Extremism banning orders and disruption orders suggested by the Government would be difficult to enforce in reality; the fear would be that such a net would be cast very wide. Simon Cole, the police lead for the Government's own Prevent anti-radicalisation programme, said that the plans may not be enforceable and could risk making police officers judges of 'what people can and cannot say'.[32]

Draconian measures of the type suggested in the counter-extremism bill will not help in the pushback against extremism. Instead they could worsen the problem.

Salafi-Islamists have seized on the Government's poor communication in furthering their anti-Western and victimhood narrative. I believe that most British Muslims would welcome engagement and discourse with the Government, but not always on matters of security and extremism.

Undermining the Salafi-Islamist narrative

Islamists regularly purport that Muslim values are not compatible with British values. Professor Hossein Askari at George Washington University countered this by stating a view that may seem outlandish at first sight. He asked whether it might be the case that many Muslim majorities countries had drifted away from core Islamic values and thus left some western countries closer to the original principles of Islam. He ranked Ireland and Denmark as being more Islamic than Malaysia and Kuwait.

We must emphasise that many countries that profess Islam and are called Islamic are unjust, corrupt and underdeveloped and are in fact not Islamic by any stretch of the imagination.[33]

Thousands of Muslims today are helping to support and shape British democracy through their involvement in local councils, schools, health bodies, civil society groups and the voluntary sector. They enjoy the opportunities to speak their mind and practise their faith that, shamefully, do not always exist in Muslim majority countries. As long as violence, hatred or discrimination are not advocated, their religious views, and even their standpoint on contentious issues like the Palestine-Israel conflict, should not preclude an acceptance of British values. As defined by the Government, these include influencing decision-making through the democratic process, and accepting that other faiths and views are protected by law and that discriminatory behaviour is not permissible

The British values of tolerance and non-discrimination have to be enforced on non-Muslims too. These values cut both ways. Anti-Muslim attacks rose by 70 per cent in London from July 2014 to July 2015, according to Metropolitan Police figures.[34] Tell MAMA, the project monitoring hate incidents against Muslims, noted that women were the primary targets. After the Paris attacks in November 2015, attacks on Muslims tripled in London, though the police also noted that, over the previous twelve months, attacks on Jewish people and property had doubled.[35]

Police forces across the UK are doing more to record anti-Muslim hate crime. The Metropolitan Police attributes some of the rising figures to a growing willingness by Muslims to report attacks. Fiyaz Mughal, the head of Faith Matters and Tell MAMA, believes the actions of terrorists are deliberately intended to fuel anti-Muslim hatred and foster division. The fact that the authorities in Britain take this kind of crime seriously, Fiyaz believes, shows that this is a country where Muslims can expect the law to protect them.

However, there are those within British Islam who blame the

Government for the rise in anti-Muslim hate crime. In November 2015, the Islamic Human Rights Commission (IHRC) produced a report called 'Environment of Hate: The New Normal for Muslims in the UK'. This claimed that Britain was turning into a 'Stasi state' (a reference to the secret police of communist-era East Germany) subjecting Muslims to ever-increasing levels of repression.[36] Under the headline 'British government responsible for alarming rise in Islamophobia' it argued that the UK expects Muslims to show more deference than any other group in society. It blamed Prevent for 'demonising' Muslims and said that the Government was forcibly corralling Muslims into being obedient citizens.

> *Muslims are subject to discriminatory policies that are at once punitive and also designed to drag them to the state's politically expedient notions of what constitutes national identity.*[37]

This gives rise to the question of whether Britain is an inherently 'Islamophobic' country that despises Muslims; if so, it would leave little room for reconciling Muslim and British values. This report certainly painted a grim picture of the UK. Prevent was presented as a structurally racist strategy socialising hate and helping to create a police state. The media and politicians were united in fostering a 'hate environment', with the Muslim minority in the UK being the victims of the social attitudes of the majority in Britain.

The report's authors talked about Muslims being turned into 'the other'. The risk with this line of argument is that Muslims are effectively invited to 'self-other' – to admit that they will never be accepted as an integral part of British society. Even though the statistics show that hate crime is perpetrated by a small minority in society, Muslims are being asked to believe that most of the British population have been socialised by the media and establishment into despising all Muslims. This is surely a recipe for disaffection among young Muslims. Why bother to integrate, the logic might follow, when society absolutely hates you?

British values can be compatible with Muslim values. The rule of law, an ancient right in Britain, applies universally, giving Muslims the same access to justice as other Britons. Freedom of expression and worship allows Muslims to build mosques, of which there are just under 2,000 in Britain, and worship freely, a right won by past generations of religious dissenters in England but now a protection for today's Muslim population. Freedom of the press allows 5Pillars and Islam21c to publish their views without fear of reprisal or being shut down. If we champion British values, our democracy and plural society, then we benefit British Muslims by protecting their rights. Speaking out against Salafi-Islamists who oppose British Islam is therefore in the interest of British Muslims.

Building an inclusive movement

In the 2005 7/7 bombings, four British-born Muslims blew themselves up on London's transport system. Fifty-two people were murdered. Just over ten years later we see third-generation British Muslims, some as young as thirteen, packing their bags in the hope of either joining jihadist organisations or seeking to live in ISIS's caliphate. Others have been convicted of attempting to carry out ISIS-inspired plots in our country. It is difficult to predict the trajectory of Islamist extremism in the next ten years. But it goes without saying that we cannot simply stand by.

Muslims are the main victims of Islamist-inspired terrorism around the globe. ISIS and other Islamist extremist groups have killed thousands of Muslims across the Middle East, including Sunnis who have refused to pledge loyalty. Its members have even executed imams who have denounced their activities.[38] Their sectarianism has spawned deadly attacks on civilians simply because they are Shi'i. These extremists have determinedly created divisions to wipe out the 'grey zone' of reason and tolerance. They have conflated religion and politics and thereby poisoned Islam.[39]

Islamist extremism rejects British identity, insisting that Muslims declare their first and only loyalty to the *ummah*. Like the counter-jihadist movement on the far Right, Islamists assume that a 'clash of civilisations' is in some way inevitable. Muslims, they argue, must detach themselves from man-made nation states and democracies and share the pain of their brothers and sisters around the world while striving to create a caliphate of the righteous.

British Muslims are of course entitled to be moved or angered, and to speak out about unjust policies in Muslim countries, especially if the injustices are sanctioned by their governments. But the answer does not come through joining a jihadist organisation, made up to a large degree of foreign fighters, whose victims are mainly local Muslims.

If we are to have any hope of defeating Islamist extremism, we must all protect the middle ground. Confronting any type of extremism lies in championing genuine human rights and embracing democracy, none of which are antithetical to Islam's teachings. Solidarity with those Muslims doing just that is desperately needed to achieve the common good.

Sometimes the hardest battle we fight is the battle within. This is certainly the case for Muslims and the struggle within contemporary Islam. Muslims have to ask themselves what kind of an Islam they would like to champion in the world. Islam can be a religion of violence, as much as a religion of peace. It can be a religion that discriminates against non-Muslims and minority voices, but it can also be a faith that advocates genuine equality and respect for all.

A responsibility lies on Muslims to define and shape British Islam. It is not an issue of 'bad Muslims' and 'good Muslims', though it has often been debated in such terms. It is about countering extremism, hatred and discrimination. Challenging anti-Muslim discrimination must continue, but young Muslims cannot allow that to distort their view of life in Britain. It is disempowering and can discourage Muslims from recognising the opportunities available to them in the UK. Succumbing to anti-western or anti-Islam discourses can only hinder them from fulfilling their potential.

Dina al Raffie at George Washington University has grappled with the question of Islamist extremism, trying to identify how different sections of society can push back. One of her most striking pieces of advice is that it 'takes a network to defeat a network'.

> *In CVE [countering violent extremism] this means creating a wide network of partners from the grassroots to the state-level, as opposed to a few select organisations that are not representative of all stakeholders involved.*[40]

I entirely agree. Who, then, should be part of this network of partners? And how can our shared aims be achieved, for the good of all in British society?

The network must certainly involve parents promoting a reconciled British Muslim identity to their children. They must bridge the generational divide widened by extremism. Imams and religious figures are needed as theological role models, guiding Muslims away from distorted interpretations of Islam. It will be a challenge for them to puncture the 'jihadi cool' of the online extremists, but they must find a voice that speaks with real impact to young people.

Developing a strong British Muslim identity can defeat terrorist and extremist ideology. It is something that Muslims and non-Muslims must work together to achieve.

> *Helping British Muslims to feel as much a part of British society as other ethnic and faith minorities, while getting the worried-but-not-prejudiced members of the mainstream non-Muslim public to a similar place, should be the top priority for those committed to inclusive citizenship and tackling prejudice in British society today.*[41]

The extremist narratives that create a climate in which radicalisers can thrive should be deconstructed. The constant refrain that Muslims can never fit into British society – whether promoted by Salafi-Islamists or those on the far Right – must be openly challenged.

However, as we have seen, the battle is not solely a Muslim issue.

The political Left and Right must recognise the harmful role played by identity politics in favouring Islamists over Muslims who are seeking to champion a British Islam. While many anti-racist movements are more than happy to counter far-Right narratives, a significant number have refused to address Islamist extremism in the misguided belief that such action would be Islamophobic. This stems from the erroneous assumption that Islamism is Islam. This must change. Too much ground has been ceded to the Salafi-Islamists, who have dominated online channels and social media, toured the country tirelessly with their messages and built disturbingly effective networks at local level.

Salafi-Islamism continues to play an influential role, not only within Muslim communities but within our society as a whole. Individuals and organisations espousing such ideology have partnered with teachers, universities and human rights groups, often talking the language of liberalism to hide their illiberal and anti-western outlook. If this continues then we have little hope of defeating Islamist extremism in the near future.

Building an inclusive movement against Islamist extremism has never been more important. Already hundreds of Muslim civil society groups across the United Kingdom are doing incredible work in such areas as youth safeguarding and building cohesive communities. They reject the Islamist worldview and as a result find themselves being undermined by Islamists who are spreading a gospel of disenchantment and suspicion in Muslim communities.

A united civil society movement backed by liberals and the Left would be one major step forward. This movement would recognise the need to respond in unison to Salafi-Islamism and support those Muslims who are on the front-line. The more civil society speaks out against Islamist extremism, the more we normalise our opposition to bigotry, discrimination and regressive ideologies. The more we challenge the Islamist worldview, the greater are the chances of fermenting a comfortable British Muslim identity which will help young Muslims become resilient to extremist narratives.

The Government has understood the threat posed by Islamist extremism. It has engaged with hundreds of mosques and faith groups, taken down online extremist content and worked with civil society groups in producing counter-narrative videos.

The truth is, however, that diktats from Whitehall will not defeat extremism. That goal can be achieved by a re-energised civil society movement on the ground, but this movement needs to be cultivated and invested in. Partners are needed at every level in society – teachers, activists, feminists, for example, who can help build the united Britain that all of us want.

Both Islamist and far-Right extremists seek to extinguish the 'grey zone', the middle ground of compassionate co-existence. However, our greatest strength lies in the defence of our shared values. The choices and decisions we make today impact the battle for British Islam.

ABOUT THE AUTHORS

Sara Khan is one of the UK's leading Muslim female voices on countering Islamist extremism and a long-standing human rights campaigner. In 2008, she co-founded Inspire, a non-governmental women's rights and counter-extremism organisation, of which she is currently director. Selected as one of BBC Woman's Hour's Top 10 Influencers in 2015, and listed in Debrett's 500 most influential people in Britain in the 'War and Peace' category in 2016, Sara is regularly called on for her expertise by the Government, the European Parliament, the Metropolitan police, schools, local communities and the media. She has written for numerous magazines and newspapers and has been interviewed on BBC Radio 4's Today Programme, CNN's Amanpour, Sky News and Channel 4 News, among others.

Tony McMahon is an independent consultant working with the UK Government and civil society groups on counter-extremism projects. For the last fifteen years, he has advised Government, global companies and community groups on communications strategies. He is a former *Financial Times* magazine news editor and BBC news producer. He has been a Labour Party activist for thirty-five years, selected as a candidate in Hammersmith on two occasions. His other publications include *Original Rude Boy* and *No Place To Hide*, which was shortlisted for the 2011 Best Sports Biography prize and longlisted for the 2010 William Hill prize.

NOTES

Introduction

1. 'Islamic State releases "al-Baghdadi message"', BBC News, 14 May 2015, http://www.bbc.co.uk/news/world-middle-east-32744070
2. 'Muslims in Britain: What figures tell us', BBC News, 12 February 2015, http://www.bbc.co.uk/news/uk-31435929
3. 'UK Mosque statistics', Muslims in Britain, 23 September 2015, http://www.muslimsinbritain.org/resources/masjid_report.pdf
4. 'London's Mecca rich: the rise of the Muslim multi-millionaires splashing their cash', *Evening Standard*, 30 October 2013, http://www.standard.co.uk/lifestyle/london-life/londons-mecca-rich-the-rise-of-the-muslim-multi-millionaires-splashing-their-cash-8913153.html
5. 'Muslims are Britain's "top charity givers"', *The Times*, 20 July 2013 http://www.thetimes.co.uk/tto/faith/article3820522.ece
6. *A Place for Pride*, Max Wind-Cowie and Thomas Gregory, Demos, 2011 http://www.demos.co.uk/files/Place_for_pride_-_web.pdf?1321618230
7. 'So, what do British Muslims really think?' Kenan Malik, 11 April 2016 https://kenanmalik.wordpress.com/2016/04/12/so-what-do-british-muslims-really-think/
8. 'The majority of voters doubt that Islam is compatible with British values', YouGov, 30 March 2015, https://yougov.co.uk/news/2015/03/30/majority-voters-doubt-islam-compatible-british-val/
9. Richard Dawkins Twitter, October 2014, https://twitter.com/richarddawkins/status/518671362286964736
10. *Reasoning with God: Reclaiming Shari'ah in the Modern Age*, Khaled Abou El Fadl, Rowman & Littlefield

Chapter One

1. Interview with Leila (name changed), a Channel intervention provider, December 2015
2. 'Anzac Day ISIS terror plot', *The Independent*, 23 July 2015, http://www.independent.co.uk/news-14-0/anzac-day-isis-terror-plot-british-15-year-old-boy-pleads-guilty-to-involvement-10409761.html
3. 'Britain's youngest terrorist planned to behead his teachers, court hears', *Daily Telegraph,* 1 October 2015
4. 'Burning the earth: ISIS and the threat to Britain', *New Statesman*, 16 November 2015, http://www.newstatesman.com/politics/uk/2015/11/burning-earth-isis-and-threat-britain
5. 'This snake of an Aussie jihadist got promoted to be new head recruiter for Islamic State', *Daily Telegraph* (Australia), 25 February 2015, http://www.dailytelegraph.com.au/news/nsw/this-snake-of-an-aussie-jihadist-got-promoted-to-be-new-head-recruiter-for-islamic-state/news-story/805107841b37caed9fc5f973b98a7f99
6. 'Neil Prakash, most senior Australian fighting with Isis, killed in Iraq airstrike', *The Guardian,* 4 May 2016, http://www.theguardian.com/australia-news/2016/may/05/neil-prakash-most-senior-australian-fighting-with-isis-killed-in-iraq-airstrike
7. 'Neil Prakash aka Abu Khaled al-Cambodi', Counter Extremism Project, http://www.counterextremism.com/extremists/neil-prakash-aka-abu-khaled-al-cambodi
8. 'Chilling transcript revealed', *The Age Victoria*, 3 June 2015, http://www.theage.com.au/victoria/chilling-transcript-revealed-alleged-secret-communications-between-14yearold-english-boy-and-sevdet-besim-20150603-ghfrwf.html
9. 'Blackburn boy sentenced to at least five years in custody after plotting terror "massacre"', *Lancashire Telegraph*, 2 October 2015, http://www.lancashiretelegraph.co.uk/news/13799799.Blackburn_boy_sentenced_to_at_least_five_years_in_custody_after_plotting_Anzac_Day_terror__massacre_/
10. 'Anzac Day terror plot: Blackburn boy sentenced to life', BBC, http://www.bbc.co.uk/news/uk-34423984
11. Poem by Muneera, late 2015
12. 'Anzac Day terror plot: Blackburn boy sentenced to life', BBC, 2 October 2015
13. 'ISIS supporters "offering cash to British girls as young as 14 to become jihadi brides in Syria"', *The Independent*, 19 December 2014, http://www.independent.co.uk/news/uk/home-news/isis-supporters-

offering-cash-to-british-girls-as-young-as-14-to-become-jihadi-brides-in-syria-9935047.html

14. 'Female jihadist Twitter activity', Quilliam, 18 December 2014, http://www.quilliamfoundation.org/blog/female-jihadist-twitter-activity-discussed-by-quilliam-intern-ruth-manning/

15. 'Women of the Islamic State', translation by Quilliam, Februray 2015, https://www.quilliamfoundation.org/wp/wp-content/uploads/publications/free/women-of-the-islamic-state3.pdf

16. Ibid: 'Women of the Islamic State'

17. Ibid: 'Women of the Islamic State'

18. 'Till Martyrdom Do Us Part', Institute for Strategic Dialogue, 2015, http://www.strategicdialogue.org/wp-content/uploads/2016/02/Till_Martyrdom_Do_Us_Part_Gender_and_the_ISIS_Phenomenon.pdf

19. 'Women and Islamic Militancy', Dissent, Winter 2015, https://www.dissentmagazine.org/article/why-women-choose-isis-islamic-militancy

20. 'Isis's Al-Khansaa Brigade kills woman for breast-feeding baby in public in Raqqa', International Business Times, 28 December 2015, http://www.ibtimes.co.uk/isiss-al-khansaa-brigade-kills-woman-breast-feeding-baby-public-raqqa-1535110

21. 'Bride to be? The Tumblr Recruitment Blogs of ISIS', The Digital Human blog, 11 September 2015, http://thedigitalhuman.net/politics/bride-to-be-the-tumblr-recruitment-blogs-of-isis/

22. 'Family of Aqsa Mahmood 'sickened" by Tunisia blog post', BBC, 29 June 2015, http://www.bbc.co.uk/news/uk-scotland-glasgow-west-33316076

23. 'Convert or die: ISIS chief's former slave says he beat her, raped US hostage', CNN, 11 September 2015, http://edition.cnn.com/2015/09/09/middleeast/al-baghdadi-isis-slave/

24. 'Isis releases "abhorrent" sex slaves pamphlet, The Independent, 10 December 2014, http://www.independent.co.uk/news/world/middle-east/isis-releases-abhorrent-sex-slaves-pamphlet-with-27-tips-for-militants-on-taking-punishing-and-9915913.html

25. 'Isis: Austrian teen "poster girl" reportedly beaten to death for trying to leave Raqqa', International Business Times, 24 November 2015, http://www.ibtimes.co.uk/isis-teen-austrian-poster-girl-reportedly-beaten-death-trying-leave-raqqa-1530343

26. 'The roots of radicalisation? It's identity stupid', The Guardian, 17 June 2015,http://www.theguardian.com/commentisfree/2015/jun/17/roots-radicalisation-identity-bradford-jihadist-causes

27. Mental Health in the War on Terror, Columbia University Press, 2015.

28. 'A public health approach to understanding and preventing violent radicalization', *BMC Medicine*, 14 February 2012, http://bmcmedicine. biomedcentral.com/articles/10.1186/1741-7015-10-16

29. 'Plymouth bomber Nicky Reilly regrets attempt to blow up restaurant for Islam, mum says', *Plymouth Herald*, 9 May 2014, http://www. plymouthherald.co.uk/Plymouth-bomber-Nicky-Reilly-regrets-attempt-blow/story-21079540-detail/story.html

30. 'How did Michael Piggin become radicalised?', BBC, 30 May 2014, http://www.bbc.co.uk/news/uk-england-leicestershire-27328590

31. 'Do certain mental disorders put people more at risk of being radicalised?', University of Salford, 15 March 2016, http://hub.salford. ac.uk/salfordpsych/2016/03/15/certain-mental-disorders-put-people-risk-radicalised/

32. 'Mental health and violent radicalisation', *Mental Health Today*, July/ August 2013, http://www.culturalconsultation.org.uk/wp-content/ uploads/2011/11/Mental-Health-Today-Mental-Health-and-Violent-Radicalisation.pdf

33. 'Islamists actively seek prison sentences to radicalise other convicts, say officers', *The Guardian*, 12 December 2015, http://www.theguardian. com/society/2015/dec/12/islamists-radicalise-convicts-prison-officers

34. *Radicalisation in Prisons*, Criminal Justice Inspectorates, https://www. justiceinspectorates.gov.uk/hmiprisons/wp-content/uploads/ sites/4/2014/02/Radicalisation-in-prisons.pdf

35. *Operation of police powers under the Terrorism Act 2000 and subsequent legislation*, Home Office, 17 March 2016, https://www.gov.uk/ government/publications/operation-of-police-powers-under-the-terrorism-act-2000-quarterly-update-to-december-2015/operation-of-police-powers-under-the-terrorism-act-2000-and-subsequent-legislation-arrests-outcomes-and-stop-and-search-great-britain-quarterly-u

36. 'Lee Rigby murderer Michael Adebolajo will die in prison after having appeal attempt quashed', *The Independent*, 3 December 2014, http:// www.independent.co.uk/news/uk/crime/lee-rigby-murderer-michael-adebolajo-will-die-in-prison-after-having-appeal-attempt-quashed-9900515.html

37. 'Six admit planning to bomb English Defence League rally', BBC, 30 April 2013, http://www.bbc.co.uk/news/uk-22344054

38. 'Teenager jailed for 22 years for plotting to copy Lee Rigby beheading', *The Guardian*, 20 March 2015, http://www.theguardian.com/uk-news/2015/mar/20/brusthom-ziamani-jailed-plot-behead-soldier-lee-rigby

39. 'Brusthom Ziamani, 19, guilty of plotting to behead soldier', ITV

News, 19 February 2015, http://www.itv.com/news/story/2015-02-19/brusthom-ziamani-19-guilty-of-plotting-to-behead-solider/

40. 'Video: Ex-girlfriend of Brusthom Ziamani on how he revealed his plans to "recreate the murder of Lee Rigby"', ITV News, 19 February 2015,http://www.itv.com/news/2015-02-19/ex-girlfriend-of-brusthom-ziamani-on-how-he-revealed-his-plans-recreate-the-murder-of-lee-rigby/

41. 'Brusthom Ziamani: London Muslim convert convicted of plot to behead British soldier in Lee Rigby copycat killing', Evening Standard, 19 February 2015, http://www.standard.co.uk/news/crime/london-teenager-brusthom-ziamani-guilty-of-plot-to-behead-british-solider-in-lee-rigby-copycat-10057050.html

42. '"You want war, you got it": terror suspect Brusthom Ziamani's chilling letter to the British government', Daily Telegraph, 9 February 2015, http://www.telegraph.co.uk/news/uknews/terrorism-in-the-uk/11400672/You-want-war-you-got-it-terror-suspect-Brustholm-Ziamanis-chilling-letter-to-the-British-government.html

43. 'Islamic extremist who plotted to behead a soldier is confronted by Britain First', Britain First, http://videos.britainfirst.org/islamic-extremist-who-plotted-to-behead-a-soldier-is-confronted-by-britain-first/

44. Ibid: 'Ex-girlfriend of Brusthom Ziamani on how he revealed his plans to "recreate the murder of Lee Rigby"', ITV News, 19 February 2015

45. Interview with prison chaplain Ahmed, December 2015

46. 'How many people convert to Islam?', The Economist, 29 September 2013, http://www.economist.com/blogs/economist-explains/2013/09/economist-explains-17

47. 'We can't prevent all attacks, warns EU anti-terror chief', Agence France Press (The National), 14 January 2015, http://www.thenational.ae/world/europe/we-cant-prevent-all-attacks-warns-eu-anti-terror-chief

48. 'From convert to extremist: new Muslims and terrorism', The Conversation, 24 March 2013, http://theconversation.com/from-convert-to-extremist-new-muslims-and-terrorism-14643 and Islamist Terrorism, The Centre for Social Cohesion, July 2010, http://conservativehome.blogs.com/files/1278089320islamist_terrorism_preview.pdf

49. 'The Role of Converts in Al Qa'ida Related Terrorism Offenses in the United States', Combating Terrorism Center at West Point, Vol.6 Issue 3, March 2013, https://www.ctc.usma.edu/v2/wp-content/uploads/2013/03/CTCSentinel-Vol6Iss32.pdf

50. 'Samantha Louise Lewthwaite', Interpol, http://www.interpol.int/notice/search/wanted/2013-52018

51. 'The group of Walsall converts who became Britain's largest group of ISIL fanatics', *Daily Telegraph*, 24 February 2016, http://www.telegraph.co.uk/news/uknews/terrorism-in-the-uk/12168612/The-group-of-Walsall-friends-who-became-Britains-largest-group-of-Isil-fanatics.html

52. 'Syria wife Lorna Moore "abused" by fighter husband', BBC, 17 February 2016, http://www.bbc.co.uk/news/uk-35597294

53. 'Bristol student guilty of bomb plot', *Bristol Post*, 17 July 2009, http://www.bristolpost.co.uk/Bristol-student-guilty-bomb-plot/story-11301056-detail/story.html

54. 'Thomas Evans: British Al-Shabaab fighter's body will not be brought home', *Daily Telegraph*, 16 June 2015, http://www.telegraph.co.uk/news/uknews/terrorism-in-the-uk/11677317/Thomas-Evans-British-al-Shabaab-fighters-body-will-not-be-brought-home.html

55. '"Why I joined Islamic State": Chatham mum Sally Jones speaks of jihadist mission after moving to Syria with husband Junaid Hussain', *Kent Online*, 8 September 2014, http://www.kentonline.co.uk/medway/news/jihadist-sally-jones-23110/

56. 'The British Punk Rocker Widow who wants to run ISIS's hackers', *The Daily Beast*, 28 September 2015, http://www.thedailybeast.com/articles/2015/09/27/the-british-woman-who-wants-to-run-isis-hackers.html

57. 'Chatham mum-of-two Sally Jones "who wants to behead Christians joins Islamic State with new British jihadi husband Junaid Hussain"', *Kent Online*, 26 March 2016, http://www.kentonline.co.uk/medway/news/chatham-jihadi-mum-sally-jones-22722/

58. 'Le blog de Thomas Piketty', *Le Monde*, 24 November 2015, http://piketty.blog.lemonde.fr/2015/11/24/le-tout-securitaire-ne-suffira-pas-2/?utm_campaign=Echobox&utm_medium=Social&utm_source=Twitter#link_time=1448362144

59. 'Woolwich attack: If the whole world's a battlefield, that holds in Woolwich as well as Waziristan', *The Guardian*, 20 December 2013, http://www.theguardian.com/commentisfree/2013/dec/20/woolwich-attack-muslim-world-islamophobia

60. Ibid: 'Woolwich attack: If the whole world's a battlefield, that holds in Woolwich as well as Waziristan'

61. 'Now the truth emerges: how the US fuelled the rise of ISIS in Syria and Iraq', *The Guardian*, 3 June 2015, http://www.theguardian.com/commentisfree/2015/jun/03/us-isis-syria-iraq

62. 'The trouble with radicalisation', Peter Neumann, *International Affairs*, 2013, http://rudar.ruc.dk/bitstream/1800/17678/3/Appendix.pdf

63. 'Social Identity Theory for Investigating Islamic Extremism in the Diaspora', *Journal of Strategic Security*, Vol.6 Number 4, Winter 2013, http://scholarcommons.usf.edu/cgi/viewcontent.cgi?article=1242&context=jss

64. *Joining the cause: Al-Muhajiroun and radical Islam*, Quintan Wiktorowicz, Department of International Studies, Rhodes College, http://insct.syr.edu/wp-content/uploads/2013/03/Wiktorowicz.Joining-the-Cause.pdf

65. 'What the jihadists who bought "Islam for Dummies" on Amazon tell us about radicalization', *New Statesman*, 21 August 2014, http://www.newstatesman.com/religion/2014/08/what-jihadists-who-bought-islam-dummies-amazon-tell-us-about-radicalisation

66. 'MI5 report challenges views on terrorism in Britain', *The Guardian*, 20 August 2008, http://www.theguardian.com/uk/2008/aug/20/uksecurity.terrorism1

67. 'The west's Islamophobia is only helping the Islamic State', *Washington Post*, 23 March 2016, https://www.washingtonpost.com/posteverything/wp/2016/03/23/the-wests-islamophobia-is-only-helping-the-islamic-state/?tid=sm_tw

68. 'The secret world of ISIS brides', *The Guardian*, 24 June 2015, http://www.theguardian.com/world/2015/jun/24/isis-brides-secret-world-jihad-western-women-syria

69. 'ISIS taps into a mass culture of violence', *Middle East Eye*, 8 November 2015,http://www.middleeasteye.net/columns/how-isis-taps-our-new-appetite-violence-1185583344

70. 'On social media, ISIS uses modern cultural images to spread anti-modern values', Brookings Institution, 24 September 2015, http://www.brookings.edu/blogs/techtank/posts/2015/09/24-isis-social-media-engagement

71. 'A Drowned Syrian Boy as ISIS Propaganda', *The Atlantic*, 11 September 2015,http://www.theatlantic.com/international/archive/2015/09/aylan-kurdi-isis-propaganda-dabiq/404911/

Chapter Two

1. *The System of Islam*, Taqiuddin an-Nabahani, Al-Khilafah Publications

2. *Princeton Readings in Islamist Thought*, Princeton University Press, 2009

3. 'European Colonialism and the Emergence of Modern Muslim States', Oxford Islamic Studies, http://www.oxfordislamicstudies.com/article/book/islam-9780195107999/islam-9780195107999-chapter-13

4. 'Islamist Recruitment and Antisemitism on British Campuses', RUSI, 23 January 2006; and 'Islamic political radicalism in Britain: the case of

Hizb ut-Tahrir', Sadek Hamid, https://www.academia.edu/498553/Islamic_political_radicalism_in_Britain_the_case_of_Hizb-ut-Tahrir

5. 'Media Statement regarding ISIS's declaration in Iraq', Hizb ut-Tahrir , 2July2014,http://www.hizb.org.uk/current-affairs/media-statement-regarding-isiss-declaration-in-iraq

6. 'Al Muhajiroun and Islam4UK: The group behind the ban', ICSR, 2010, http://icsr.info/wp-content/uploads/2012/10/1276697989Catherine ZaraRaymondICSRPaper.pdf

7. 'Radical Islamist group al-Muhajiroun linked to half of British terror attacks', *The Independent*, 23 March 2015, http://www.independent.co.uk/news/uk/crime/radical-islamist-group-al-muhajiroun-linked-to-half-of-british-terror-attacks-in-past-20-years-10128492.html;   and *We Love Death as You Love Life*, Raffaello Pantucci, C. Hurst & Co, 2015

8. 'Muslim Brotherhood Review: Main Findings', December 2015, House of Commons, https://www.gov.uk/government/uploads/system/uploads/attachment_data/file/486932/Muslim_Brotherhood_Review_Main_Findings.pdf

9. Ibid: 'Muslim Brotherhood Review: Main Findings', December 2015, House of Commons

10. 'Understanding the Origins of Wahhabism and Salafism', The Jamestown Foundation, 15 July 2005, http://www.jamestown.org/programs/tm/single/?tx_ttnews%5Btt_news%5D=528#.VvPY95OLQoQ

11. 'The Nour Party goes Dim', Foreign Policy, 21 November 2015, http://foreignpolicy.com/2015/11/21/the-nour-party-goes-dim-egypt/

12. *Global Salafism: Islam's New Religious Movement*, Roel Meijer (Editor), C. Hurst & Co, 2009

13. Interview with Usama Hasan, September 2015

14. Interviews with Abu Muntasir between November 2014 and March 2016

15. *Islam in Transition: Religion and Identity among British Pakistani Youth*, Jessica Jacobson, Routledge, 1998

16. 'Recruitment and Mobilisation for the Islamist Movement in Europe', King's College London, 2007, http://ec.europa.eu/home-affairs/doc_centre/terrorism/docs/ec_radicalisation_study_on_mobilisation_tactics_en.pdf

17. Interview with Usama Hasan, 20 April 2016

18. Usama Hasan, BBC, 30 August 2007, http://news.bbc.co.uk/1/hi/programmes/hardtalk/6970298.stm

19. Interview with Usama Hasan, 15 May 2016

20. 'War on terror "threatens" UK Muslims', BBC News, 23 December 2002, http://news.bbc.co.uk/1/hi/uk/2600059.stm

21. '"The West needs to understand it is inevitable: Islam is coming back"', *The Guardian*, 11 November 2004, http://www.theguardian.com/uk/2004/nov/11/religion.islam

22. 'Islamist Recruitment and Antisemitism on British Campuses', RUSI, 23 January 2006; and 'Recruitment and Mobilisation for the Islamist Militant Movement in Europe', King's College, December 2007, http://ec.europa.eu/home-affairs/doc_centre/terrorism/docs/ec_radicalisation_study_on_mobilisation_tactics_en.pdf

23. 'What is the "British Islam" debate all about?', Hizb ut-Tahrir, 9 February 2016,http://www.hizb.org.uk/current-affairs/what-is-the-british-islam-debate-all-about

24. 'Dr Abdul Wahid on the Recent Events in Paris', Hizb ut-Tahrir, 8 January2015,http://www.hizb.org.uk/current-affairs/dr-abdul-wahid-on-the-recent-events-in-paris

25. '"Extremist is the secular word for heretic"', *The Guardian*, 24 July 2015,http://www.theguardian.com/uk-news/2015/jul/24/david-cameron-extremism-struggle-generation-abdul-wahid

26. 'UK Government seeks to convert Muslim children with latest witch-hunt', *The Khilafah*, 29 November 2014, http://www.khilafah.com/uk-government-seeks-to-convert-muslim-children-with-latest-witch-hunt/

27. 'HT urges Muslims not to compromise their Islam post-Woolwich', 5Pillars,10June2013,http://5pillarsuk.com/2013/06/10/ht-urges-muslims-not-to-compromise-their-islam-post-woolwich/

28. 'No Platform policy', National Union of Students, 4 November 2013, http://www.nus.org.uk/Documents/NEC_131120_No%20Platform%20policy.pdf

29. *Prevent Strategy*, Home Office, 2011, ISBN: 978 0 10 180922 1

30. Off-the-record interview with NUS source, January 2016

31. FOSIS Facebook announcement, 20 April 2016, https://www.facebook.com/fosischannel/photos/a.123542467683002.9082.121280397909209/1000814566622450/?type=3

32. 'Islam21c departure from the Foundation', MRDF, 1 September 2015, http://www.mrdf.co.uk/islam21c-com-departure-from-the-foundation/

33. 'Growing use of Sharia by UK Muslims', BBC, 16 January 2012, http://www.bbc.co.uk/news/uk-16522447

34. 'Thousands sign petition to stop anti-gay scholar Haitham al-Haddad from speaking day before National Student Pride festival', *The Independent*, 23 February 2015, http://www.independent.co.uk/

student/news/thousands-sign-petition-to-stop-anti-gay-scholar-haitham-al-haddad-from-speaking-day-before-national-10066017.html

35. 'After Kent Uni's last minute intervention, how did the extremist preacher nearly get through?', *The Tab*, http://thetab.com/uk/kent/2015/03/15/students-raise-questions-hate-preacher-event-5420;   and 'University of Kent bans extremist Islamic preacher Haitham al-Haddad from giving talk on shari'ah law', Kent Online, 16 March 2016, http://www.kentonline.co.uk/canterbury/news/haitham-al-haddad-33512/

36. 'Standing up against Homosexuality and LGBTs', Islam21c, 30 March 2012, http://www.islam21c.com/politics/4670-standing-up-against-homosexuality-and-lgbts/

37. 'Haitham al-Haddad supports female genital mutilation', YouTube, https://www.youtube.com/watch?v=qRTyLhRFXpk

38. 'Anger as preacher who supports FGM speaks at SOAS campus debate', *Evening Standard*, 19 February 2014, http://www.standard.co.uk/news/london/anger-as-preacher-who-supports-fgm-speaks-at-soas-campus-debate-9137997.html

39. '"FGM": The Latest Attempt to Dehumanise Muslims', Islam21c, 21 February2014,http://www.islam21c.com/politics/fgm-the-latest-attempt-to-dehumanise-muslims/

40. Video: Haitham al-Haddad, 'The Islamic Far-Right in Britain', https://tifrib.com/haitham-al-haddad/

41. Ibid: Video: Haitham al-Haddad, 'The Islamic Far-Right in Britain'; and 'Radical Islam on UK campuses', The Centre for Social Cohesion, 2010, http://henryjacksonsociety.org/wp-content/uploads/2013/01/RADICAL-ISLAM-ON-CAMPUS.pdf

42. 'Dr Haitham al-Haddad Press Conference in Norway', Islam Net video, 22 December 2012, https://www.youtube.com/watch?v=4aQrx9L79yM

43. Huda TV, http://www.huda.tv/about-huda

44. Op. Cit. Video: Haitham al-Haddad, 'The Islamic Far-Right in Britain'

45. Op. Cit. Video: Haitham al-Haddad, 'The Islamic Far-Right in Britain'

46. 'Evangelising Hate', Council of Ex-Muslims of Britain, 2014, http://ex-muslim.org.uk/wp-content/uploads/2014/05/EvangelisingHate_Report_Web.pdf

47. 'Is Islam the Cause or Solution to Extremism', iERA, YouTube video, https://www.youtube.com/watch?v=Jahx01Wo9Gw

48. 'Peter Tatchell insists panellists answer Qs at iERA', YouTube, 17 October 2015, https://www.youtube.com/watch?v=5DweO9ABOgo

49. Op. Cit. Video: Abdur Raheem Green, 'The Islamic Far-Right in Britain'

50. Op. Cit. Video: Abdur Raheem Green, 'The Islamic Far-Right in Britain'

51. Abdur Raheem Green, 'Stoning', YouTube, 11 September 2012, https://www.youtube.com/watch?v=X1sfqpOlujA

52. Abdur Raheem Green, 'Stoning', YouTube, 11 September 2012

53. '"Terror link" charities get British millions in Gift Aid', *Daily Telegraph*, 29 November 2014, http://www.telegraph.co.uk/news/uknews/terrorism-in-the-uk/11263309/Terror-link-charities-get-British-millions-in-Gift-Aid.html

54. Hope not Hate website, 7 November 2014, http://www.hopenothate.org.uk/debate/should-hope-not-hate-differentiate-between-violent-and-non-violent-extremism-when-deciding-how-to-confront-islamist-extremists-4114

55. 'iERA responds to recent report about the death of Portsmouth men in Syria', iERA website, 27 October 2014, http://www.iera.org/media/press-releases/iera-responds-recent-report-death-portsmouth-men-syria

56. MEND aims and objectives, http://mend.org.uk/community/aims-and-objectives/

57. Summary of MEND manifesto on Mayor of London and London Assembly elections 2016, MEND, 2016, http://mend.org.uk/wp-content/uploads/2016/04/GLA-Summary-2016.pdf

58. MEND, Media toolkit, http://mend.org.uk/wp-content/uploads/2015/03/MEND_Media_Toolkit_v2.pdf

59. 'A Momentous Occasion', Independent report produced on behalf of the All Parliamentary Group on Islamophobia, 2011, http://conservativehome.blogs.com/files/appg-islamophobia-allen-2011-2.pdf

60. Ibid: 'A Momentous Occasion'

61. 'Fighting hatred together or setting communities apart', Community Security Trust, 15 April 2015, https://cst.org.uk/news/blog/2015/04/15/fighting-hatred-together-or-setting-communities-apart

62. 'Setting the record straight: comments at Cheadle mosque, 2014', Sufyan Ismail blog, 4 January 2016, http://www.sufyanismail.com/blog/setting-the-record-straight-comments-at-cheadle-mosque-2014/

63. 'You are nothing till you are everything', Sufyan Ismail, http://sufyanismail.com/biography.html

64. 'Islam under attack – seminar at Zakariyaa Masjid', YouTube, https://www.youtube.com/watch?v=Cxs7uDclXDY&feature=youtu.be&t=51m58s

65. Ibid: 'Islam under attack – seminar at Zakariyaa Masjid', YouTube, https://www.youtube.com/watch?v=Cxs7uDclXDY&feature=youtu.be&t=51m58s

66. 'MEND CEO Sufyan Ismail lying', HurryUpHarry, 4 April 2015

67. 'Muslims say thank you to Muswell Hill shul', The Jewish Chronicle, 13

November 2014, http://www.thejc.com/community/community-life/125443/muslims-say-thank-you-muswell-hill-shul

68. 'Cameron will not engage with the only people able to stop the IS narrative', *Middle East Eye*, 30 June 2015, http://www.middleeasteye.net/columns/david-cameron-refusing-engage-only-people-who-can-stop-1982739573

69. 'The short, violent life of Abu Musab al-Zarqawi', *The Atlantic*, July/August 2006, http://www.theatlantic.com/magazine/archive/2006/07/the-short-violent-life-of-abu-musab-al-zarqawi/304983/

70. 'A virulent ideology in mutation: Zarqawi upstages Maqdisi', Hudson, 12 September 2005, http://www.hudson.org/content/researchattachments/attachment/1368/kazimi_vol2.pdf

71. 'Jordan releases anti-ISIL Salafi leader', Al Jazeera, 17 June 2014, http://www.aljazeera.com/news/middleeast/2014/06/jordan-releases-anti-isil-Salafi-leader-2014617121457552506.html

72. (Released in Arabic by Al-Sahab Establishment for Media Production; translated by BBC Monitoring, 'Al-Qa'idah leader praises Charlie Hebdo attacks, urges more', 1 December 2015) https://cst.org.uk/news/blog/2016/02/29/abu-qatada-no-longer-in-britain-but-still-preaching-jihad-and-antisemitism

73. 'Abu Qatada: No longer in Britain, but still preaching jihad and anti-Semitism', CST, 29 February 2016, https://cst.org.uk/news/blog/2016/02/29/abu-qatada-no-longer-in-britain-but-still-preaching-jihad-and-antisemitism

74. Moazzam Begg Facebook page, https://www.facebook.com/moazzam.begg/posts/10153480746567915

75. 'Gita Sahgal's dispute with Amnesty International puts human rights group in the dock', *The Guardian*, 25 April 2010, http://www.theguardian.com/world/2010/apr/25/gita-sahgal-amnesty-international

76. 'Amnesty International responds to questions about CAGE', Amnesty International, 12 March 2015, https://www.amnesty.org.uk/amnesty-international-responds-questions-about-cage

77. 'CAGE's Asim Qureshi on BBC This Week', YouTube, 5 March 2015

78. '"Jihadi John"': Mohammed Emwazi was "extremely kind, gentle, beautiful young man", says Cage director', *The Independent*, 26 February 2015, http://www.independent.co.uk/news/uk/home-news/jihadi-john-mohammed-emwazi-was-an-extremely-kind-gentle-beautiful-young-man-says-cage-director-10073338.html

79. Op. Cit. 'Amnesty International responds to questions about CAGE', Amnesty International, 12 March 2015

80. 'A united front against the criminalisation of Islam', 5Pillars, 6 January

2014, http://5pillarsuk.com/2014/01/06/a-united-front-against-the-criminalisation-of-islam/

81. 'Event Review: Is Islam being criminalized?', *Asian Image*, 10 January 2014, http://www.asianimage.co.uk/columnists/10928609.Event_Review__Is_Islam_being_criminalised_/

82. Ibid: 'Event Review: Is Islam being criminalized?', *Asian Image*, 10 January 2014

83. 'Our Team', 5Pillars, http://5pillarsuk.com/about/our-team/

84. 'ITV's documentary on "charities behaving badly" was a political ploy', 5Pillars, 20 February 2015, http://5pillarsuk.com/2015/02/20/itvs-documentary-on-charities-behaving-badly-was-a-political-ploy/

85. 'Council deny attempts to derail "extremist" Quizz-a-Muslim event', *Bedfordshire on Sunday*, 12 November 2015, http://www.bedfordshire-news.co.uk/Council-deny-attempts-derail-extremist-Quizz/story-28163423-detail/story.html

86. '5Pillars presents "Quiz a Muslim"', YouTube, 20 November 2015, https://www.youtube.com/watch?v=ir7Veizz9NY

87. 'Thank you Maajid Nawaz, but why did Bedford's Quiz a Muslim cause such outrage?', 5Pillars, 17 November 2015, http://5pillarsuk.com/2015/11/17/thank-you-maajid-nawaz-but-why-did-bedfords-quiz-a-muslim-cause-such-outrage/

88. 'Paris massacre: At least 128 killed in gunfire and blasts, French officials say', CNN, 14 November 2015, http://edition.cnn.com/2015/11/13/world/paris-shooting/

89. Home Affairs Committee, 17 November 2015, http://data.parliament.uk/writtenevidence/committeeevidence.svc/evidencedocument/home-affairs-committee/countering-extremism/oral/24795.pdf

90. 'ISIL terror suspect Tarik Hassane offered place at top UK university', *Daily Telegraph*, 8 October 2014, http://www.telegraph.co.uk/news/uknews/terrorism-in-the-uk/11148113/Isil-terror-suspect-Tarik-Hassane-offered-place-at-top-UK-university.html

91. 'Tarik Hassane: CAGE concerned by alarmist reporting and violence', CAGE, 9 October 2014, http://cageuk.org/article/tarik-hassane-cage-concerned-alarmist-reporting-and-violence

92. 'Justice for Tarik Hassane', 5Pillars, 10 October 2014, https://web.archive.org/web/20150507012746/http://5pillarsuk.com/2014/10/10/justice-for-tarik-hassane-a-politically-motivated-arrest-by-a-police-state/

93. Author Archives: Amar Alam, Islam21c, http://www.islam21c.com/author/amar-alam/

94. Op. Cit. 'Justice for Tarik Hassane', 5Pillars, 10 October 2014

95. Tweets under #JusticeforTarik, https://twitter.com/search?q=justicefor

tarik&src=typd

96. 'Police or soldier "target in IS inspired moped plot"', BBC, 18 January 2016, http://www.bbc.co.uk/news/uk-35343843

97. 'Man accused of London shootings plot changes plea to guilty', Press Association/*The Guardian*, 12 February 2016, http://www.theguardian.com/uk-news/2016/feb/12/accused-london-shootings-plot-changes-plea-guilty

98. 'Two British students jailed for plotting Isis-style drive-by shootings', *The Guardian*, 22 April 2016, http://www.theguardian.com/uk-news/2016/apr/22/british-students-jailed-plotting-isis-style-drive-by-shootings-tarik-hassane-suhaib-majeed

99. 'Muslim Community Writes to the House of Lords over the CTS Bill', Hizb ut-Tahrir, 26 January 2015, http://www.hizb.org.uk/current-affairs/muslim-community-writes-to-the-house-of-lords-over-the-new-cts-bill

100. 'Is Islam being criminalized? Abdullah al-Andalusi', YouTube, 9 January 2014, https://www.youtube.com/watch?v=-3Rd29tMczM

101. 'Is Islam being criminalised? Nasir Hafezi', YouTube, 10 January 2014, https://www.youtube.com/watch?v=WGqIzGS7LQ8

102. 'Is Islam being criminalised? Mohammed Jahangir', YouTube, 8 January 2014, https://www.youtube.com/watch?v=4Ev8n-naaw4

103. Ibid. 'Is Islam being criminalised? Mohammed Jahangir'

104. 'Project Shanaz', Shanaz website, http://shanaznetwork.weebly.com/shanaz-what-we-stand-for.html

105. 'Jahangir Mohammed: Andrew Gilligan's "sexed up" story about me', 5Pillars, 11 February 2016, http://5pillarsuk.com/2016/02/11/jahangir-mohammed-andrew-gilligans-sexed-up-story-about-me/

106. 'The Prevent Strategy: A Cradle to Grave Police State', CAGE, 2013, http://cageuk.org/report.pdf

107. Ibid: 'The Prevent Strategy: A Cradle to Grave Police State', CAGE, 2013

108. 'Cameron will not engage with the only people able to stop the IS narrative', *Middle East Eye*, 30 June 2015, http://www.middleeasteye.net/columns/david-cameron-refusing-engage-only-people-who-can-stop-1982739573

109. '"Jihadi John"': Mohammed Emwai was "extremely kind, gentle, beautiful young man", says Cage director', *The Independent*, 26 February 2015, http://www.independent.co.uk/news/uk/home-news/jihadi-john-mohammed-emwazi-was-an-extremely-kind-gentle-beautiful-young-man-says-cage-director-10073338.html

110. 'Jihadi John: "Radicalised" by Britain', CAGE, 26 February 2015, http://www.cageuk.org/press-release/jihadi-john-radicalised-britain

111. Ibid: 'Jihadi John: "Radicalised" by Britain', CAGE, 26 February 2015

112. Ibid: 'Jihadi John: "Radicalised" by Britain', CAGE, 26 February 2015

113. 'CAGE's Asim Qureshi on BBC This Week', YouTube, 5 March 2015, https://www.youtube.com/watch?v=afdeFuJbK3E

114. 'MohammedEmwazi',CAGE,http://www.cageuk.org/case/mohammed-emwazi

115. Ibid: 'Mohammed Emwazi', CAGE, http://www.cageuk.org/case/mohammed-emwazi

116. 'Jihadi John radicalised after meeting al-Qaeda chief, Kuwaiti sources say', *Daily Telegraph*, 1 March 2015, http://www.telegraph.co.uk/news/11442904/Jihadi-John-radicalised-after-meeing-al-Qaeda-chief-Kuwaiti-sources-say.html

117. 'Islamic State: Profile of Mohammed Emwazi aka "Jihadi John"', 13 November 2015, http://www.bbc.co.uk/news/uk-31641569

118. 'British Muslims on safari "stopped by MI5"', *The Independent*, 30 April 2010, http://www.independent.co.uk/news/uk/home-news/british-muslims-on-safari-stopped-by-mi5-1959610.html

119. 'Mohammed Emwazi: Tanzanian officer recalls airport arrest', BBC, 8 March 2015, http://www.bbc.co.uk/news/uk-31785820

120. Dabiq, January 2016 edition, ISIS

121. 'Muslim converts who hacked British soldier to death jailed for life', Reuters, 26 February 2014, http://uk.reuters.com/article/uk-britain-soldier-idUKBREA1P1KG20140226

122. 'Return to old-style terror', *The Economist*, 25 May 2013, http://www.economist.com/news/britain/21578453-shocking-killing-reminder-disorganised-jihadists-are-harder-stop-organised

123. *Report on the intelligence relating to the murder of Fusilier Lee Rigby*, Intelligence and Security Committee of Parliament, November 2014

124. 'Arrest extremist marchers, police told', *The Guardian*, 6 February 2006, http://www.theguardian.com/uk/2006/feb/06/raceandreligion.muhammadcartoons

125. 'Woolwich murder suspect: Michael Adebolajo held in Kenya in 2010', BBC News, 26 May 2013, http://www.bbc.co.uk/news/uk-22673164

126. 'Jeremiah Adebolajo comments on Woolwich – ISC Report', CAGE, 25November2014,http://cageuk.org/article/jeremiah-adebolajo-comments-woolwich-isc-report

127. 'Don't criminalise the innocent', CAGE, 13 May 2015, http://www.cageuk.org/article/don%E2%80%99t-criminalise-innocent

128. Ibid: 'Don't criminalise the innocent', CAGE, 13 May 2015

129. 'BBC interviewee Abu Nusaybah faces three terror charges', BBC News, 31 May 2013, http://www.bbc.co.uk/news/uk-22732630

130. 'Newsnight's dramatic interview with Abu Nusaybah minutes before

214 | The Battle for British Islam

he was arrested', BBC Newsnight, YouTube, https://www.youtube.com/watch?v=BqL5d1IWu9s

131. 'Ibrahim Hassan and Shah Hussain plead guilty to terror charges', BBC News, 24 March 2014, http://www.bbc.co.uk/news/uk-england-26716152

132. 'Tackling extremism in the UK: An ideological attack on Muslim communities', CAGE, 2012, http://www.cageuk.org/sites/files/reports/CAGE_REPORT_Extremism_In_The_UK.pdf

133. 'PM: New counter-extremism strategy is a clear signal of the choice we make today', Prime Minister's Office, 19 October 2015, https://www.gov.uk/government/news/pm-new-counter-extremism-strategy-is-a-clear-signal-of-the-choice-we-make-today

134. 'Terrorism adviser warns of counter-extremism bill "backlash"', Politics Home, 17 September 2015, https://www.politicshome.com/news/uk/home-affairs/news/61234/terrorism-adviser-warns-counter-extremism-bill-backlash

135. Ibid: 'Terrorism adviser warns of counter-extremism bill "backlash"', Politics Home, 17 September 2015

Chapter Three

1. 'The Eco Warrior', Prevent Watch, May 2015, http://www.preventwatch.org/incident-the-eco-warrior/

2. 'Anti-radicalisation strategy "alienating pupils"', Sky News, 14 December 2015, http://news.sky.com/story/1605240/anti-radicalisation-strategy-alienating-pupils

3. 'School questioned Muslim pupil about ISIS after discussion on eco-activism', *The Guardian*, 22 September 2015, http://www.theguardian.com/education/2015/sep/22/school-questioned-muslim-pupil-about-isis-after-discussion-on-eco-activism

4. Prevent Watch website, http://www.preventwatch.org/

5. Op. Cit. 'School questioned Muslim pupil about ISIS after discussion on eco-activism'

6. High Court of Justice Queen's Bench Division, Salaahudeen Smith v Secretary of State for Education, Secretary of State for the Home Dept and Headteacher and Governors of Central Foundation Boys' School, CO/4064/2015, October 2015

7. Op. Cit. 'School questioned Muslim pupil about ISIS after discussion on eco-activism'

8. Op. Cit. High Court of Justice Queen's Bench Division, Salaahudeen Smith v Secretary of State for Education, Secretary of State for the Home Dept and Headteacher and Governors of Central Foundation

Boys' School, CO/4064/2015, October 2015

9. Op. Cit. High Court of Justice Queen's Bench Division, Salaahudeen Smith v Secretary of State for Education, Secretary of State for the Home Dept and Headteacher and Governors of Central Foundation Boys' School, CO/4064/2015, October 2015

10. Op. Cit. http://www.preventwatch.org/incident-the-eco-warrior/

11. Institute of Race Relations, http://www.irr.org.uk/wp-content/uploads/2016/01/IRR_Prevent_Submission.pdf

12. *The United Kingdom's Strategy for Countering International Terrorism*, March 2009, HM Government, ISBN: 9780101754729

13. Home Office, Freedom of Information request, 2016

14. Prevent Duty Guidance for Higher Education, HM Government, 16 July 2015, file:///Users/tonymcmahon/Desktop/Prevent_Duty_Guidance_For_Higher_Education_England_Wales_.pdf

15. Interview with Will Baldet, March 2016

16. Prevent Community Q&A, March 2016, Home Office, obtained through a Freedom of Information request

17. 'Prevent, Police and Schools', Association of Chief Police Officers, June 2013, http://www.londonscb.gov.uk/files/2010/mash/prevent_police_and_schools_2013.pdf

18. Ibid: 'Prevent, Police and Schools', Association of Chief Police Officers, June 2013

19. Seminars launched to help protect young people against radicalisation, Association of School and College Leaders, 6 May 2015, http://www.ascl.org.uk/news-and-views/news_news-detail.seminars-launched-to-help-protect-young-people-against-radicalisation.html

20. 'Lancashire "terrorist house" row "not a spelling mistake"', BBC News, 20 January 2016, http://www.bbc.co.uk/news/uk-england-lancashire-35354061

21. 'Commissioner condemns mis-reporting of so called "Terrorism" incident', Lancashire PCC, 20 January 2016, http://lancashire-pcc.gov.uk/latest-news/commissioner-condemns-mis-reporting-of-so-called-terrorism-incident/

22. 'BBC criticised by Lancashire Police for "terrorist house" story', Prolific North, 22 January 2016, http://www.prolificnorth.co.uk/2016/01/bbc-criticised-by-lancashire-police-for-terrorist-house-story/

23. 'The Prevent Duty', June 2015, Department for Education, https://www.gov.uk/government/uploads/system/uploads/attachment_data/file/439598/prevent-duty-departmental-advice-v6.pdf

24. 'Age SIX and groomed for jihad in British suburbia', *Daily Mail*, 23 January 2016, http://www.dailymail.co.uk/news/article-3413806/Age-SIX-

groomed-jihad-British-suburbia-Shocking-image-UK-extremism-taken-little-boy-s-Muslim-convert-father.html

25. Waltham Forest Against Prevent, 3 February 2016, https://www.eventbrite.co.uk/e/waltham-forest-against-prevent-tickets-20742107201

26. 'David Cameron steps up racism against Muslims', *Socialist Worker*, 5 January2016,https://socialistworker.co.uk/art/41949/David+Cameron+steps+up+racism+against+Muslims

27. 'The Extremist Reaction to the UK's Prevent Strategy', Hudson Institute, 18 October 2011, http://www.hudson.org/research/9862-the-extremist-reaction-to-the-uk-s-prevent-strategy

28. Ibid: 'The Extremist Reaction to the UK's Prevent Strategy', Hudson Institute

29. Ibid: 'The Extremist Reaction to the UK's Prevent Strategy', Hudson Institute

30. 'The Prevent Strategy: A Cradle to Grave Police State', CAGE, 2013, http://cageuk.org/report.pdf

31. Report of the Independent Reviewer, David Anderson QC, September 2015, https://terrorismlegislationreviewer.independent.gov.uk/wp-content/uploads/2015/09/Terrorism-Acts-Report-2015_web-version.pdf

32. 'Prevent will have a chilling effect on open debate, free speech and political dissent', *The Independent*, 10 July 2015, http://www.independent.co.uk/voices/letters/prevent-will-have-a-chilling-effect-on-open-debate-free-speech-and-political-dissent-10381491.html

33. Ibid: 'Prevent will have a chilling effect on open debate, free speech and political dissent', *The Independent*, 10 July 2015

34. 'Government deradicalisation plan will brand Muslims with beards as terrorists, say academics', *The Independent*, 10 July 2015, http://www.independent.co.uk/news/uk/politics/government-deradicalisation-plan-will-brand-muslims-with-beards-as-terrorists-say-academics-10381796.html

35. *Channel Duty Guidance*, https://www.gov.uk/government/uploads/system/uploads/attachment_data/file/425189/Channel_Duty_Guidance_April_2015.pdf

36. 'Fighting the Prevent Agenda', CAGE, 15 July 2015, http://www.cageuk.org/article/fighting-prevent-agenda

37. Op. Cit. 'The Prevent Strategy: A Cradle to Grave Police State', CAGE, 2013

38. 'Taking Away Our Children: The Counter-Terrorism and Security Bill 2014',CAGE,http://cageuk.org/article/taking-away-our-children-counter-terrorism-and-security-bill-2014

39. Ibid: 'Taking Away Our Children: The Counter-Terrorism and Security Bill 2014', CAGE
40. 'Cage's lies over new anti-terror laws', *Daily Mail*, 11 April 2015, http://www.dailymail.co.uk/news/article-3035188/Cage-s-lies-new-anti-terror-laws-Terrorism-apologists-accused-scaremongering-warning-Muslims-police-children-away.html#ixzz40dhBGaTB
41. 'Missing Bradford sisters: Fathers appeal over "Syria" family', BBC News, 17 June 2015, http://www.bbc.co.uk/news/uk-33156712
42. *Newsnight*, BBC TV, 16 June 2015: from transcript of broadcast
43. 'Muslim Council of Britain Parliamentary Briefing on introducing "Prevent" as a statutory duty for all public bodies', MCB, 18 January 2015, http://www.mcb.org.uk/wp-content/uploads/2015/01/MCB-Briefing-on-introducingPrevent-as-a-statutory-duty-for-all-public-bodies.pdf
44. Ibid: 'Muslim Council of Britain Parliamentary Briefing on introducing "Prevent" as a statutory duty for all public bodies'
45. 'Muslim Council of Britain says government hampering anti-Isis efforts', *The Guardian*, 16 June 2015, http://www.theguardian.com/uk-news/2015/jun/16/muslim-council-of-britain-says-government-hampering-anti-isis-efforts
46. 'Shuja Shafi, head of the Muslim Council of Britain: "We've never claimed to speak for everyone"', *The Guardian*, 30 January 2015, http://www.theguardian.com/world/2015/jan/30/shuja-shafi-head-muslim-council-britain-interview
47. 'Muslim Council says Prevent anti-terror scheme has "failed"', BBC News, 26 August 2014, http://www.bbc.co.uk/news/uk-28934992
48. 'British Muslim leader urged to quit over Gaza', *The Guardian*, 8 March 2009, http://www.theguardian.com/world/2009/mar/08/daud-abdullah-gaza-middle-east; and 'Jewish leaders attack Muslim Council "deal"', *Jewish Chronicle*, 21 January 2010, http://www.thejc.com/news/uk-news/26266/jewish-leaders-attack-muslim-council-deal
49. 'Government anti-terrorism strategy "spies" on innocent', *The Guardian*, 16 October 2009, http://www.theguardian.com/uk/2009/oct/16/anti-terrorism-strategy-spies-innocents
50. 'Muslim teachers fear objecting to Prevent strategy', Islam21c, 31 March 2016,http://www.islam21c.com/special/web-posts/muslim-teachers-fear-objecting-to-prevent-strategy/
51. Op. Cit. 'The Prevent Strategy: A Cradle to Grave Police State', CAGE, 2013
52. 'Who are ISIL', *Leicester Prevent*, 17 July 2015, http://www.leicesterprevent.co.uk/author/will_baldet/
53. Motion 517, National Union of Students Conference 2015, https://s3-eu-west-1.amazonaws.com/nusdigital/document/documents/15469/

84ddb0975328cbf3209bda92be723d8f/CD13_NC2015_Final%20
Resolutions%20DRAFT%201.pdf

54. Ibid: Motion 517, National Union of Students Conference 2015

55. 'Challenging the Prevent Agenda', UCU Left, 27 September 2015, http://uculeft.org/2015/09/challenging-the-prevent-agenda/

56. 'Misleading stories in the media – why NUS does not work with CAGE', NUS Connect, 7 May 2015, http://www.nusconnect.org.uk/articles/misleading-stories-in-the-media-why-nus-does-not-work-with-cage

57. 'National Union of Students refuses to condemn ISIS due to fears it would be "Islamophobic"', *Daily Mail*, 15 October 2014, http://www.dailymail.co.uk/news/article-2794183/national-union-students-refuses-condemn-isis-fears-islamophobic.html

58. Recording at 'Students not Suspects' meeting, Birmingham University, 15 October 2015

59. Ibid: Recording at 'Students not Suspects' meeting

60. 'Preventing Prevent at Strathclyde', Strath Union YouTube channel, https://www.youtube.com/watch?v=UQgvniRAKAk&app=desktop

61. 'Preventing Prevent', NUS black students, December 2015, http://nus-digital.s3-eu-west-1.amazonaws.com/document/documents/20353/20e0c6d0960aa7836fcc4e1dd2aa8320/2015_Preventing_PREVENT_handbook_BSC.

62. Speech by the Prime Minister, David Cameron on 20 July 2015: https://www.gov.uk/government/speeches/extremism-pm-speech

63. Ibid: Speech by the Prime Minister, David Cameron on 20 July 2015

64. 'David Cameron tears into NUS for links with CAGE – the group accused of being Jihadi John Apologists', Huffington Post, 20 July 2015, http://www.huffingtonpost.co.uk/2015/07/20/david-cameron-shames-nus-links-with-cage-anti-terrorism_n_7831632.html

65. *Preventing Prevent?*, Rupert Sutton, The Henry Jackson Society, 2015

66. 'Student David Souaan jailed for Syria jihad plan', BBC News, 3 February 2015, http://www.bbc.co.uk/news/uk-31117843

67. 'Prevent isn't making anyone safer. It is demonising Muslims and damaging the fabric of trust in society', *The Guardian*, 10 February 2016, http://www.theguardian.com/politics/2016/feb/10/prevent-isnt-making-anyone-safer-it-is-demonising-muslims-and-damaging-the-fabric-of-trust-in-society

68 'Open Letter – urgent call to repeal the Prevent legislation', Students not Suspects, 10 February 2016, http://studentsnotsuspects.com/2016/02/10/guardian-open-letter-urgent-call-to-repeal-the-prevent-legistlation/

69. National Union of Teachers conference agenda 2016, https://www.teachers.org.uk/sites/default/files2014/nut-final-agenda-2016.PDF

70. 'Tackling Islamophobia today', YouTube, 29 July 2015, https://www.

youtube.com/watch?v=u-2vP-FmVYA

71. Ibid: 'Tackling Islamophobia today', YouTube, 29 July 2015

72. 'Challenging the Prevent Agenda', UCU Left, 27 September 2015, http://uculeft.org/2015/09/challenging-the-prevent-agenda/

73. 'I dissent from Prevent', UCU union website, https://www.ucu.org.uk/media/316/I-dissent-from-prevent-poster-1-Nov-15/pdf/ucu_dissentfromprevent_poster1_nov15.pdf

74. 'Strikes loom as UCU urges rebuff', *Times Higher Education*, 28 May 2015, https://www.timeshighereducation.com/content/strikes-loom-ucu-urges-rebuff

75. 'Ofsted starts talks over more anti-extremism teacher training', Schools Week,14November2015,http://schoolsweek.co.uk/ofsted-starts-talks-over-more-anti-extremism-teacher-training/

76. Home Office, Freedom of Information request, 2016

77. 'How do we prevent radicalisation?', Shenaz Bunglawala, Theos Thinktank, http://www.theosthinktank.co.uk/comment/2014/09/24/how-do-we-prevent-radicalisation-by-shenaz-bunglawala

78. Data provided under a Freedom of Information request to Home Office – submitted in February 2015

79. 'The Observer view on the radicalisation of young British Muslims', *The Guardian*, 24 January 2016, http://www.theguardian.com/commentisfree/2016/jan/24/islam-radical-young-politics

80. Ibid: 'The Observer view on the radicalisation of young British Muslims', *The Guardian*

81. 'HASC: Countering Extremism 2015–2016', Independent Reviewer of TerrorismLegislation,3February2016,https://terrorismlegislationreviewer.independent.gov.uk/hasc-countering-extremism-2016/

82. '21st century McCarthyism – a "Prevent" cheat-sheet', Scotland Against Criminalising Communities, 17 September 2015, http://www.sacc.org.uk/articles/2015/21st-century-mccarthyism-prevent-cheat-sheet

83. 'That latest video from Islamic State was its most menacing warning to Britain yet', *New Statesman*, 30 January 2016, http://www.newstatesman.com/politics/uk/2016/01/latest-video-islamic-state-was-its-most-menacing-warning-britain-yet

84. 'Revealed: Britain has foiled seven terror attacks in one year', *Daily Telegraph*, 16 November 2015, http://www.telegraph.co.uk/news/uknews/terrorism-in-the-uk/11997853/Revealed-Britain-foils-seven-terror-attacks-in-just-six-months.html

85. 'Islamic State planning mass attack on Britain, warns head of MI5', *Daily Telegraph,* 29 October 2015, http://www.telegraph.co.uk/news/uknews/terrorism-in-the-uk/11962037/Islamic-State-planning-mass-

attack-on-Britain-warns-head-of-MI5.html

Chapter Four

1.   'Marginalised voices are the first victims of no-platforming', Politics, 16 March 2016, http://www.politics.co.uk/comment-analysis/2016/03/16/marginalised-voices-are-the-first-victims-of-no-platforming
2.   '"Free speech is a left-wing value"', *Spiked*, 21 March 2016, http://www.spiked-online.com/newsite/article/free-speech-is-a-left-wing-value/18166#.VvmRKRIrJxg
3.   'NUS criticized in open letter for its safe space and no-platform policies as free speech campaigners plan protest', *The Independent*, 29 February 2016, http://www.independent.co.uk/student/news/nus-criticised-in-open-letter-for-its-safe-space-and-no-platform-policies-as-free-speech-campaigners-a6903576.html
4.   Protest against safe spaces and no-platform at NUS, 17 March 2016
5.   'Peter Tatchell: snubbed by students for free speech stance', *The Guardian*, 13 February 2016, http://www.theguardian.com/uk-news/2016/feb/13/peter-tatchell-snubbed-students-free-speech-veteran-gay-rights-activist
6.   'We cannot allow censorship and silencing of individuals', *The Observer*, 15 February 2015, http://www.theguardian.com/theobserver/2015/feb/14/letters-censorship?CMP=twt_gu
7.   'Islam and the "culture of offence": missing the point', Open Democracy, 12 February 2015, https://www.opendemocracy.net/5050/maryam-namazie/islam-and-culture-of-offence-missing-point
8.   'Maryam Namazie speaks at the Phil after cancelled SOFIA talk', *Trinity News*,21October2015,http://trinitynews.ie/maryam-namazie-speaks-at-the-phil-after-cancelled-sofia-talk/
9.   'News from Warwick Atheists, Secularists and Humanists', Warwick Student Union, September 2015, https://www.warwicksu.com/news/article/WarwickAtheists/Maryam-Namazie-barred-from-speaking-at-The-University-of-Warwick/
10.   'What's a "safe space"?', Fusion, 11 November 2015, http://fusion.net/story/231089/safe-space-history/
11.   'Staff Assembly passes motions against green paper and Prevent', The Boar,11March2016,https://theboar.org/2016/03/staff-assembly-pass-motions-green-paper-prevent/
12.   'Report: Maryam Namazie speaks at Warwick University', Student Rights, 29 October 2015, http://www.studentrights.org.uk/article/2317/report_maryam_namazie_speaks_at_warwick_university
13.   'Goldsmiths ISOC fails to intimidate and silence dissenters',

Freethought Blogs, November 2015, http://freethoughtblogs.com/maryamnamazie/2015/12/01/goldsmith-isoc/

14. Ibid: 'Goldsmiths ISOC fails to intimidate and silence dissenters', Freethought Blogs, November 2015

15. '"Death threats and intimidation" at controversial Goldsmiths lecture with speaker Maryam Namazie', London Student, 3 December 2015, http://londonstudent.coop/death-threats-goldsmiths-speaker-maryam-namazie/

16. Video: 'Maryam Namazie shouts at Muslim student telling him to "shutup!"',5Pillars,9January2016,http://5pillarsuk.com/video/video-maryam-namazie-shouts-at-muslim-students-telling-them-to-get-out/

17. Goldsmiths College student union policy on Safe Space, http://www.goldsmithssu.org/pageassets/yourunion/governance/policies/Safe-Space-Policy.pdf

18. Goldsmiths Feminist Society, Tumblr account, 2 December 2015, http://goldfemsoc.tumblr.com/post/134396957048/goldsmiths-feminist-society-stands-in-solidarity?utm_content=bufferco96f&utm_medium=social&utm_source=facebook.com&utm_campaign=buffer

19. Goldsmiths LGBTQ+ Society Facebook post, 4 December 2015, https://m.facebook.com/story.php?story_fbid=933160130085501&id=422404244494428

20. 'Campus Activists Weaponize "Safe Space"', The Atlantic, 10 November 2015,http://www.theatlantic.com/politics/archive/2015/11/how-campus-activists-are-weaponizing-the-safe-space/415080/

21. 'Is university free speech under threat?', BBC News, 26 February 2016, http://www.bbc.co.uk/news/education-35661362

22. 'London School of Economics free speech society faces ban threat', The Independent, 4 February 2016, http://www.independent.co.uk/student/news/london-school-of-economics-free-speech-society-faces-ban-threat-after-student-files-motion-a6853496.html

23. 'Can student radicals please just publish a League Table of Oppression?', Daily Telegraph, 25 March 2016, http://www.telegraph.co.uk/education/universityeducation/12204717/Can-student-radicals-please-just-publish-a-League-Table-of-Oppression.html

24. 'The NUS says gay men are not oppressed enough to have LGBT+ representatives', The Tab, March 2016, http://thetab.com/2016/03/23/gay-men-arent-oppressed-enough-according-nus-81622

25. ExeterFemSoc on Twitter, @ExeterFemSoc, 14 March 2016

26. https://worldtomorrow.wikileaks.org/episode-5.html

27. 'Outcry at "gender apartheid" in new guidance for UK universities', The Independent, 11 December 2013, http://www.independent.co.uk/student/news/outcry-at-gender-apartheid-in-new-guidance-for-uk-

universities-8997861.html

28. *External speakers in higher education institutions*, Universities UK, 2013, ISBN: 978-1-84036-315-9

29. 'The "Segregation" Debate and Muslim Female Empowerment', Huffington Post, 2 February 2014, http://www.huffingtonpost.co.uk/camillia-khan/segregation-women-muslim-empowerment_b_4379317.html

30. 'London School of Economics Islamic Society holds segregated dinner', *Daily Mail*, 15 March 2016, http://www.dailymail.co.uk/news/article-3492872/LSE-Islamic-Society-holds-segregated-event-veil-room-separate-male-female-students.html

31. 'Segregation and the Useful Idiot Paradigm', Islam21c, 13 December 2013, http://www.islam21c.com/politics/segregation-and-the-useful-idiot-paradigm/

32. 'Universities UK report vindicates iERA policies', iERA, 26 November 2013,http://www.iera.org/media/press-releases/universities-uk-report-vindicates-iera-policies-on-separate-seating-at-events

33. Ibid: 'Universities UK report vindicates iERA policies', iERA, 26 November 2013

34. 'iERA event at UCL on 9 March', UCL News, 11 March 2013, https://www.ucl.ac.uk/news/news-articles/0313/11032013-meeting

35. Video: 'Lawrence Krauss walkout over gender segregation at iERA event at UCL', YouTube, 10 March 2013, https://www.youtube.com/watch?v=iRrSmwqUxtk

36. Op. Cit. 'Universities UK report vindicates iERA policies', iERA, 26 November 2013

37. 'Commission tackles gender segregation in universities', Equality and Human Rights Commission, 18 July 2014, http://www.equalityhuman rights.com/commission-tackles-gender-segregation-universities

38. 'Globalising Capitalism and the Rise of Identity Politics', *Socialist Register*, http://socialistregister.com/index.php/srv/article/view/5652#.V0LPfOlm2JU

39. *Siding with the Oppressor: The Pro-Islamist Left*, Maryam Namazie, One Law for All, 2013, ISBN: 978-0-9566054-6-7

40. *Double Bind*, Meredith Tax, Centre for Secular Space, 2012, ISBN: 978-0-9888303-0-1

41. 'Stop Scapegoating Muslims', Stop the War Coalition public meeting, London, 10 March 2016

42. 'About Stop the War', Stop the War website, http://stopwar.org.uk/index.php/about

43. 'Stop the War patrons, officers and steering committee', Stop the War

website, http://stopwar.org.uk/index.php/officers

44. 'Why did we withdraw? A statement by Moayed Ahmad and Dashti Jamal, previous members of StWC Interim Steering Committee', 28 October 2001, http://www.hartford-hwp.com/archives/51/253.html

45. Op. Cit. 'Stop Scapegoating Muslims', Stop the War Coalition public meeting, London, 10 March 2016

46. Martin Niemoller: 'First they came for the socialists...', Holocaust Encyclopedia, https://www.ushmm.org/wlc/en/article.php?ModuleId= 10007392

47. *The Prophet and the Proletariat*, Chris Harman, Socialist Workers Party

48. Ibid: *The Prophet and the Proletariat*, Chris Harman

49. Ibid: *The Prophet and the Proletariat*, Chris Harman

50. *History and Class Consciousness*, Georg Lukacs, MIT Press, ISBN: 978-0262620208

51. Op. Cit. *The Prophet and the Proletariat*, Chris Harman

52. 'Qaradawi et al. fatwa against 9/11', Charles Kurzman, 2001, http:// kurzman.unc.edu/islamic-statements-against-terrorism/qaradawi/

53. Video: 'Yousef al-Qaradawi – his position on suicide bombings', YouTube, 29 December 2010, https://www.youtube.com/watch?v= w2PSbGLJjV4

54. 'Qaradawi on Homosexuals', Memri TV, 27 January 2013, https://www. youtube.com/watch?v=NxnVSnnZsoQ

55. 'Yusuf al-Qaradawi praises Hitler and the Holocaust', YouTube, 19 November 2009, https://www.youtube.com/watch?v=VcB_DZ4YQYQ

56. 'Mayor's Dodgy Dossier on Dr. Qaradawi', Peter Tatchell website, 22 February 2005, http://www.petertatchell.net/religion/qaradawidossier. htm

57. 'If Qaradawi is an extremist, who is left?', *The Guardian*, 9 July 2004, http://www.theguardian.com/world/2004/jul/09/religion. politics?INTCMP=ILCNETTXT3487

58. 'Ken Livingstone on Yusuf Al-Qaradawi', Dave Hill, YouTube, 19 April 2008, https://www.youtube.com/watch?v=Vh1ep7jC_oQ

59. 'Mayor justifies cleric's welcome', BBC News, 11 January 2005, http:// news.bbc.co.uk/1/hi/4165691.stm

60. 'Livingstone exposed over al-Qaradawi', Indymedia, 15 February 2005, https://www.indymedia.org.uk/en/2005/02/305315.html

61. 'Anti-Islam hate crimes triple in London after Paris attacks', BBC News, 4 December 2015, http://www.bbc.co.uk/news/uk-england-london-34995431

62. *Double Bind*, Meredith Tax, Centre for Secular Space, 2012, ISBN: 978-0-9888303-0-1

63. 'Malcolm X: The House Negro and the Field Negro', Malcolm X Network, https://www.youtube.com/watch?v=znQe9nUKzvQ

64. 'A Nation challenged: The First Lady: Mrs Bush cites women's plight under Taliban', *New York Times*, 18 November 2001, http://www.nytimes.com/2001/11/18/us/a-nation-challenged-the-first-lady-mrs-bush-cites-women-s-plight-under-taliban.html

65. *(En)Gendering the War on Terror: War Stories and Camouflaged Politics (Gender in a Global/Local World)*, Kym Rygiel, ed. Krista Hunt, Routledge, 2007, ISBN: 978-0754673231

66. 'Imperialist feminism: a response to Meredith Tax', Deepa Kumar, Open Democracy, 17 December 2014, https://www.opendemocracy.net/deepa-kumar/imperialist-feminism-response-to-meredith-tax

67. Op. Cit. *Double Bind*, Meredith Tax

68. 'The Antis: anti-imperialist or anti-feminist?', Open Democracy, 19 November 2014, https://www.opendemocracy.net/5050/meredith-tax/antis-antiimperialist-or-antifeminist-0

69. Saadia Toor, College of Staten Island, http://www.csi.cuny.edu/faculty/TOOR_SAADIA.html

70. Ibid: Saadia Toor, College of Staten Island

71. 'Islam belongs in people's lives, not in politics, says Karima Bennoune', *The Guardian*, 28 October 2013, http://www.theguardian.com/global-development/2013/oct/28/islam-politics-karima-bennoune-fatwa-fundamentalism

72. *Your Fatwa does not apply here*, Karima Bennoune, W.W. Norton & Company, 2013, ISBN: 978-0393081589

73. *Gender, National Security, and Counter-Terrorism*, ed. Margaret L. Satterthwaite & Jayne Huckerby, Routledge, 2013, ISBN: 978-0-203-08139-6

74. *Can the Subaltern speak?*, ed. Rosalind Morris, Columbia University Press, 2010, ISBN: 9780231143851

75. *Women and Gender in Islam: Historical Roots of a Modern Debate*, Leila Ahmed, Yale University Press, 1993, ISBN: 978-0300055832

76. *Do Muslim Women Need Saving?*, Lila Abu-Lughod, Harvard University Press, 2013, ISBN: 978-0-674-08826-9

77. 'The Rise of the Islamic Feminists', *The Nation*, 4 December 2013, http://www.thenation.com/article/rise-islamic-feminists/

78. *Inside the Gender Jihad*, Amina Widud, Oneworld Publications, 2006, ISBN: 978-1851684632

79. Ziba Mir-Hosseini, http://www.zibamirhosseini.com/

80. *Men in charge? Rethinking Authority in Muslim Legal Tradition*, Ziba Mir-Hosseini, Oneworld Publications, 2014, ISBN: 978-1780747163

81. Musawah, http://www.musawah.org/

82. 'British Muslim women 71% more likely to be unemployed', *The Independent*, 15 April 2015, http://www.independent.co.uk/news/uk/home-news/british-muslim-women-71-more-likely-to-be-unemployed-due-to-workplace-discrimination-10179033.html

83. 'Strand Campus in King's College the centre of an Islamophobic hate incident', Tell MAMA, 5 March 2016, http://tellmamauk.org/strand-campus-in-kings-college-the-centre-of-an-islamophobic-hate-incident/

84. 'The Law Society provides guidance on Sharia wills', *The Gazette*, https://www.thegazette.co.uk/wills-and-probate/content/160

85. 'Law Society withdraws sharia wills practice note', Southall Black Sisters, 24 November 2014, http://www.southallblacksisters.org.uk/law-society-withdraws-sharia-wills-practice-note/

86. Press Release: 'Wills without bigotry – protest against the Law Society', One Law for All, 28 April 2014, http://www.onelawforall.org.uk/wills-without-bigotry-%E2%80%93-protest-against-the-law-society/

87. 'Law Society retracts Islamic wills guidance note', MEND, 27 November 2014 http://mend.org.uk/law-society-retracts-islamic-wills-guidance-note/

88. 'Muslims in Europe: A crisis of liberalism, not a clash of civilizations', Informed Comment, 14 February 2016, http://www.juancole.com/2016/02/muslims-in-europe-a-crisis-of-liberalism-not-a-clash-of-civilizations.html

89. 'A Neo-Nationalist Network: the English Defence League and Europe's Counter-Jihad movement', Alexander Meleagrou-Hitchens, The International Centre for the Study of Radicalisation and Political Violence, 2013, http://icsr.info/wp-content/uploads/2013/03/ICSR-ECJM-Report_Online.pdf

90. Ibid: 'A Neo-Nationalist Network', Alexander Meleagrou-Hitchens

91. 'Knights Templar 2083 by Anders Behring Breivik', YouTube, 2012, https://www.youtube.com/watch?v=gcu4HNkF3QM

92. Stop Islamisation of Europe website, about us, https://sioeeu.wordpress.com/about/

93. 'Why Jihad Watch?', Jihad Watch, http://www.jihadwatch.org/why-jihad-watch

94. *Islam Unveiled*, Robert Spencer, Encounter Books, 2003, ISBN: 978-1893554771

95. Pamela Geller website, biography, http://pamelageller.com/about/

96. 'Texas shooting: Who is Pamela Geller?', CNN, 4 May 2015, http://edition.cnn.com/2015/05/04/us/texas-shooting-who-is-pamela-geller/

97. 'ISIS claims responsibility for Texas shooting but offers no proof', CNN,6May2015,http://edition.cnn.com/2015/05/05/us/garland-texas-prophet-mohammed-contest-shooting/

98. 'Muslims defend Pam Geller's Right to Hate', Daily Beast, 4 May 2015, http://www.thedailybeast.com/articles/2015/05/04/muslims-defend-pam-geller-s-right-to-hate.html

99. 'London "Draw Mohamed" exhibition cancelled due to "real possibility people could be killed"', *The Independent*, 20 August 2015, http://www.independent.co.uk/arts-entertainment/art/news/london-draw-mohamed-exhibition-cancelled-due-to-real-possibility-people-could-be-killed-10464019.html

100. 'Warning – Muhammad Cartoon provocations would not serve our cause', Knights Templar International, 13 June 2015, https://www.knightstemplarinternational.com/warning-muhammad-cartoon-provocations-would-not-serve-our-cause/#

101. 'Culture matters more', *The Economist*, 11 August 2012, http://www.economist.com/node/21560294

102. 'Anti-Muslim prejudice "is moving to the mainstream"', *The Guardian*, 5December2015,http://www.theguardian.com/world/2015/dec/05/far-right-muslim-cultural-civil-war

103. 'Pegida UK: What does Tommy Robinson's "anti-Islam" group want?' *Newsweek*,5February2016,http://europe.newsweek.com/tommy-robinson-edl-pegida-uk-423623

104. 'Tommy Robinson brings Pegida to Britain', Channel 4 News, 3 December 2015, https://www.facebook.com/Channel4News/videos/10153369684221939/

105. 'The Battle of Liverpool – Review and Action Report', National Action,February2016,http://national-action.info/2016/03/19/the-battle-of-liverpool-review-action-report/

106. National Action Year Review 2014, http://national-action.info/wp-content/uploads/2014/08/NA2014.pdf

107. Ibid: National Action Year Review 2014

108. National Action website, http://national-action.info/

109. 'We could have seen Europe's Muslim rape crisis coming', algemeiner, 21January2016,http://www.algemeiner.com/2016/01/21/we-could-have-seen-europes-muslim-rape-crisis-coming/#

110. 'Sweden fights back: Muslim rape epidemic, refugee crimes fuel vigilante justice', *Examiner*, 30 January 2016, http://www.examiner.com/article/badass-swedish-men-mount-vigilante-justice-after-refugee-kills-soial-worker

111. 'Islamski gwałt na Europie', *wSieci*, February 2016, http://www.wsieci.pl/wsieci-islamski-gwalt-na-europie-pnews-2681.html

112. Ibid: 'Islamski gwałt na Europie'

113. *Pointing the Finger: Islam and Muslims in the British Media*, Julian Petley & Robin Richardson, Oneworld Publications, 2011, ISBN: 978-1851688128

114. The Reporter, *The Guardian*, 29 October 2005, http://www.theguardian.com/money/2005/oct/29/moneysupplement

115. 'No, there is no "Muslim campaign" to ban Peppa Pig', *Indy100*, 2014, http://indy100.independent.co.uk/article/no-there-is-no-muslim-campaign-to-ban-peppa-pig--x1A-NdcEEl

116. 'British Muslim faces backlash after starting campaign to ban Peppa Pig', *Daily Star*, 6 September 2014, http://www.dailystar.co.uk/news/latest-news/398413/British-Muslim-campaign-ban-Peppa-Pig

117. 'The Media and Muslims in the UK', Centre for Ethnicity and Racism Studies, University of Leeds, March 2012, http://www.ces.uc.pt/projectos/tolerace/media/Working%20paper%205/The%20Media%20and%20Muslims%20in%20the%20UK.pdf

118. 'British media coverage of refugee and migrant crisis is the most polarised and aggressive in Europe', Cardiff School of Journalism, 14 March 2016, http://www.jomec.co.uk/blog/new-report-finds-british-media-coverage-of-refugee-and-migrant-crisis-is-the-most-polarised-and-aggressive-in-europe/

119. 'Video! Migrants think it is normal to rape people if they need sex', Britain First, 10 February 2016, https://www.britainfirst.org/video-migrants-think-it-is-normal-to-rape-people-if-they-need-sex/

120. 'Welcome to East London', *Daily Mail*, 25 July 2015, http://www.dailymail.co.uk/news/article-3174610/Welcome-East-London-gang-slashes-tyres-immigration-raid-van-officers-showered-eggs-high-rise.html

121. 'Mehdi Hasan tells Wilderness Festival the "hysterical" British Press is encouraging Islamophobia', Huffington Post, 11 August 2014, http://www.huffingtonpost.co.uk/2014/08/08/mehdi-hasan-wilderness-festival-islamophobia-british-press_n_5661667.html

122. 'Intelligent Design: An Ambiguous Assault on Evolution', Live Science, 21 September 2005, http://www.livescience.com/9355-intelligent-design-ambiguous-assault-evolution.html

123. *The God Delusion*, Richard Dawkins, Black Swan, 2007

124. 'Fundamentalist Atheism and its Intellectual Failures', Jeff Nall, Humanity & Society/Florida Atlantic University, 2008, https://www.academia.edu/191087/Fundamentalist_Atheism_and_its_Intellectual_Failures

125. 'Richard Dawkins goes on anti-Islam rant', Salon, 7 January 2015, http://www.salon.com/2015/01/07/richard_dawkins_goes_on_

anti_islam_rant_blames_charlie_hebdo_massacre_on_entire_
religion/

126. 'Three-quarters of Muslims say Islam and British values compatible',
     SkyNews, 25 November 2015, http://news.sky.com/video/1462054/april-
     survey-reveals-common-ground

Chapter Five

1. *#notinmyname*, Active Change Foundation, ACF website
2. 'President Obama mentioning the #notinmyname campaign in UN
   General Assembly speech', Active Change Foundation YouTube, 24
   September 2014, https://www.youtube.com/watch?v=aPXMMp2z6X0
3. Ibid: 'President Obama mentioning the #notinmyname campaign in
   UN General Assembly speech'
4. 'The Muslim Blame Game "Not In My Name"', Huffington Post, 18
   August 2014, http://www.huffingtonpost.co.uk/dilly-hussain/the-
   muslim-blame-game_b_5682830.html
5. 'I know the actions of Isis are #NotInMyName, and I won't be pressured to
   apologise for them', *The Guardian*, 25 September 2014, http://www.
   theguardian.com/commentisfree/2014/sep/25/i-know-the-actions-
   of-isis-are-notinmyname-and-i-wont-be-pressured-to-apologise-for-them
6. Interview with Fiyaz Mughal, December 2015
7. Ibid: Interview with Fiyaz Mughal, December 2015
8. 'Tell Mama director says Muslims should unite with gays to combat
   prejudice', 5Pillars, 7 April 2014, http://5pillarsuk.com/2014/04/07/tell-
   mama-director-says-muslims-should-unite-with-gays-to-combat-
   prejudice/
9. 'Tell Mama is nearing its sell-by date', 5Pillars, 7 January 2016, http://
   5pillarsuk.com/2016/01/07/tell-mama-is-nearing-its-sell-by-date/
10. 'Don't be fooled by Islamophobia', Community Security Trust, 30
    November 2009, https://cst.org.uk/news/blog/2009/11/30/dont-be-
    fooled-by-islamophobia
11. Ibid: 'Don't be fooled by Islamophobia'
12. 'Fighting hatred together or setting communities apart', Community
    Security Trust, 15 April 2015, https://cst.org.uk/news/blog/2015/04/15/
    fighting-hatred-together-or-setting-communities-apart
13. 'Setting the record straight: comments at Cheadle mosque, 2014',
    Sufyan Ismail blog, 4 January 2016, http://www.sufyanismail.com/
    blog/setting-the-record-straight-comments-at-cheadle-mosque-2014/
14. 'Radical Islamist group al-Muhajiroun linked to half of British terror

attacks in past 20 years', *The Independent*, 23 March 2015, http://www.independent.co.uk/news/uk/crime/radical-islamist-group-al-muhajiroun-linked-to-half-of-british-terror-attacks-in-past-20-years-10128492.html

15. 'Proscribed Terrorist Organisations', Home Office, 2016, https://www.gov.uk/government/uploads/system/uploads/attachment_data/file/509003/20160318proscription.pdf

16. 'Tehmina Kazi on Religion, Religious Freedom and Secularism', Internal Association for Religious Freedom, https://iarf.net/tehmina-kazi-religion-religious-freedom-and-secularism/

17. 'Those who threaten "Twitter blasphemy"', *The Guardian*, 17 February 2012, http://www.theguardian.com/commentisfree/belief/2012/feb/17/twitter-blasphemy-hamza-kashgari-islam

18. 'Saudi "blasphemy" prisoner Hamza Kashgari tweets for first time after release', Gulf News Saudi Arabia, 29 October 2013, http://gulfnews.com/news/gulf/saudi-arabia/saudi-blasphemy-prisoner-hamza-kashgari-tweets-for-first-time-after-release-1.1248548

19. 'Tehmina Kazi: "Abuse against female activists occurs through a gendered lens"', *Marie Claire*, 1 February 2016, http://www.marieclaire.co.uk/blogs/551727/tehmina-kazi-abuse-against-female-activists-occurs-through-a-gendered-lens.html

20. 'Knowledge regained', *The Guardian*, 11 September 2008, http://www.theguardian.com/commentisfree/2008/sep/11/religion.darwinbicentenary

21. 'The Veil: Between Tradition and Reason, Culture and Context', Usama Hasan, 2011, https://www.academia.edu/4386604/Islam_and_the_Veil_-_Usama_Hasan

22. 'Imam who believes in evolution retracts statements', BBC News, 7 March 2011, http://www.bbc.co.uk/news/uk-12661477

23. 'Tawhid Mosque – statement', Unity, 5 March 2011, https://unity1.wordpress.com/2011/03/03/tawhid-mosque-statement/ ; and 'London imam subjected to death threats for supporting evolution', *The Guardian*, 6 March 2011, http://www.theguardian.com/world/2011/mar/06/usama-hasan-london-imam-death-threats-evolution

24. 'A further clarification and retraction', Unity, 4 March 2011, https://unity1.wordpress.com/2011/03/04/a-further-clarification-and-retraction/

25. 'Why Defend Usama Hasan?', Muslim Institute, 2011, http://www.musliminstitute.org/blogs/culture/why-defend-usama-hasan

26. Interviews with Usama Hasan in 2015 and 2016

27. 'Usama Hasan – The Trinity: Father, Son and Unholy Views', 5Pillars, 12 February 2014, http://5pillarsuk.com/2014/02/12/usama-hasan-the-trinity-

father-son-and-unholy-views/

28. 'A night with the Quilliam Foundation', Quilliam, 12 February 2016, http://www.quilliamfoundation.org/blog/a-night-with-the-quilliam-foundation-by-jodie-satterley/

29. Op. Cit. 'Usama Hasan – The Trinity: Father, Son and Unholy Views'

30. 'University Islamic Society tries to stop talk because speaker didn't condemn Maajid Nawaz', National Secular Society, 29 January 2014, http://www.secularism.org.uk/news/2014/01/university-islamic-society-tries-to-stop-talk-because-speaker-didnt-condemn-maajid-nawaz

31. Yusuf Chambers Facebook post on Plymouth University protest, 29 January 2014, https://www.facebook.com/OfficialYusufChambers/posts/682030935153008

32. Letter from the Fawcett Society to Professor Wendy Purcell, 27 January 2014,http://www.islamophobiawatch.co.uk/wp-content/uploads/Fawcett-Plymouth-letter.png

33. 'Have You Stopped Beating Your Wife? The Quran, Hadith and Domestic Violence', Usama Hasan, Unity blog, https://unity1.wordpress.com/2011/01/03/have-you-stopped-beating-your-wife-the-quran-hadith-and-domestic-violence/

34. Interview with Mina Topia, December 2015

35. Ibid: Interview with Mina Topia, December 2015

36. 'Islamic State: Young British Muslims debate Caliphate', BBC News,14 August 2014, http://www.bbc.co.uk/news/uk-28772646

37. 'Speculation that ISIS executioner "could be Walthamstow jihadi"', report claims', Waltham Forest Guardian, 4 January 2016, http://www.guardian-series.co.uk/news/14180820.Speculation_that_ISIS_executioner_
_could_be_Walthamstow_jihadi___report_claims/?ref=mr&lp=4

38. Op. Cit. 'Islamic State: Young British Muslims debate Caliphate'

39. 'How "Jihadi Sid" was arrested six times on terror offences', Daily Mail, 6 January 2016, http://www.dailymail.co.uk/news/article-3385722/Police-wrote-Jihadi-Sid-explaining-bail-conditions-SIX-weeks-fled-Britain-Syria.html

40. 'How a bounce-house salesman became an alleged ISIS executioner', Time,5January2016,http://time.com/4167480/isis-isil-executioner-jihadi-john-abu-rumaysah/

41. Tweet from @DillyHussain88 at 09:46 on 17 August 2014; and 'The World According to Dilly Hussain', Homo economicus weblog, 23 August 2014,https://homoeconomicusnet.wordpress.com/2014/08/23/the-world-according-to-dilly-hussain/

42. 'British imams visit Iraq in bid to counter ISIS propaganda in the UK', The Independent, 28 February 2016, http://www.independent.co.uk/

news/uk/home-news/isis-propaganda-terrorism-british-imams-visit-iraq-yazidi-community-a6902051.html

43. 'Prayer for the Nation', Faiths Forum for London, 19 November 2015, http://www.faithsforum4london.org/2015/11/prayer-for-the-nation/

44. Interview with Mustafa Field, December 2015

45. Ibid: Interview with Mustafa Field, December 2015

46. Ibid: Interview with Mustafa Field, December 2015

47. 'ISIS killing of three Iraqi truck drivers', YouTube, 16 June 2014, https://www.youtube.com/watch?v=PC3aZ2qPcAs

48. 'Isis accused of ethnic cleansing as story of Shia prison massacre emerges', *The Guardian*, 25 August 2014, http://www.theguardian.com/world/2014/aug/25/isis-ethnic-cleansing-shia-prisoners-iraq-mosul

49. 'We highlight the possible roots of anti-Shia bigotry in Yorkshire', Tell MAMA,22June2015,http://tellmamauk.org/we-highlight-the-possible-roots-of-anti-shia-bigotry-in-yorkshire/

50. Ibid: 'We highlight the possible roots of anti-Shia bigotry in Yorkshire'

51. 'Hate leaflets calling for killing of Ahmadi Muslims distributed across London', *International Business Times*, 8 April 2016, http://www.ibtimes.co.uk/hate-leaflets-calling-killing-ahmadi-muslims-distributed-across-london-1553591

52. 'Terrorism trial puts focus on Sparkhill and Sparkbrook', BBC News, 21February2013,http://www.bbc.co.uk/news/uk-england-birmingham-21458869

53. Interview with Mohammed Ashfaq, Kikit, 22 October 2015

54. 'A New Synthetic Drug Is Making British Prisoners Attack Walls and Shit Themselves', Vice News, 15 April 2015, http://www.vice.com/en_uk/read/fake-weed-mamba-in-uk-prisons-596

Conclusion

1. 'London will shortly get a Muslim mayor but I can't find a Muslim who cares', 5Pillars, 4 May 2016, http://5pillarsuk.com/2016/05/04/london-will-shortly-get-a-muslim-mayor-but-i-cant-find-a-muslim-who-cares/

2. 'Britain First's Paul Golding Turned his back on Sadiq Khan during London mayoral election speech', Huffington Post, 7 May 2016, http://www.huffingtonpost.co.uk/entry/britain-firsts-paul-golding-turns-his-back_uk_572d2f48e4b0e6da49a6523f

3. 'How Zac Goldsmith imported Donald Trump's politics into Britain', *Middle East Eye*, 21 April 2016, http://www.middleeasteye.net/

columns/london-mayor-race-conservatives-game-religious-and-racial-divisions-538083247; and 'Tories step up attempts to link Sadiq Khan to extremists', *The Guardian*, 20 April 2016, http://www.theguardian.com/politics/2016/apr/20/tory-claims-sadiq-khan-alleged-links-extremists

4. 'London mayor Sadiq Khan', *Time*, 9 May 2016, http://time.com/4322562/london-mayor-sadiq-khan-donald-trump/
5. 'New Polling of British Muslims', Survation, November 2015, http://survation.com/new-polling-of-british-muslims/
6. 'Muslims add over £31bn to UK economy', Huffington Post, 29 October 2013, http://www.huffingtonpost.co.uk/2013/10/29/uk-muslims-economy_n_4170781.html
7. 'The Muslim Pound', Muslim Council of Britain, 2013, http://www.mcb.org.uk/wp-content/uploads/2014/10/The-Muslim-Pound-FINAL.pdf
8. 'British Muslims: integration and segregation are about economics, not values', *Daily Telegraph*, 13 February 2015, http://www.telegraph.co.uk/news/uknews/immigration/11409181/British-Muslims-integration-and-segregation-are-about-economics-not-values.html
9. 'Why the survey of British Muslim attitudes is so profoundly disconcerting', *The Independent*, 25 February 2015, http://www.independent.co.uk/voices/comment/why-the-survey-of-british-muslim-attitudes-is-so-profoundly-disconcerting-10070358.html
10. 'Islamic State's goal: "Eliminating the grayzone" of coexistence between Muslims and the West, The Intercept, 17 November 2015, https://theintercept.com/2015/11/17/islamic-states-goal-eliminating-the-grayzone-of-coexistence-between-muslims-and-the-west/
11. *Dabiq VII* feature article: 'The world includes only two camps', Memri, February 2015, http://www.memrijttm.org/dabiq-vii-feature-article-there-is-no-longer-any-gray-zone-the-world-includes-only-two-camps-that-of-isis-and-that-of-its-enemies.html
12. 'Women in Society', Pew Research Center, 30 April 2013, http://www.pewforum.org/2013/04/30/the-worlds-muslims-religion-politics-society-women-in-society/
13. 'Who creates harmony the world over? Women. Who signs peace deals? Men', *The Guardian*, 20 September 2012, http://www.theguardian.com/global-development/2012/sep/20/harmony-women-peace-deals
14. 'Home Secretary supports #MakingAStand campaign', Home Office, 24 September 2014, https://www.gov.uk/government/news/home-secretary-supports-makingastand-campaign
15. Women interviewed during the 'Making A Stand' roadshows in 2014
16. Letter to Kamal Hanif from Ofsted, 12 May 2014

17. Waverley School, Stonewall, http://www.waverley.bham.sch.uk/about-us/Stonewall-1

18. 'Meeting the needs of Muslim pupils in state schools', Muslim Council of Britain, 2007, http://www.religionlaw.co.uk/MCBschoolsreport07.pdf

19. Ibid: 'Meeting the needs of Muslim pupils in state schools', Muslim Council of Britain, 2007, http://www.religionlaw.co.uk/MCBschools report07.pdf

20. *War and Peace in Islam: The Uses and Abuses of Jihad*, ed. HRH Prince Ghazi bin Muhammad, Professor Ibrahim Kalin, Professor Mohammad Hashim Kamali, The Islamic Texts Society, ISBN: 978-1-903682-83-8

21. Interview on an Inspire programme

22. 'Shaykh bin Bayyah carries the message of peace to the world at the United Nations', Abdallah bin Bayyah, http://binbayyah.net/english/2015/10/09/shaykh-bin-bayyah-carries-the-message-of-peace-to-the-world-at-the-united-nations/

23. Ibid: 'Shaykh bin Bayyah carries the message of peace to the world at the United Nations'

24. 'Ministers call on Muslim faith leaders to challenge extremism', Department for Communities and Local Government, 19 January 2016,https://www.gov.uk/government/news/ministers-call-on-muslim-faith-leaders-to-challenge-extremism

25. 'Muslim Council of Britain responds to Eric Pickles letter', Muslim CouncilofBritain,19January2015,http://www.mcb.org.uk/muslim-council-britain-responds-eric-pickles-letter/

26. 'Cameron backs Pickles' letter to Muslim leaders', *The Guardian*, 19 January2015,http://www.theguardian.com/uk-news/2015/jan/19/david-cameron-backs-eric-pickles-letter-muslim-leaders

27. 'Why Eric Pickles' letter to mosques was right and wrong', *The Guardian*, 25 January 2015, http://www.theguardian.com/uk-news/2015/jan/25/eric-pickles-letter-to-mosques-right-and-wrong

28. '"Passive tolerance" of separate communities must end, says PM', Prime Minister's Office, 18 January 2016, https://www.gov.uk/government/news/passive-tolerance-of-separate-communities-must-end-says-pm

29. Ibid: '"Passive tolerance" of separate communities must end, says PM', Prime Minister's Office

30. 'Cameron has alienated the very people he must ally with: Muslim women', *The Guardian*, 18 January 2016, http://www.theguardian.com/commentisfree/2016/jan/18/david-cameron-muslim-women-anti-women

31. 'The Queen's Speech 2016', HM Government, https://www.gov.uk/government/uploads/system/uploads/attachment_data/

file/524040/Queen_s_Speech_2016_background_notes_.pdf

32. 'Anti-radicalisation chief says ministers' plans risk creating "thought police"', *The Guardian*, 24 May 2016, http://www.theguardian.com/uk-news/2016/may/24/anti-radicalisation-chief-says-ministers-plans-risk-creating-thought-police

33. 'Muslim Prof: West leads the world in "Islamic Values"', Frontpage Mag,19June2014,http://www.frontpagemag.com/fpm/234437/muslim-prof-west-leads-world-islamic-values-ali-sina

34. 'Islamophobic crime in London "up by 70%"', BBC News, 7 September 2015, http://www.bbc.co.uk/news/uk-england-london-34138127 ; and 'Latest crime figures for London', Metropolitan Police, http://www.met.police.uk/crimefigures/#

35. 'Targeting of London Muslims triples after Paris attacks', *The Guardian*, 4 December 2015, http://www.theguardian.com/uk-news/2015/dec/04/attacks-against-london-muslims-triple-in-wake-of-paris-attacks

36. 'UK: British government responsible for alarming rise in Islamophobia', Islamic Human Rights Commission, 11 November 2015, http://www.ihrc.org.uk/activities/press-releases/11560-press-release-uk-british-government-responsible-for-alarming-rise-in-islamophobia

37. Ibid: 'UK: British government responsible for alarming rise in Islamophobia', IHRC

38. 'Report on the Protection of Civilians in Armed Conflict in Iraq', United Nations Assistance Mission for Iraq, 2014, http://www.ohchr.org/Documents/Countries/IQ/UNAMI_OHCHR_POC_Report_FINAL_6July_10September2014.pdf

39. 'How politics has poisoned Islam', Mustafa Akyol, *New York Times*, 3 February 2016, http://www.nytimes.com/2016/02/04/opinion/how-politics-has-poisoned-islam.html

40. 'The Identity-Extremism Nexus: Countering Islamist Extremism in the West', Dina Al Raffie, George Washington University, 2015, https://cchs.gwu.edu/sites/cchs.gwu.edu/files/downloads/AlRaffiePaper-Final.pdf

41. 'Making integration work', British Future, 18 January 2016, http://www.britishfuture.org/artic

BIBLIOGRAPHY

Books

Abu-Lughod, Lila, *Do Muslim Women Need Saving?*, Harvard University Press, Massachusetts, USA, 2013

Aggarwal, Neil Krishan, *Mental Health in the War on Terror: Culture, Science, and Statecraft*, Columbia University Press, New York, 2015

Ahmed, Leila, *Women and Gender in Islam: Historical Roots of a Modern Debate*, Yale University Press, Connecticut, USA, 1993

Akyol, Mustafa, *Islam without Extremes: A Muslim Case for Liberty*, W. W. Norton & Company, New York, 2013

An-Nabahani, Taqiuddin *The System of Islam*, Al-Khilafah Publications, London, 2002

Begg, Moazzam, *Enemy Combatant*, Pocket Books, London, 2007

Bennoune, Karima, *Your Fatwa Does not Apply Here: Untold Stories from the Fight Against Muslim Fundamentalism*, W.W. Norton & Company, New York, 2013

Bin Muhammad, Ghazi (Prince), Ibrahim Kalin, Mohammad Hashim Kamali, *War and Peace in Islam: The Uses and Abuses of Jihad*, The Islamic Texts Society, Cambridge, UK, 2013

Bokhari, Kamran, Farid Senzal, *Political Islam in the Age of Democratization*, Palgrave Macmillan, New York, 2013

Bowen, Innes, *Medina in Birmingham Najaf in Brent*, Hurst and

Company, London, 2014

Dawkins, Richard, *The God Delusion*, Black Swan, London, 2007

El-Affendi, Abdelwhab, *Who Needs an Islamic State?*, Malaysia Think Tank, London, 2008

El Fadl, Khaled Abou, *Speaking in God's Name: Islamic Law, Authority and Women*, Oneworld Publications, Oxford, UK, 2001

El Fadl, Khaled Abou *The Great Theft: Wrestling Islam from the Extremists*, HarperOne, New York, 2007

El Fadl, Khaled Abou, *The Place of Tolerance in Islam*, Beacon Press, Boston, Massachusetts, 2002

El Fadl, Khaled Abou, *Reasoning with God: Reclaiming Shari'ah in the Modern Age*, Rowman and Littlefield, Lanham, Maryland, 2014

Euben, L., Roxanne and Muhammad Qasim Zaman, *Princeton Readings in Islamist Thought: Texts and Contexts from al-Banna to Bin Laden*, Princeton University Press, Princeton, New Jersey, 2009

Glazov, Jamie *United in Hate: The Left's Romance with Tyranny and Terror*, WND Books, Los Angeles, 2009

Harman, Chris, *The Prophet and the Proletariat*, Bookmarks, London, 1994

Hasan, Usama (contributor), *Islam and the Veil*, Continuum-3PL, London, 2011

Hathout, Maher, *In Pursuit of Justice: The Jurisprudence of Human Rights in Islam*, Muslim Public Affairs Council, Washington DC, 2006

Herbert, Matthew, 'Hizb ut-Tahrir Rise of the Virtual Caliphate', VDM Verlag Dr Muller, Saarbrücken, 2011

Hussain, Dilwar, and Mohammad Siddique Seddon, Nadeem Malik, *British Muslims Between Assimilation and Segregation: Historical, Legal and Social Realities*, The Islamic Foundation, Markfield, Leicestershire, UK 2004

Jacobson, Jessica, *Islam in Transition: Religion and Identity among British Pakistani Youth*, Routledge, London, 1998

Kamali, Mohammad Hashim, *Freedom, Equality and Justice in Islam*, Islamic Texts Society, Cambridge, UK, 2002

Kundnani, Arun, *The Muslims are Coming!: Islamophobia, Extremism, and the Domestic War on Terror*, Verso Books, London, 2014

Kurzman, Charles, *Liberal Islam*, Oxford University Press, Oxford, UK, 1998

Lean, Nathan, *The Islamophobia Industry: How the Right Manufactures Fear of Muslims*, Pluto Press, London, 2012

Lewis, Christopher, Dan Cohn-Sherbok, *Sensible Religion*, Routledge, Oxford, UK, 2016

Lukács, Georg *History and Class Consciousness: Studies in Marxist Dialectics*, MIT Press, Cambridge, Massachusetts, 1972

Malik, Kenan, *From Fatwa to Jihad: The Rushdie Affair and its Legacy*, Atlantic Books, London, 2009

Meijer, Roel, *Global Salafism: Islam's New Religious Movement*, C. Hurst & Co, New York, 2009

Mernissi, Fatema, *Islam and Democracy: Fear of the Modern World*, Basic Books, New York, 1992

Namazie, Maryam, *Siding with the Oppressor: The Pro-Islamist Left*, One Law for All, London, 2013

Pantucci, Raffaello, *We Love Death as You Love Life: Britain's Suburban Terrorists*, C. Hurst & Co, London, 2015

Petley, Julian, and Robin Richardson, *Pointing the Finger: Islam and Muslims in the British Media*, Oneworld Publications, London, 2011

Poloni-Staudinger, Lori, and Candice D. Ortbals, *Terrorism and Violent Conflict: Women's Agency, Leadership and Responses*, Springer, New York, 2013

Sardar, Ziauddin, *Reading the Qur'an: The Contemporary Relevance of the Sacred Text in Islam*, Oxford University Press, New York, 2011

Rygiel, Kim, and Krista Hunt, *(En)Gendering the War on Terror: War Stories and Camouflaged Politics (Gender in a Global/Local World)*, Routledge, Abingdon, Oxon, UK 2007

Sachedina, Abdulaziz, *The Islamic Roots of Democratic Pluralism*, Oxford University Press, New York, 2007

Spencer, Robert *Islam Unveiled: Disturbing Questions about the World's Fastest Growing Faith*, Encounter Books, New York, 2003

Spivak, Gayatri Chakravorty, *Can the Subaltern speak? Marxism and the Interpretation of Culture*, University of Illinois Press, Champaign, Illinois, 1987

Tax, Meredith, *Double Bind: The Muslim Right, the Anglo-American Left, and Universal Human Rights*, Centre for Secular Space, New York, 2012

Wadud, Amina, *Inside the Gender Jihad*, Oneworld Publications, Oxford, UK, 2006

Wagemakers, Joas, *A Quietist Jihadi, The Ideology and Influence of Abu Muhammad al-Maqdisi*, Cambridge University Press, New York, 2012

Yuksel, Edip, Arnold Yasin Mol and Farouk A Peru, *Critical Thinkers for Islamic Reform*, Brainbow Press, New York, 2009

Ziba Mir-Hosseini, *Men in charge? Rethinking Authority in Muslim Legal Tradition*, Oneworld Publications, London, 2014

Journals

Al Raffie, Dina, 'Social Identity Theory for Investigating Islamic Extremism in the Diaspora', *Journal of Strategic Security*, Vol. 6 No. 4, Winter 2013, pp. 67-91

Bhui, Professor Kamaldeep,'Mental Health and Violent Radicalization', *Mental Health Today*, July/August 2013, pp. 24-26

Ghajar-Khosravi, S., 'Quantifying Salient Concepts Discussed in Social Media Content: A Case Study using Twitter Content Written by Radicalized Youth', *Journal of Terrorism Research*. Volume 7 No 2, May, 2016, pp.79–90

Nall, Jeff, 'Fundamentalist Atheism and its Intellectual Failures', *Humanity & Society* Vol. 32, 2008, pp. 263-280

Neumann, Peter, 'The Trouble with Radicalization', *International*

Affairs 4, Volume 89 No 4, 2013, pp. 873-893

Osman, Mohamed Nawab, 'The Caliphate of Hizb-ut-Tahrir', *Critical Muslim*, No. 10, April-June 2014, pp. 75-87

Simcox, Robin and Emily Dyer, 'The Role of Converts in Al Qa'ida Related Terrorism Offenses in the United States', *CTC Sentinel* Combating Terrorism Center at West Point, Vol. 6 Issue 3, March 2013, pp. 20-24

Magazines

Bhui, Kamaldeep S., Madelyn H. Hicks, Myrna Lashley and Edgar Jones, 'A Public Health Approach to Understanding and Preventing Violent Radicalization', *BMC Medicine*, 14 February 2012,

Dabiq VII Feature Article: 'The World Includes Only Two Camps', *Memri*, February 2015,

Dabiq III Feature Article: 'The Call to Hijra', *Clarion Project*, August, 2014

Fox Piven, Frances, 'Globalizing Capitalism and the Rise of Identity Politics', *Socialist Register*, Vol. 31, 1995

Kazi, Tehmina, 'Tehmina Kazi: "Abuse against Female Activists Occurs through a Gendered Lens"', *Marie Claire*, 1 February 2016

Zakaria, Rafia, 'Women and Islamic Militancy', *Dissent*, Winter 2015

Websites

Ali, Rashad, Hannah Stuart, 'A Guide to Refuting Jihadism: Critiquing Radical Islamist Claims to Theological Authenticity', *The Henry Jackson Society*, 2014, Web

Allely, Clare, 'Do Certain Mental Disorders Put People More at Risk of Being Radicalised?', *University of Salford*, 15 March 2016, Web

Al Raffie, Dina, 'The Identity-Extremism Nexus: Countering Islamist Extremism in the West', *The George Washington University*,

Program on Extremism, 2015, Web

Bari, Dr Muhammad Abdul Bari, Tahir Alam, 'Meeting the Needs of Muslim Pupils in State Schools', *Religion Law UK*, Muslim Council of Britain, 2007, Web

Benotman, Noman, 'Muslim Communities: Between Integration and Securitisation', *Quilliam Foundation*, 2012, Web.

Bunglawala, Shenaz, 'How Do We Prevent Radicalisation?', *Theos Thinktank*, 2014, Web

'Channel Duty Guidance', *HM Government*, April 2015, Web

'Evangelising Hate', *Council of Ex-Muslims of Britain*, 2014, Web.

'External Speakers in Higher Education Institutions', *Universities UK*, Universities UK, 2013, Web

Hamid, Sadek, 'Islamic Political Radicalism in Britain: The Case of Hizb ut-Tahrir', *Academia*, 2007, Web

Hasan, Usama, 'Have You Stopped Beating Your Wife? The Quran, Hadith and Domestic Violence', Unity blog, 2011, Web

'HASC: Countering Extremism 2015–2016', *Independent Reviewer of Terrorism Legislation*, 3 February 2016, Web

Kazi,Tehmina, 'Religion, Religious Freedom and Secularism', *Internal Association for Religious Freedom*, March 2013. Web

Lesaca, Javier, 'On Social Media, ISIS Uses Modern Cultural Images to Spread Anti-Modern Values', *Brookings Institution*, 24 September 2015, Web

'Making Integration Work', *British Future*, 18 January 2016, Web

'Martin Niemoller: "First They Came for the Socialists...", *United States Holocaust Memorial Museum*, Holocaust Encyclopedia, 2016, Web

Meleagrou-Hitchens, Alexander, Hans Brun, 'A Neo-Nationalist Network: the English Defence League and Europe's Counter-Jihad movement', *The International Centre for the Study of Radicalisation (ICSR)*, 2013, Web

Motion 517, National Union of Students Conference 2015, *Amazon S3*, NUS, 2015, Web

'Muslim Brotherhood Review: Main Findings', *Gov.UK*, House of Commons, December 2015, Web

'Muslim Council of Britain Parliamentary Briefing on Introducing "Prevent" as a Statutory Duty for All Public Bodies', *Muslim Council of Britain*, MCB, 18 January 2015, Web

Nasr, S.V.R., 'European Colonialism and the Emergence of Modern Muslim States', *Oxford Islamic Studies*, 1999, Web

'National Union of Teachers Conference Agenda 2016', *Teachers.org.uk*, National Union of Teachers, 2016, Web

Neumann, Peter, Brooke Rogers, *EC.Europa*, 'Recruitment and Mobilisation for the Islamist Movement in Europe', King's College London, 2007, Web

'Operation of Police Powers under the Terrorism Act 2000 and Subsequent Legislation', *Gov.uk*, Home Office, 17 March 2016, Web

'Oral Evidence: Countering Extremism', *Data.Parliament,UK*, Home Affairs Committee, 17 November 2015, Web

'Prevent Duty Guidance for Higher Education', *Gov.UK*, HM Government, 16 July, 2015, Web

'Prevent, Police and Schools', *London safeguarding children board*, Association of Chief Police Officers, June 2013, Web.

'Prevent Strategy', *HM Government*, Home Office, 2011, Web

'Preventing Prevent? Challenges to Counter-Radicalisation Policy on Campus', *The Henry Jackson Society*, Student Rights, 2015, Web

'Proscribed Terrorist Organisations', *Gov.UK*, Home Office, 18 March, 2016, Web

'Radicalisation in Prisons', *Criminal Justice Inspectorates*, 2014, Web.

Raymond, Catherine Zara,'Al Muhajiroun and Islam4UK: The Group behind the Ban', *The International Centre for the Study of Radicalisation (ICSR)*, 2010, Web

'Report of the Independent Reviewer', *Independent Reviewer of Terrorist Legislation*, David Anderson QC, September 2015, Web

'Report on the Intelligence Relating to the Murder of Fusilier Lee Rigby', *Open Government License*, House of Commons, November 2014, Web

'Report on the Protection of Civilians in Armed Conflict in Iraq', *United Nations Human Rights Office of the High Commissioner*,

United Nations Assistance Mission for Iraq, 2014, Web

Saltman, Erin Marie and Melanie Smith, 'Till Martyrdom Do Us Part', *Institute for Strategic Dialogue,* 2015, Web

Sian, Katy, Ian Law and S. Sayyid, 'The Media and Muslims in the UK', *Centro de Estudos Sociais Universidade de Coimbra,* Centre for Ethnicity and Racism Studies, University of Leeds, March 2012, Web

'The Battle of Liverpool – Review and Action Report', *National Action,* February 2016, Web

'The Muslim Pound', *Muslim Council of Britain,*MCB, 2013, Web

'The Prevent Duty', *Gov.UK,* Department for Education, June 2015, Web

'The Prevent Strategy: A Cradle to Grave Police State', *Cage,* CAGE, 2013, Web

'The United Kingdom's Strategy for Countering International Terrorism', *Gov.UK,* HM Government, March 2009, Web

Whine, Michael, 'Islamist Recruitment and Antisemitism on British Campuses', *RUSI,* 23 January 2006, Web

'Why did we withdraw? A statement by Moayed Ahmad and Dashti Jamal, previous members of StWC Interim Steering Committee', *World History Archives,* Hartford Web Publishing, 28 October 2001, Web

Wiktorowicz, Quintan, 'Joining the Cause: Al-Muhajiroun and Radical Islam', *Institute for National Security and Counter-Terrorism, Syracuse University* Web

'Women of the Islamic State', *Quilliam Foundation,* translation by Quilliam, February 2015, Web

INDEX